# Children Learning to Read:
## International Concerns

### Volume 1

## Emergent and Developing Reading:
### Messages for Teachers

Children Learning to Read: International Concerns Volume 2

Curriculum and Assessment Issues: Messages for Teachers

*Edited by* Pamela Owen and Peter Pumfrey

# Children Learning to Read:
## International Concerns

Volume 1

Emergent and Developing Reading:
Messages for Teachers

*Edited by*

Pamela Owen and Peter Pumfrey

 The Falmer Press

(A member of the Taylor & Francis Group)
London • Washington, D.C.

**UK**  The Falmer Press, 4 John Street, London WC1N 2ET
**USA** The Falmer Press, Taylor & Francis Inc., 1900 Frost Road, Suite 101, Bristol, PA 19007

First published in 1995

**A catalogue record for this book is available from the British Library**

**Library of Congress Cataloging-in-Publication Data are available on request**

ISBN 0 7507 0363 6 cased
ISBN 0 7507 0364 4 paper

Jacket design by Caroline Archer

Typeset in 10/12pt Garamond by
Graphicraft Typesetters Ltd., Hong Kong.

*Printed in Great Britain by Burgess Science Press, Basingstoke on paper which has a specified pH value on final paper manufacture of not less than 7.5 and is therefore 'acid free'.*

# Contents

*Acknowledgments*                                                         vii

*List of Tables and Figures*                                             viii

*List of Abbreviations*                                                     x

Introduction: International Concerns and Controversies                      1
          *P. Pumfrey and P. Owen*

**Part 1: The Importance of Phonological Awareness**                       7

*Chapter 1*     The Emergence of Word Reading in Beginning
                Reading                                                     9
                *L. Ehri*

*Chapter 2*     Some Effects of Phonics Teaching on Early Reading
                Development                                                32
                *R. Johnston, V. Connelly and J. Watson*

*Chapter 3*     Making Sense of Writing                                    43
                *P. Papoulia-Tzelepi*

*Chapter 4*     Some Effects of Context on Reading                         57
                *R. Stainthorp*

*Chapter 5*     Phonemic Awareness and Balanced Reading
                Instruction                                                67
                *A. Adamik-Jászó*

*Chapter 6*     Children Learn to Read by Being Taught                     80
                *M. Turner*

**Part 2: Wider Concerns**                                                 93

*Chapter 7*     New Moves in Early-literacy Learning in Europe             95
                *H. Dombey*

*Chapter 8*     What Do Children Know About Reading Before
                They Go to School?                                        104
                *P. Munn*

*v*

*Contents*

*Chapter 9*    Teacher Decision-making in Early-literacy Teaching    115
          *R. Fisher*

*Chapter 10*    The Importance of the Teacher    126
          *R. Campbell*

*Chapter 11*    Stance, Meaning and Voluntary Reading    137
          *M. Hunter-Carsch*

*Chapter 12*    A Conceptual Basis for a Literacy Curriculum    161
          *M. Reed, A. Webster and M. Beveridge*

*Notes on Contributors*    181

*Index*    185

# Acknowledgments

The editors are indebted to the University College of St Martin's, Lancaster, for hosting the 1993 International Reading Conference 'How Do Children Learn To Read?' in response to the International Association for the Evaluation of Educational Achievement (IEA) Reading Literacy Study.

The conference, following from the preceding Lancaster Conference on '*What Counts As Being Able To Read?*', brought together professionals from many different countries and disciplines. The aims of these meetings included sharing information on common concerns and engaging in dialogues focused on advancing an understanding of the nature of literacy, its emergence, related pedagogic concerns and assessment issues.

The importance of integrating theory, research and practice was underlined. In order to help improve practice, each contributor was asked to provide a concluding section identifying 'Messages for Teachers'. The present two volume series is an outcome of the above process. Each contributor's considerable investment of his or her time and expertize is acknowledged.

In conclusion, the editors gratefully acknowledge the professional skill, commitment and hard work of Libby Osborn, secretary to the English Department at St Martin's College, and Jackie Day and Jocelyne Cox of Falmer Press, in preparing the manuscripts.

# List of Tables and Figures

**Tables**

Table 1.1    Ways that words and pseudowords might be read
             by readers                                                    14

Table 1.2    Set of rime spellings that can be used to derive
             nearly 500 primary-grade words                               16

Table 3.1    Frequency of pictoriality–non-pictoriality in
             younger and older kindergarteners' attempted writing         48

Table 3.2    Frequency of horizontality in younger and older
             kindergarteners' attempted writing                           48

Table 3.3    Percentage of conventional letters in the written
             production of younger and older kindergarteners              48

Table 3.4    Number of written signs used to represent words
             by younger and older kindergarteners                         49

Table 3.5    Maximum of written signs used to represent words
             in younger and older kindergarteners                         49

Table 3.6    Variety of signs used in the whole written
             production: mean of children's sign repertoire               49

Table 3.7    Towards internal variation in writing words:
             percentage of writing patterns                               50

Table 3.8    Phonetic differentiation of phonetically-related
             words in the written production of younger and
             older kindergarteners                                        52

Table 3.9    Semantically influenced differentiation in written
             production of younger and older kindergarteners              53

Table 4.1    Mean percentage of acceptable pronunciation of
             the target non-words made by the children when
             they were age 9 years                                        63

Table 4.2    Mean percentage of acceptable pronunciation of
             the target non-words made by the children when
             they were age 10 years                                       63

Table 9.1    Teachers' interview results over five sessions              118

Table 12.1   Teachers' concepts of literacy                              175

Table 12.2   Differences in primary and secondary teachers'
             concepts of literacy                                        176

**Figures**

Figure 1.1   Interactive model: sources of knowledge operating
             in parallel when text is read                                   11
Figure 1.2   Guessing words from context cues                                17
Figure 1.3   Reading task demonstrating that words are
             processed automatically when known                             19
Figure 4.1   Mean percentage of non-words read with a regular
             pronunciation singly and in the two contexts                   64
Figure 4.2   Mean percentage of non-words read with an
             exception pronunciation singly and in the two
             contexts                                                        64
Figure 5.1   Reading methods in Hungary                                      77
Figure 6.1   Corrective reading gains January–June 1990 for
             fourteen pupils year 7 (11–12 years)                           86
Figure 11.1  Initial student teachers' views of what counts as
             being able to read (views at beginning of training
             course)                                                        143
Figure 11.2  Jansen's model                                                 146
Figure 11.3  Guidelines and emphases                                       151
Figure 11.4  Levels of experience and modes of experiencing
             as strata of cognition                                        153
Figure 12.1  Adult–child proximation through literacy learning             172

# Abbreviations

| | |
|---|---|
| ALE | Apprentissage Langue Ecrite |
| ANOVA | Analysis of Variance |
| APU | Assessment of Performance Unit |
| AT | Attainment Target |
| BAS | British Ability Scales |
| CATE | Council for the Accreditation of Teacher Education |
| DARTS | Directed Activities Related to Text |
| DDPT | Differential Diagnosis Prescriptive Teaching |
| DES | Department of Education and Science |
| DfE | Department for Education |
| DISTAR | Direct Instruction System for Teaching Arithmetic and Reading Program |
| DPR | Diagnostic Prescriptive Remediation |
| EC | European Council |
| ESRC | Economic and Social Science Research Council |
| FRG | Family Reading Group |
| HMI | Her Majesty's Inspectorate |
| IEA | International Association for the Evaluation of Educational Achievement |
| IEDPE | L'Institut Européen pour le Développement des Potentialités de tous les Enfants |
| ITPA | Illinois Test of Psycholinguistic Abilities |
| IQ | Intelligence Quotient |
| LINC | Language in the National Curriculum |
| NFER | National Foundation for Educational Research |
| LEA | Local Educational Authority |
| NCC | National Curriculum Council |
| PAS | Phonic-Analytic-Synthetic |
| PGCE | Post Graduate Certificate of Education |
| P/L | Perceptual-Linguistic |
| RA | Reading Ability |
| SCAA | School Curriculum and Assessment Authority |
| SD | Standard Deviation |
| SEAC | Schools Examinations and Assessment Council |
| SED | Scottish Education Department |

SRA       Science Research Association
TV        Television
UK        United Kingdom
USA       United States of America
VAKT      Visual, Auditary, Kinaesthetic, Tactile
ZPD       Zone of Proximal Development

# Introduction: International Concerns and Controversies

*P. Pumfrey and P. Owen*

## Summary

The perceived importance of literacy in general and reading in particular is common in societies across the world. Despite contextual differences, there are numerous common concerns and controversies. From these, three areas are identified. The first is developing an improved understanding of the nature of children's early reading development. The second is the consideration of ways in which children's reading can be encouraged. Finally, issues of assessment in the context of accountability are addressed. The first of these concerns is addressed under the heading of 'The Importance of Phonological Awareness' and 'Wider Concerns', in Volume 1. (The other two issues of curriculum and assessment, respectively are addressed in Volume 2.)

How much is the ability to read worth? To be illiterate in most contemporary societies is to be marginalized and disadvantaged. Anyone who arrives in a country where lack of knowledge of the language prevents their reading the most basic written signs, will appreciate the metaphorical imprisonments attributable to their ignorance of the language. Literacy is both a contributor to, and an amplifier of, human abilities. To argue that, in the era of information technology, learning to read is preparing children for the nineteenth rather than the twenty-first century, is to misunderstand the nature of human thought and its development. Literacy liberates.

In countries across the world, standards of literacy and the processes underpinning them are of central interest to politicians, parents, professionals and pupils. The editors and contributors to this series are well aware of the controversial, complex, interrelated and changing nature of views held concerning the receptive and expressive aspects of language involved in the emergence and development of literacy. Our focus on reading does not deny the importance of other modes of language. Reading is but one facet of literacy;

literacy merely one component of communication and communication one part of child development.

Optimizing pupils' reading attainments depends crucially on professionals' understanding of child development and the conditions that facilitate reading as a thinking process. In this there are reciprocal relationships between advances in theory, research and practice. Mutual benefits are likely to accrue when professionals from different countries and disciplines are able to identify literacy-related issues of common concern and share experiences of promising developments. For all teachers, knowing *why* we use particular methods and materials and their effectiveness in specified circumstances, integrates theory, its applications and their evalution.

Moves towards an interactive model integrating the unjustifiably polarized 'top-down' versus 'bottom-up' positions concerning the nature of emergent reading, its development, teaching and assessment are taking place. In respect of the first two of these, Chapter 1 in Volume 1 provides a constructive synthesis. This does not mean that important controversies do not continue. In the advancement of knowledge in all fields, the dialectic involving hypothesis, antithesis and synthesis is ever alive. The liveliness of the continuing debate on, for example, emergent and developing reading is immediately apparent when one compares the stances represented in Chapters 6 and 7 in Volume 1. The same is true in relation to assessment issues addressed in Chapters 7 to 12 in Volume 2.

In considering the merits of the cases presented in each of the chapters in both volumes, it is important to identify the author's implicit or explicit assumptions concerning the nature of reading, its development, teaching and assessment (for example, Volume 2, Chapter 2). The theoretical coherence of a contributor's case can also be considered in relation to the quality and extent of evidence adduced in support. Further, in the interests of reaching a balanced judgment, a consideration of the contributions made by different authors based on alternative theoretical stances and from different professional specialisms cannot be ignored.

Some of the chapters are based on researches carried out over many years and with considerable numbers of subjects; others report recent findings from smaller scale studies. Some chapters are descriptive of what is deemed promising practice. For example, Chapter 9, Volume 1 describes how much can be gained from careful observation of the practices of experienced classroom teachers followed by discussion and reflection. This approach requires a spirit of mutual cooperation and sensitivity but no formal research design or sophisticated data analysis in the statistical sense. Teachers can be their own best mentors. The simple strategy outlined is an excellent means whereby the expertise of experienced teachers can be communicated to colleagues. Similarly, students in initial training can benefit whether in the role of teacher or observer.

With confidence, we assert that no individual has a freehold on validity. The words of Bacon (1561–1626) continue to give important messages.

Read not to contradict and confute, nor to believe and take for granted, nor to find talk and discourse, but to weigh and consider. (Bacon 1561–1626: Essay 50 'Of Studies')

There are three major common concerns of those professionals involved in how children become literate and by what means such achievements can be appraised. These are:

- developing understanding of the nature of children's emergent reading;
- considering ways in which children's emergent and subsequent reading can be developed; and
- the assessment of reading standards.

From these major concerns, evidence drawn from the work of colleagues in many countries suggests that shared understandings are gradually emerging from research and practice. Inevitably, there are also ongoing theoretical controversies that have important implications for practice in the classroom. As noted above, the 'top–down' versus 'bottom–up' theories of reading development exemplify one controversy that appears to be nearing a resolution in an interactive model. These (inevitably partial) understandings cannot be ignored if we are to increase our ability to conceptualize, control and optimize the development of children's standards of literacy in general and reading in particular.

There is no claim that collectively the specific topics addressed by contributors represent a comprehensive coverage of critical issues. However, to remain unaware of the work being done in countries other than one's own would be irresponsibly insular. There is a growing consensus that, irrespective of the country, culture or language, the topics identified above merit inclusion in both the initial training of teachers and in continuing professional development.

This series is distinctive on the combined basis of four major counts. Firstly, it is internationally oriented. It provides a somewhat overlooked international perspectives on the three issues identified above. Evidence drawn from the following countries is presented: Australia; Canada; Denmark; England; France; Germany; Greece; Guam; Hungary; Israel; Italy; Jamaica; Japan; New Zealand; Northern Ireland; Scotland; Spain; and the USA. Reports on reading attainments across the thirty-two school systems and twenty-one language groups included in the International Association for the Evaluation of Educational Achievement (IEA) reading-literacy study are also reported and discussed.

Secondly, it is interdisciplinary. Professionals from complementary fields describe promising developments from their respective viewpoints: teachers; teacher-trainers; psychologists; advisers; inspectors; administrators; statisticians; and research workers.

Thirdly, it contains messages for teachers and mentors concerning their regular work with pupils on encouraging literacy. In relation to improving and assessing reading, it combines *what* can profitably be done with *why* this is the case.

Fourthly, it addresses international issues of accountability. Research studies and promising classroom practice from around the world are reported highlighting implications for the design, implementation, improvement and evaluation of reading programmes.

With the increasingly multicultural character of societies across the world, the two volumes are planned to appeal to an international readership, although predominantly in English-speaking countries. It is expected that the contents of both books will be of interest, albeit differentially, to the following groups.

- Teachers in mainstream primary schools;
- Teachers in special schools and units;
- LEA advisory and support staff;
- Educational and child psychologists;
- Students on initial teacher-training courses;
- Teacher-trainers and school-based mentors; and
- Research workers.

The strength of the two volumes is that they bring together, under the three international concerns identified, the work of professionals in different countries. Volumes 1 and 2 provide complementary information from colleagues with similar professional concerns working in different cultural contexts. The aim is to build bridges between theory, research and practice.

The genesis of this two-volume series derives from the editors' longstanding involvements in seeking to understand more fully, and thereby improve, the learning and teaching of literacy in general and reading attainments and progress in particular, of pupils in schools. Our work as teachers in mainstream secondary and primary schools, special schools and units, language and reading specialists in support services, research workers, academics and authors provides the basis for our involvements. Our contributions to initial training courses taken by teachers, coupled with the provision of courses of advanced training for qualified and experienced teachers, underline our personal commitments.

Over many years, our activities have led to the establishment of extensive professional contacts with colleagues in many countries engaged in similar work. Reflecting on our wide network of contacts and on common professional concerns and controversies, led to the present two volumes.

In the twenty-four chapters comprising this series, we have presented a selection of articles that provide information on research and practice. Each book is in two parts. Part 1 in Volume 1 concerns the importance of phonological awareness. Part 2 addresses wider concerns related to the development of children's reading. In Volume 2, Part 1 focuses on curriculum concerns and Part 2 deals with aspects of accountability and assessment. These contributions bear on some of the most important current concerns and controversies from the broad fields constituting emergent and developing reading and curriculum and assessment issues. Each of the chapters has a common structure. All authors have identified from their contributions a number of important 'messages for teachers'.

In Volume 1, the six chapters in part 1 focus on the importance of phonological awareness in emergent and early reading. In part 2 six contributions address wider concerns, including new moves towards early literacy learning in Europe, children's understanding of reading prior to attending school, the role of the teacher and contrasting conceptions of literacy in primary and secondary schools.

*Part 1*

# *The Importance of Phonological Awareness*

# Chapter 1

# The Emergence of Word Reading in Beginning Reading

*L. Ehri*

**Summary**

There are various ways to read words: by sight, by phonological or orthographic 'recoding', by analogizing, and by contextual guessing. This chapter considers the processes that beginners use to read words and how these processes change as the reader's general phonological and orthographic knowledge grows. Evidence is presented indicating that in order for sight word reading to develop into a mature form, learners must acquire and apply knowledge of the alphabetic system.

**Introduction**

Whole language instruction has gained a strong following among primary-grade teachers in today's schools (Gursky, 1991). One feature making whole-language instruction attractive is that the reading and writing activities are meaningful and interesting not only to students but also to teachers. However, a weakness of this approach is the absence of systematic phonics instruction during the first year of reading instruction.[1] Some attention is paid to letter–sound relationships as students attempt to invent spellings during journal writing and as teachers read big books and stop to point out initial letters and sounds in salient words. However, care is not taken to insure that each student masters the alphabetic system by learning all the letter shapes and names, learning which sounds they typically symbolize in words, learning how to segment words into sounds, and learning how to blend the sounds of letters to form words. Studies indicate that students who fall behind in learning to read often do so because they have not acquired sufficient, working knowledge of the alphabetic system. Because this learning is difficult for them, they do not pick it up simply by being exposed to print (Juel, Griffith and Gough, 1986; Stanovich, 1986; Wagner and Torgeson, 1987; Juel, 1988).

This chapter suggests that to become effective instructors of beginning reading, kindergarten and first-grade teachers need to understand the course of development that beginners follow when they learn to read, and how to assess whether these processes are developing adequately in individual students. With this knowledge, teachers are in a better position to make instructional decisions. Very recently our knowledge about reading processes and their development has advanced significantly as a result of research investigating these processes. (For summaries of this research, see Anderson *et al.*, 1985; Adams, 1990; Barr, Kamil, Mosenthal and Pearson, 1991; Brady and Shankweiler, 1991; Gough, Ehri and Treiman, 1992). The chapter below reviews what we have learned from research about the development of reading processes, including the various ways that words are read, how word reading fits into text reading, and what processes are needed in order for novices to make progress in learning to read.

One all-too-common approach to educating teachers about how to teach reading is to give them a list of do's and don'ts. For example, whole language advocates tell teachers that instruction in reading should be meaning-based, students should write daily in journals, and they should do lots of silent and oral reading of real literature. Students should not read words in isolation on flash cards, and they should never read non-words. Also prohibited are worksheets, phonics drills, memorization, direct instruction and practice on component processes of reading, and giving tests to see what students have learned about reading and its components. Likewise, advocates of phonics instruction offer lists of do's and don'ts. They may tell teachers that students should never hear letter–sound relations pronounced in isolation but only in the context of words. Or they may assert that students should not be allowed to guess words they are reading in text but should always stop and sound them out. Typically prescriptions and proscriptions are presented dogmatically without a full explanation of how these practices are related to the development of reading processes and without any research evidence. This 'do–don't' approach makes teachers heavily dependent upon authority for making instructional decisions, and it discourages them from relying upon their own knowledge, experience and judgment.

A better approach to educating teachers of reading is to help them acquire working knowledge about many aspects of reading acquisition. This knowledge should include processes that develop in learners, informal tests to observe whether these processes are developing in individual students, various instructional approaches, methods, and activities, and how they promote the development of processes (Ehri and Williams, in press). Teachers who have extensive knowledge about reading have a much greater chance of success. Moreover, teaching becomes a highly interesting challenge when you know what to expect from learners as they make progress, what problems might develop, and the best ways to resolve them. This chapter discusses some of the processes that I think teachers should know about indicating ways to assess their development in readers, and offering a sampling of instructional activities that hold promise of promoting their development.

*Figure 1.1: Interactive model: sources of knowledge operating in parallel when text is read*

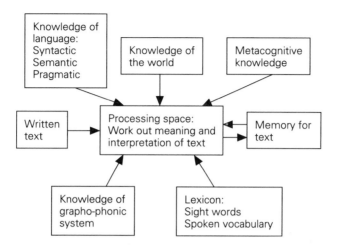

*Source*: adapted from Rumelhart (1977).

## Reading Processes and Their Development

When skilled readers read and understand text, many cognitive and linguistic processes operate concurrently and automatically in synchrony. The interactive model presented in Figure 1.1 depicts these mental processes. The centre box represents a central processor that receives and interprets information coming in from the eyes as lines of text are scanned. The boxes around the centre depict the various sources of information that are stored in memory and that enable readers to recognize and interpret text.

Knowledge of language enables readers to process sentences and their meanings. Knowledge of the world, including both encyclopedic and experiential knowledge, supplies readers with the background for understanding ideas and filling in parts that are left implicit and assumed known rather than stated explicitly in the text. Readers use their metacognitive knowledge to monitor the quality of their comprehension and to verify that the information makes sense and that it meets specific purposes. If problems are detected, corrective strategies may be implemented, such as re-reading or self-questioning (Baker and Brown, 1984). Memory for the text read up to that point enables readers to interpret incoming text in terms of previously processed meanings. Lexical knowledge refers to the reader's dictionary of words held in memory, those known in speech and those known in print by sight (Ehri, 1991, 1992). Accessing sight words in lexical memory is the principal way that readers recognize most words in text. Knowledge of the grapho-phonic system involves knowing how the spelling system symbolizes speech, including how letters can be transformed into blends of sounds to approximate known words

(Venezky, 1970). Readers use sounding out and blending processes to decode unfamiliar words.

Knowledge of language and knowledge of the world begin to develop during the preschool years before children move into independent reading (Goelman, Oberg and Smith, 1984; McGee and Richgels, 1990). The experience of listening to storybooks enables children to practise and become familiar with several reading processes, including the process of applying their linguistic knowledge and their world knowledge to understand text, the process of retaining text meanings in memory and drawing from this to interpret subsequent text. For books heard many times, children may learn to pretend to read the stories by memorizing the text and using pictures as prompts to recall text on each page (Sulzby, 1985). This may teach them about the structure of sentences that appear more frequently in text than in speech. There is evidence that young children's vocabularies grow from listening to storybooks (Robbins and Ehri, 1994). The development of metacognitive strategies is apparent when children ask questions to clarify the meanings of stories being read to them. It is important to recognize that even though preschoolers cannot read print on their own, the experience of listening to storybooks allows them to practise many of the processes that they will need in the future when they do learn to read print independently.

Various experiences may acquaint preschoolers with the squiggles constituting written language. When adults read books to children, they may slide their finger under the lines of print they are reading, and they may explain how print is structured. This shows children where book language comes from, and it corrects the misconception that adults are reading the pictures. Another source for learning about written language comes from environmental print. As preschoolers travel with parents to supermarkets, shopping malls, and restaurants, labels and signs that distinguish among stores and products may be pointed out, helping children learn what written forms of words look like (Mason, 1980; Masonheimer, Drum and Ehri, 1984). Letter knowledge emerges as adults name and point to alphabet letters in storybooks, alphabet books, and signs, and as they have children practise naming plastic magnetic letters clinging to the doors of their refrigerators and writing their own names (Mason, 1980).

Although bits and pieces of reading may appear in preschoolers, the bulk of reading skill of the sort that involves reading print independently emerges when reading is taught formally in the primary grades. By independent reading, is meant the ability to read words and text from written forms without the aid of pictures or other non-alphabetic prompts. This involves acquiring the two knowledge sources depicted at the bottom of Figure 1.1, and learning to integrate all the knowledge sources in Figure 1.1 to read text fluently (Chall, 1983).

### Ways to Read Words

When beginners learn to read English, their eyes encounter three types of structural units that make contact with their knowledge of language: letters, words, and sentences. During the course of learning to read, the eyes come to favour written words. The advantage of words over sentences is that words can be assimilated in one glance. The advantage of words over letters is that written words correspond more reliably to spoken words than letters correspond to sounds. Many years ago, Cattell (1886) found that skilled readers can recognize a whole word as quickly as they can recognize a single letter, and in fact they can name a word faster than a letter. Since words are the primary units of written language for learners, it is essential for teachers to understand how words are read and how word-reading skill develops.

At least five ways to read words can be distinguished: by sight, by sounding out and blending letters, by analogizing to known words, by pronouncing common spelling patterns, and by using context cues. In each case the processes differ (Ehri, 1991, 1994). As readers attain skill, they learn to read words in all five ways.

When readers read words *by sight* they access information about the words stored in lexical memory from previous experiences of reading the words. This process is used to read words that have been read several times before. Sight of the written word triggers its spelling, pronunciation and meaning immediately in memory without any sounding out or blending required. Reitsma (1983) found that on average, beginning readers in first grade needed four experiences of reading the individual words to store them as sight words in memory. You can tell when readers are reading words by sight because they read the words as whole units, with no pauses between sounds, and they read the words within one second of seeing them.

My research demonstrates that the traditional way of viewing sight word learning, as rote memorization of the visual forms of words, is incorrect (Ehri and Wilce, 1979, 1980a and b, 1983, 1985, 1987a, 1987b). Skilled readers do not read sight words by memorizing associations between the shapes of words and their meanings. This view is incapable of explaining how skilled readers can recognize in an instant any one of the thousands of words that they know by sight and how they can learn to read new sight words with very little practice (Ehri, 1992).

These findings indicate that sight words are secured in memory through the application of letter-sound knowledge. The process of learning individual sight words involves forming associations between particular spellings of words and their pronunciation–meaning amalgams by applying knowledge of letter-sound relations. Readers remember how to read a specific word by interpreting letters they see in a spelling as symbols for sounds they detect in the pronunciation of the word. For example, the initial letter G in 'giggle' gets remembered as the sound /g/ rather than /j/ because the pronunciation of the word specifies /g/; I is remembered as /i/, GG as /g/, LE as /ul/.[2] In this way, the spelling is bonded to a pronunciation–meaning amalgam and stored in memory.[3] The next time the reader sees the word, he or she can retrieve the spelling–pronunciation–meaning amalgam from memory to read it. Knowledge of letter-sound relations provides the powerful mnemonic system that

Table 1.1: Ways that words and pseudowords might be read by readers

| By Sight[a] | By Sounding out/Blending[b] | By Analogy[c] | By Spelling pattern[d] |
|---|---|---|---|
| break | goan | greak | tain |
| busy | taich | fusy | goach |
| sugar | soag | tugar | joal |
| none | vep | jone | sug |
| prove | fiss | brove | vess |
| yacht | jul | bacht | fip |
| calf | paig | dalf | chail |
| suede | chol | nuede | pog |
| react | leck | leact | juck |
| island | juf | disland | lef |
| tongue | choub | fongue | foud |
| depot | fod | nepot | chob |
| bouquet | paf | souquet | vag |
| fiance | veeg | riance | peef |
| guitar | haip | fuitar | hain |
| chauffeur | foon | mauffeur | foop |
| rhythm | vud | chythm | jub |
| heights | jeeb | beights | veed |

Notes:
[a] Words from Adams and Huggins (1985) list.
[b] Pseudowords with uncommon spelling patterns (Treiman et al., 1990)
[c] Pseudowords created by changing the initial letter of sight words in Column 1. Analogy and sounding out strategies yield different pronunciations.
[d] Pseudowords with common spellings patterns (Treiman et al., 1990)

bonds the written forms of specific words to their pronunciations in memory. Once the system is known, readers can learn to read words and build a lexicon of sight words easily.

Adams and Huggins (1985) studied sight word reading by selecting fifty words that had to be known by sight to be read correctly, words such as 'ocean', 'bouquet', 'aisle', and 'busy', which could not be sounded out because of their irregular spellings. The words were ordered by frequency of occurrence in text so that easier words preceded harder words. Examples of the words are listed in the first column in Table 1.1. Adams and Huggins found that students in Grades 2–5 typically read words accurately until they reached a point in the list where the words became unfamiliar (i.e., not in their sight vocabularies). At this point readers shifted from sight word reading to sounding out and blending which caused them to hesitate and often misread the words (e.g., pronouncing 'tongue' as /ton/-/gyu/ ). These findings document the process of sight word reading. Readers use this approach to read not just irregular words but all words that have been practised sufficiently to become established in their lexical memory. Assessing readers' store of sight words can be used to decide whether a specific text is within their reading ability. Texts that contain 90 per cent of sight words can be read by children independently (Johns, 1978).

Another way to read words is by *sounding out letters and blending them into pronunciations that approximate real words* (also referred to as phonological recoding) (Venezky, 1970; Venezky and Johnson, 1973; Marsh *et al.*, 1981; Beck, 1981; Ehri, 1991). This is a strategy that readers can employ to read words they have never seen before. To use this strategy requires knowing how letters typically symbolize sounds in words, not only single letters but digraphs such as TH, SH, EA, OU. Phonological recoding is a slower way of reading words than sight word reading and tends to emerge later during development (Ehri and Wilce, 1983) although this may depend upon how reading is taught (Wimmer and Hummer, 1990). Disabled readers have special difficulty learning to recode words phonologically (Ehri and Wilce, 1983; Rack, Snowling and Olson, 1992). The best way to assess readers' recoding ability is to have them read pseudowords which cannot be read by sight because they have never been read before. Table 1.1 also lists pseudowords with uncommon spelling patterns taken from a study by Treiman, Goswami and Bruck (1990).

An alternative way to read unfamiliar words is to read them *by analogy to known words*, that is, by recognizing spelling similarities between new and known words (Marsh *et al.*, 1981; Goswami, 1986; Goswami and Bryant, 1990). In looking at a word never read before, readers may notice that a part of it resembles a known sight word. They access the similar sight word in their lexicons and then adjust the pronunciation to accommodate the new word, for example, reading 'peak' by analogy to 'beak' or 'fight' by analogy to 'night'. This is an easier way for beginners to read words than phonological recoding because it requires blending fewer subword units to make the word, P plus -EAK, rather than P + EA + K.

To read words by analogy to known sight words requires that beginners have some rudimentary decoding skill (Ehri and Robbins, 1992). They have to have enough knowledge so that they can recognize how letters correspond to sounds in the known and new words and how to blend the subunits (e.g., P + EAK). Also they need sufficient letter-sound knowledge to be able to store the sight words in memory by bonding spellings to pronunciations in the way described above.

In the third column of Table 1.1 appears a list of pseudowords that if read by analogy to real words are pronounced one way and if read by sounding out and blending are pronounced another way. Read them to see which way you pronounce them. The footnote in the table explains the two solutions.

Another way to read unfamiliar words is *by detecting and pronouncing familiar spelling patterns*. This process is later to emerge, after readers have learned a number of sight words. To establish spelling patterns as familiar units in memory, readers must first acquire a sight vocabulary consisting of several words exhibiting the same spelling patterns (e.g., words sharing stems such as -ICK, -ANK, -INE), and they must recognize how the common letter sequences are pronounced as single blends. Treiman *et al.* (1990) found that beginners were more accurate in reading nonwords with stems common to several other words than nonwords with uncommon stems. Examples of their common-stem nonwords are listed in the last column in Table 1.1. Stahl, Osborn

Table 1.2: Set of rime spellings that can be used to derive nearly 500 primary-grade words

| -ack | -all | -ain | -ake | -ale | -ame | -an |
| -ank | -ap | -ash | -at | -ate | -aw | -ay |
| -eat | -ell | -est | -ice | -ick | -ide | -ight |
| -ill | -in | -ine | -ing | -ink | -ip | -ir |
| -ock | -oke | -op | -ore | -or | -uck | -ug |
| -ump | -unk | | | | | |

Notes: The rimes were taken from Stahl et al. (1990). These authors in turn took the list from Wylie and Durrell (1970).

and Lehr (1990) list thirty-seven rime stems that have stable pronunciations across words and can be used to derive nearly 500 primary-grade words. These are listed in Table 1.2.

One final way to read words is *by using context cues to guess words* (Goodman, 1965, 1976). As portrayed in Figure 1.1, readers can use their knowledge about language, their knowledge of the world, and their memory for the text already read, to guess the identity of some words as they read text. You can experience the value of context cues by attempting to read the words that are missing in the text (Robinson *et al.*, 1965) displayed in Figure 1.2. It is easy to guess function words such as 'to' and 'the' but hard to guess content words unless they have appeared in prior text, for example, 'farmer' and 'truck'. This way of reading words is evident in the oral reading errors (miscues) that readers produce when they read text aloud (Biemiller, 1970; Weber, 1970; Goodman, 1976; Leu, 1982; Allington, 1984). When words are misread, the words substituted will often fit the sentence structure and meaning, indicating that context influenced how the words were read. This approach is used mainly to read unfamiliar words (Carnine, Carnine and Gersten, 1984). Familiar words are recognized so quickly and automatically by sight that contextual expectations do not have time to facilitate the process (Stanovich, 1980; Perfetti, 1985).

To summarize, there are several ways to read words: by sight, by sounding out and blending, by analogy to known sight words, by pronouncing familiar spelling patterns, and by guessing from context. Which process is the primary one for any particular word depends upon whether readers have practised reading that word. Words sufficiently familiar in print are read by sight. Words unfamiliar in print are read using the other strategies.

## Reading Words in Text

Contextual guessing does not account for the way that readers read most words in text. Studies of the predictability of words in text indicate that on average 25 per cent to 30 per cent of the words can be guessed correctly. However, the most important content words are the least predictable, only 10 per cent correct (Gough and Walsh, 1991). Thus, to guess words effectively, most of the surrounding words in a text must be known. To read these

*Figure 1.2: Pages from a basal text in which every fifth word has been deleted to illustrate processes involved in guessing words based on context cues. Illustration from* Friends Old and New *(p. 190) by H. Robinson, M. Monroe, A. Artley, C. Huck, & W. Jenkins. Copyright 1965 by Scott, Foresman. Reprinted by permission. Text from* The Christian Science Monitor. *Copyright 1961 by The Christian Science Publishing Society. All rights reserved. Reprinted by permission.*

## The Little Gray Truck

It was time for ▇▇▇ Field to pick the ▇▇ on his farm.

With ▇ bang and a bump ▇▇ big ears of corn ▇▇ into his little gray ▇▇▇. At last there was ▇ more room in it. ▇▇ Farmer Field started off ▇ town with his corn.

▇▇▇ little gray truck was ▇ a hurry. It went ▇▇▇ down the old farm ▇▇▇ just as fast as ▇▇ wheels could turn.

*Source*: Page 190 from a Basal Text in *Friends Old and New* by H. Robinson, M. Monroe, A. Artley, C. Huck and W. Jenkins; Scott, Foresman and Co. Publishers.

accurately, a reader must use processes other than contextual guessing. Hence, this is not the major way that words are identified.

During text reading, all of these ways of reading words may contribute (Perfetti, 1985; Ehri, 1987). In the skilled reader, several different processes are thought to operate together in parallel. As readers' eyes fixate on words known by sight, the first process to fire is lexical access which happens quickly and automatically. This yields recognition of the word's meaning and pronunciation. Other processes do not lie dormant, however, but are activated as well and perform a confirmatory function. Knowledge of the grapho-phonic system confirms that the pronunciation, derived from lexical access, does fit the spelling pattern on the page. Knowledge sources involving language, the world, and text memory confirm that the meaning of the word fits into the sentence and is consistent with the text's meaning up to that point. The redundancy in the system that arises from several knowledge sources operating in parallel serves to maintain highly accurate reading, to make the reader sensitive to errors, and to provide a means of self correction when errors disrupt comprehension.

Whereas skilled readers have operational use of all these processes during text reading, disabled readers do not. They are most apt to be weak in their knowledge of the grapho-phonic system and in their sight vocabulary (Liberman and Shankweiler, 1979; Perfetti, 1985; Stanovich, 1986; Juel, Griffith and Gough, 1986; Ehri, 1989). As a result, their reading is not fully supported by all the knowledge sources. Stanovich (1980) provides evidence that disabled readers *compensate* for inadequate decoding and sight word reading by relying more heavily on word-guessing strategies. It is important for teachers to insure that beginners learn to use all of these sources adequately so their text reading is fully supported.

Currently, educators who advocate a whole-language approach to teaching reading (Goodman and Goodman, 1979) claim that use of context is the major way that readers read words in text and that this is what they should be taught to do skillfully. These educators ignore and do not provide instruction for the other ways to read words. In fact, Goodman (1976) claims that readers do not read individual words when they read text but rather use context cues and guess words. Only when they cannot guess a word do readers attend to letter cues in words. According to Goodman, having to attend to individual words to read them requires too much time and effort and subtracts attention from the processing of meaning.

Results of several studies reveal that this view is flawed because it fails to consider the process of reading words by sight (Stanovich, 1980, 1986; Perfetti, 1985; Ehri, 1991). Studies show that by the end of first grade, readers can recognize words by sight automatically without expending attention or effort. Beginners can look at a word and recognize its meaning instantly, even under conditions when they try to ignore the word (Golinkoff and Rosinski, 1976; Guttentag and Haith, 1978).

To experience automatic word recognition, look at Figure 1.3 and try labelling the pictures from left to right as rapidly as you can while ignoring the

*Figure 1.3:* Reading task demonstrating that words are processed automatically when known

*Source*: From "Learning to Read and Spell Words" by L.C. Ehri, *Journal of Reading Behavior*, *19*, 5–11. Copyright 1987 by National Reading Conference. Reprinted by permission.
*Note*: The reader's task is to ignore the words and name the pictures from left to right as rapidly as possible. Use of this task in research studies has shown that readers who know the written words by sight cannot ignore them. The words are processed inadvertently and slow them down in naming the pictures, indicating that readers process the words automatically without attention or effort.

words printed on the pictures. You will find that you cannot ignore the words, indicating that your mind is processing them automatically. Reading words automatically by sight is much faster and more accurate than reading words by sampling letter cues and guessing. Also it is much less time-consuming and involves much less conscious attention. Findings of several studies (Stanovich, 1980, 1986) indicate that effective sight word reading, not effective use of context cues to guess words, lies behind effective text reading.

### The Development of Word Reading

Suppose you measured various capabilities and experiences of children entering kindergarten without any reading ability, for example, their knowledge of vocabulary words, their IQs, the number of books read to them by parents, the education level and socio-economic status of parents, their knowledge of nursery rhymes, the number of hours spent watching TV each week, their knowledge of letter names and their ability to segment spoken words into sounds. You waited for two years while they acquired reading skill in school, and then you measured their reading ability. Which of the capabilities would best predict their reading achievement? Various researchers have done this and have found that letter-name knowledge and sound-segmentation skill are the best predictors, better than all the others (Chall, 1967; Share *et al.*, 1984). These capabilities stand at the gate of reading acquisition and screen who is admitted and who is not. Although other capabilities may contribute to reading skill as well, they do not have a chance to exert an impact if beginners cannot get through the gate by knowing letters and how to segment. The reason why these two capabilities are so important is that they are needed for learning to read words in the various ways described above (Ehri, 1992).

Ehri (1991, 1994) divides the course of development of word-reading processes into four phases, (1) a visual cue phase, (2) a rudimentary alphabetic phase, (3) a mature alphabetic phase, and (4) a spelling-pattern phase. During the *visual cue phase*, readers memorize visual, contextual, or graphic features of words to remember how to read them. They do not use letter–sound relations. During the *two alphabetic phases*, readers use letter–sound correspondences to read words. Alphabetic processing is considered *rudimentary* when readers process only some of the letters and sounds in words, for example, initial and final letters. Alphabetic processing is considered *mature* when readers process all of the letters and sounds in words. The *spelling-pattern phase* emerges after readers have had sufficient experience processing words alphabetically to learn which letters combine frequently in different words and how they are pronounced. In this phase, familiar spelling patterns along with letter–sound knowledge are used to read words.

Visual cue reading portrays how emergent readers process words. It is an immature process adopted by children who know little about letter–sound relations and how to segment words into sounds (Byrne, 1992). Lacking letter knowledge, they use whatever cues are visually salient in or around words to remember how to read them, for example, the golden arches behind the sign saying 'MacDonald's', the two tall posts in the middle of the spelling of 'yellow', the tail at the end of the spelling of 'dog'. If they remember any letters in words, it is not because they interpret the letters as symbolizing sounds in the words. Masonheimer, Drum and Ehri (1984) examined visual-cue readers' awareness of letters in environmental print they could read. They found that when the youngsters were shown familiar signs with one of the letters altered (e.g., XEPSI for PEPSI), they read them as if nothing had changed. This indicates that visual-cue readers do not necessarily use letter cues to remember how to read environmental print.

Studies of visual-cue reading reveal that the associations remembered are between print and meanings rather than between print and specific pronunciations. 'Crest' might be read as 'toothpaste' or 'brush teeth', indicating that letter–sound ties in the spelling do not constrain the word accessed in memory (Harste, Burke and Woodward, 1982). Studies also indicate that visual-cue readers have trouble remembering how to read words for any length of time when the words lack distinctive context cues and are read from alphabetic print alone (Mason, 1980). When presented with words they have never read before, visual-cue readers have no way of reading them except by guessing the words from context cues. For example, if shown a picture of a car drawn above the word TIRE, visual-cue readers will guess that the word says 'car' and remain oblivious to the letter discrepancy. Visual-cue readers know how to read too few words to be able to read text other than by pretend reading through memorization.

The rudimentary alphabetic phase becomes possible when beginners learn about letter–name or letter–sound relations and about how to segment initial sounds in words. With this knowledge, they can use partial alphabetic cues to remember how to read words by sight. I have called this *phonetic-cue reading*. For example, they might remember how to read 'milk' by bonding the initial and final letters M and K to the beginning and ending sounds /m/ and /k/ in the pronunciation. Several studies (Ehri and Wilce, 1985; Scott and Ehri, 1989) show that, whereas visual-cue readers learn to read words most easily when they contain salient visual cues, phonetic-cue readers learn to read words most easily when letters symbolize salient sounds in the words. In one study, beginners were taught visually salient spellings (e.g., wBc to stand for 'giraffe') and phonetically salient spellings (e.g., LFT for 'elephant'). Results showed that the former type was easier for visual-cue readers to learn to read whereas the latter type was easier for phonetic-cue readers to learn.

Mason (1980) showed that phonetic-cue readers can remember how to read words when the words lack any context and must be read from their alphabetic forms alone. If shown words they have never read before, phonetic-cue readers may mistake the new words for known sight words if the words share some of the same letters (Ehri and Wilce, 1987a, 1987b). Phonetic-cue readers can build a sight vocabulary that is sufficient to support the reading of text composed of those words. However, unfamiliar words must be guessed from context because phonetic-cue readers lack the sounding out and blending skill needed to figure out unknown words. In recent studies, we have found that older disabled readers exhibit characteristics of phonetic-cue reading (Ehri and Saltmarsh, 1991).

When beginners acquire more complete knowledge about how the alphabetic system symbolizes speech, including how the vowel spelling system works and how digraphs such as CH, TH, EA, symbolize sounds, they advance to the mature alphabetic phase of reading words (Ehri, 1991). They become skilled at sounding out and blending unfamiliar words. They add words to their sight vocabulary by processing and remembering how all of the letters in a word's spelling symbolize sounds detected in the word's pronunciation. For example, MILK is fully analysed as M-/m/, I-/i/, L-/l/, and K-/k/ when the spelling is bonded to the pronunciation in memory.

The process of bonding spellings to pronunciations of specific words may influence the sounds that mature alphabetic readers believe constitute words (Ehri and Wilce, 1980b; 1986). For example, the spelling of PITCH may cause readers to conceptualize a /t/ sound in the pronunciation that is not thought of as being present in RICH. Learning the spelling of FAMILY may induce readers to believe that the pronunciation consists of three syllables, /fam/-/i/-/ly/ rather than two, /fam/-/ly/. To the extent that readers can justify the presence of letters in spellings by recognizing how they symbolize sounds in the word's pronunciation, they can bond the full spelling to the pronunciation and retain letter information in memory as they learn to read words by sight (Ehri, 1992).

The sight vocabulary of mature alphabetic readers grows rapidly as readers process new words in their reading. Their word reading is highly accurate and they do not often mistake similarly spelled words, unlike phonetic-cue readers. This is because fairly complete letter-based representations of the sight words are bonded to pronunciations in memory.

As more words are added to the sight vocabularies of mature alphabetic readers and as they practise sounding out and blending letter combinations, the spelling pattern phase of word reading emerges. Pronunciations of common letter sequences become known as units. These units make the task of reading unfamiliar words easier, particularly multisyllabic words. For example, fewer subunits must be blended to read the word 'infuriate' if readers recognize familiar spelling patterns within the word, such as IN, FUR, and ATE, and how to pronounce them, than if each letter must be sounded out and blended. Also fewer units are required to bond spellings to pronunciations in learning to read multisyllabic words by sight.

During this phase, readers may learn to associate some spelling patterns with meanings, for example, UN-, -TION, -ED, -ING, -ABLE. Instruction that teaches readers about roots of words, prefixes and suffixes and that distinguishes patterns in terms of language origins, for example, Greek, Latin, and Anglo-Saxon, serves to enhance the learning of spelling patterns and their utility for reading words (Henry, 1989; Templeton, 1992).

## Messages for Teachers

The four phases described above are useful for characterizing the development of word-reading processes. Knowing about these can tell teachers what to look for as signs of development and what processes need to be in place before others can be expected to emerge. In considering what teachers might do to insure that word-reading processes develop various activities are suggested. However, this should not be construed as a prescription for teaching reading. These activities illustrate some ways that objectives might be accomplished. There are other ways as well. Moreover, learning to read skilfully involves more than learning to read words.

To prepare students for the rudimentary alphabetic phase of reading, they need to learn how to name and write letters. During the preschool years, parents can contribute by reading alphabet books to children, pointing out letters in environmental print, singing the alphabet song, teaching children to name the letters and to write their own names, and so forth. Also, adults can engage children in playing sound games that involve finding rhyming words, finding words that begin with the same sounds, dividing words into sounds. In this way adults can help children learn to detach the form of language from its meaning and to focus on sounds. To the extent that such informal pre-school experiences provide children with letter knowledge and sound seg-mentation ability, they will be better prepared for learning to read independently when they begin formal instruction in school.

During the preschool years, it is important for children to experience reading in various contexts, for example, identifying environmental print, lis-tening to storybooks, hearing letters sent by relatives. In this way, children become aware of the act of reading, they learn about its purposes, they ob-serve what people do when they read, and so forth. These experiences serve to orient children so that when they receive formal instruction in school, they know where they are headed and what to expect (Dyson, 1984).

Activities performed during shared book reading can introduce preschoolers to the structure of print and how spoken language is represented in print (Holdaway, 1979). Once children are familiar with a storybook, adults can slow down their reading of the story enough to fingerpoint read the lines of text. This involves pointing to each word as it is read. Such a procedure supplemented by explanations can reveal many things to beginners: where the text begins and ends on a page, how lines of text run from left to right, how meaningful speech can be analysed into words, syllables, and punctuation marks. As a result, preschoolers may begin to grasp how written language cor-responds to spoken language. However, studies show that preschoolers who have memorized a text cannot learn to fingerpoint read that text themselves simply by watching someone else do it. In order to track speech in print at the level of words, they need to know how to segment initial sounds in words and how to represent the sounds with letters (Ehri and Sweet, 1991; Morris, 1992).

Because letter knowledge and sound awareness are so important for learn-ing to read, kindergarten and first-grade teachers need to identify and work with those children who lack this knowledge. Letter mnemonics are useful for helping children learn the shapes of letters and how to associate them with sounds. This is shown in a study where children were taught to associate each letter shape with the name of an object that was shaped like the letter and that had a name beginning with that letter's sound (e.g., S drawn like 'snake' beginning with /s/, T drawn like 'table' beginning with /t/) (Ehri, Deffner and Wilce, 1984). It was found that this procedure taught letter–sound associations more effectively than other procedures such as learning pictures unrelated to the shapes of letters or simply rehearsing the letter–sound associations. A very popular programme to teach letters in British kindergartens is 'Letterland' (Wendon, 1990, 1992) which makes extensive use of mnemonics.

It is important to recognize that if students already know the names of letters, it is easy to teach them the letter–sound relations that are present in the names, for example, /b/ in B (bee), /j/ in J (jay), /m/ in M (em). Most letters, in fact, have a relevant sound in their names. Mnemonics would not be needed to teach these associations.

Once children learn the names or sounds of several letters, then they can begin to use their letter knowledge to invent spellings of words for the purpose of conveying meaning in print (Read, 1971). Teachers can use the task of inventing spellings to get children analysing sounds in words and finding letters to symbolize those sounds. It is important for teachers to intervene and help students detect all of the sounds in words and to pick appropriate letters for those sounds. Sounds needing special attention are consonant blends, for example, /bl/, /st/, /str/, which are difficult to separate because they are pronounced together so quickly.

Children having trouble learning to read often find the task of segmenting sounds in words especially difficult. One way to ease the task is to teach students how to monitor the articulatory movements occurring in their mouths when they pronounce words, for example, recognizing that there are three mouth positions involved in saying 'bad': (1) lips closed for /b/, (2) mouth open for /a/, (3) tongue touching the roof of the mouth for /d/ (Lindamood and Lindamood, 1975). By locating the sounds of words in their mouths, beginners are provided with a basis that is more tangible and easier to scrutinize than that coming into their ears. Acoustic features of speech are ephemeral and disappear quickly.

Various researchers such as Henderson (1985) and Treiman (1993) have studied the course of development of invented spellings. In spelling the sounds they hear in words, children progress from representing only some of the sounds (e.g., YL for 'while', JRF for 'giraffe') to representing all the sounds (e.g., WIL, JERAF). The letters they choose progress from non-conventional symbols for sounds (e.g., JREM for 'dream', SGAT for 'skate') to more conventional symbols (e.g., DREM, SCAT). When children learn the regularities of the spelling system, they have a much easier time remembering the correct spellings of individual words (Ehri, 1986).

Once children have some knowledge of letter–sound relations, they can begin to build a sight vocabulary. This is done mainly by reading meaningful text that is written at their level (i.e., about 90 per cent sight words, 10 per cent unfamiliar words). As readers enounter new words in text, as they pronounce them and recognize their meanings, and as they analyse how the spellings match up to the pronunciations so that the two become bonded, they begin to establish the new words as sight words in memory. At the outset, this learning may be helped by having students keep a set of cards printed with the words they have learned to read in text. The cards can be reviewed, combined to form sentences, analysed and sorted for letter–sound similarities, and so forth. One technique used in the Reading Recovery programme (Clay, 1979, 1991) is to take selected words from stories just read and have children segment the letters to discover how they correspond to sounds in the words.

Studying newly learned words in these ways may make beginners more aware of constituent letters and may speed up sight word learning.

Teaching children the strategy of sounding out and blending words may be easier once they know how letters symbolize sounds, particularly vowel letters, and once they have learned a number of words by sight. This strategy is important for directing their attention to letter–sound relations within words. However, decoding English in this way may involve some trial and error and may not result in a recognizable word (e.g., the irregularly spelled sight words in Table 1.1). However, it is still a useful strategy to know. One skill readers must learn is how to blend consonants so that the vocalic element present when the sound is pronounced in isolation is deleted when it is blended with other sounds (e.g., pronouncing B as 'buh' in isolation vs. /b/ in 'blue').

Another strategy for reading words never read before is to teach children to look for familiar parts in the words, parts they know how to pronounce, for example, 'in', 'at', 'on'. A programme used at the Benchmark School in Pennsylvania teaches children several key words that are especially useful for decoding unknown words. These words are posted on the wall and become familiar sight words to the children (Gaskins *et al.*, 1988). Teachers can learn more about this approach by viewing a video tape obtainable from the Center for the Study of Reading at the University of Illinois.

Once beginners acquire working knowledge of the alphabetic system and once their sight-word lexicons begin to grow, then the best thing they can do to become more fluent readers is to practise reading and re-reading lots of stories and books that are appropriate for their sight-word level (Chall, 1983; Stanovich and West, 1989; Stanovich and Cunningham, 1992). Practice is also important for strengthening the strategies of sounding out/blending and reading by analogy so that both develop as effective ways to read unfamiliar words.

Assessing the various capabilities that are involved in reading words can be done with informal tests administered to individual students. In the Reading Recovery programme (Clay, 1979, 1991), informal assessment is considered an essential first step in working with a child and is called 'roaming around the known'. Periodic assessment is also important to verify that students are making the progress expected. The advantage of individual over group administered tests is that teachers can observe processes and strategies as well as products.

One important capability for teachers to examine in novices is their letter knowledge, that is, their ability to write and name both upper and lower-case letters. Whereas letter names can be elicited by presenting randomly ordered letters one at a time, this is not the best way to assess beginners' knowledge of letter–sound relations. Beginners are more apt to reveal what they know about letter-sounds in an invented spelling task. In this task, the teacher pronounces words the spellings of which are unfamiliar and asks students to write the sounds they hear in the words. The maturity of their invented spellings can be interpreted by comparing inventions to developmental examples given in

Gentry (1981), Morris and Perney (1984) and Henderson (1985). This task also reveals students' ability to segment words into constituent sounds.

To test children's sight vocabulary, teachers can use lists of words that are organized by grade level or words that their students have been exposed to in text (Harris and Jacobson, 1972). Words read within one second of seeing them are considered to be known by sight (Boder and Jarrico, 1982). Teachers can determine whether a book is within a child's reading capability by pointing to individual words selected at random on various pages and making sure that the child can read 90 per cent of the sampled words by sight.

It may be especially important to check children's ability to read high-frequency function words by sight, words such as the following: was, the, which, that, from, and, are, did, do, for, get, have, here, it, she, not, said, that, the, this, to, what, who, with. These words are crucial for reading and comprehending sentences in text. One study (Ehri and Wilce, 1980a), found that students needed to practise reading function words in meaningful text rather than in isolation on flash cards to learn to process their meanings.

Children's ability to use sounding out and analogy strategies can be assessed by giving them pseudowords containing letter–sound relations or letter parts that they are expected to know. Teachers who have not had their students practise reading words in isolation or reading pseudowords may be surprised at their students' success. This is because students do not have to practise word and pseudoword reading in isolation to develop these capabilities.

## Conclusion

This chapter has provided an overview of how word-reading processes develop during the first two grades and what this might mean for the teaching of reading. Much more could be said, not only about reading but also about spelling processes and how they contribute. In discussing how to teach reading neither a whole language nor a phonics list of do's and don'ts has been adhered to. Both lists oversimplify the solution to the problem of teaching reading effectively to all beginners, and both lists fall short in specifying how to teach all of the major processes involved in learning to read. It is important for teachers to move beyond lists and to acquire their own practice-based understanding of how reading processes develop and which instructional procedures are effective for developing which processes. Hopefully, teachers will become interested in the processes discussed above, will look further for additional information (Balmuth, 1982; Feitelson, 1988; Adams, 1990; Cunningham, 1991), and will not be put off by the technical language and jargon used in some research papers and books. One anticipates that teachers will try out some of the informal assessment tasks suggested in order to learn more about the extent of development of individual students and to detect those lagging behind and needing special help. By knowing what to expect regarding the course of development in beginners, by having tools to see whether individual readers are developing as expected, and by accumulating a repertoire of effective instructional procedures to move learners forward, teachers can achieve much success in fostering the growth of independent-reading skill in beginners.

### Notes

1.  By systematic phonics instruction, I mean instruction that follows a plan and is effective in providing students with working knowledge of the alphabetic system as it symbolizes speech so that students' word-reading competencies develop and mature. I am not subscribing to any particular way of teaching phonics. Rather in this chapter I attempt to specify the various grapho-phonic processes that students must be enabled to acquire in order to develop into mature readers. Systematic instruction may not be needed for students who enter school already knowing how to read but it must be provided for students who enter school with little of this knowledge, and teachers of beginning reading must know how to provide this instruction.
2.  I designate sounds in words by placing lower-case letters between slash marks. I represent spellings of words by placing words in quotation marks or in capital letters.
3.  It is necessary to refer to pronunciation–meaning amalgams rather than just pronunciations here. This is because the meaning dictates the pronunciation that is bonded to a spelling. To illustrate the problem, there are spellings that are pronounced in more than one way: WIND, LEAD, AFFECT. Two separate sight words are established in memory in each case to represent the two different pronunciation–meaning amalgams. For example, the sight word WIND meaning 'encircling' consists of a spelling-pronunciation bond that includes I — /iy/ (long i sound). The sight word WIND meaning 'moving air' consists of a bond that includes I — /i/ (short i sound).

(A variant of the arguments and evidence included above appears in the book *Literacy and Thinking: The Mind at Work in the Classroom*, Edited by C. Hedley, T. Antonacci and M. Rabinowitz, published by Erlbaum, Hillsdale, New Jersey.)

### References

ADAMS, M. (1990) *Beginning to Read: Thinking and Learning About Print*, Cambridge, MA, MIT Press.

ADAMS, M. and HUGGINS, A. (1985) 'The growth of children's sight vocabulary: A quick test with educational and theoretical implications', *Reading Research Quarterly*, **20**, pp. 262–81.

ALLINGTON, R. (1984) 'Oral reading', in PEARSON, P.D. (Ed) *Handbook of Reading Research*, New York, Longman, pp. 829–864.

ANDERSON, R., HEIBERT, F., SCOTT, J. and WILKINSON, I. (1985) *Becoming a Nation of Readers*, Washington DC, The National Institute of Education.

BAKER, L. and BROWN, A. (1984) 'Cognitive monitoring in reading', in FLOOD, J. (Ed) *Understanding Reading Comprehension*, Newark, DE, International Reading Association, pp. 21–144.

BALMUTH, M. (1982) *The Roots of Phonics*, New York, Teachers College Press.

BARR, R., KAMIL, M., MOSENTHAL, P. and PEARSON, P. (1991) (Eds) *Handbook of Reading Research Volume II*, New York, Longman.

BECK, I. (1981) 'Reading problems and instructional practices', in MACKINNON, G. and WALLER, T.G. (Eds) *Reading Research: Advances in Theory and Practice* (Vol. 2) New York, Academic Press, pp. 55–95.

BIEMILLER, A. (1970) 'The development of the use of graphic and contextual information as children learn to read', *Reading Research Quarterly*, **6**, pp. 75–96.

BODER, E. and JARRICO, S. (1982) *The Boder Test of Reading-Spelling Patterns*, New York, Grune and Stratton.

BRADY, S. and SHANKWEILER, D. (1991) *Phonological Processes in Literacy: A Tribute to Isabelle Y. Liberman*, Hillsdale, NJ, Erlbaum.

BYRNE, B. (1992) 'Studies in the acquisition procedure for reading: Rationale, hypotheses and data', in GOUGH, P., EHRI, L. and TREIMAN, R. (Eds) *Reading Acquisition*, Hillsdale, NJ, Erlbaum, pp. 1–34.

CARNINE, L., CARNINE, D. and GERSTEN, R. (1984) 'Analysis of oral reading errors made by economically disadvantaged students taught with a synthetic-phonics approach', *Reading Research Quarterly*, **19**, 3, pp. 343–56.

CATTELL, J.M. (1886) 'The time it takes to see and name objects', *Mind*, **11**, pp. 63–5.

CLAY, M. (1979) *The Early Detection of Reading Difficulties*, Auckland, New Zealand, Heinemann.

CLAY, M. (1991) *Becoming Literate: The Construction of Inner Control*, Auckland, NZ, Heinemann.

CHALL, J.S. (1967) *Learning to Read: The Great Debate*, New York, McGraw Hill.

CHALL, J.S. (1983) *Stages of Reading Development*, New York, McGraw Hill.

CUNNINGHAM, P. (1991) *Phonics They Use: Words for Reading and Writing*, New York, Harper/Collins.

DYSON, A.H. (1984) 'Learning to write/Learning to do school: Emergent writers' interpretations of school literacy tasks', *Research in the Teaching of English*, **18**, pp. 233–64.

EHRI, L.C. (1986) 'Sources of difficulty in learning to spell and read', in WOLRAICH, M.L. and ROUTH, D. (Eds) *Advances in Developmental and Behavioral Pediatrics*, Greenwich, CT, Jai Press, pp. 121–95.

EHRI, L.C. (1987) 'Learning to read and spell words', *Journal of Reading Behavior*, **19**, pp. 5–31.

EHRI, L.C. (1989) 'The development of spelling knowledge and its role in reading acquisition and reading disability', *Journal of Learning Disabilities*, **22**, pp. 356–65.

EHRI, L.C. (1991) 'Development of the ability to read words', in BARR, R., KAMIL, M., MOSENTHAL, P. and PEARSON, P. (Eds) *Handbook of Reading Research Volume II*, New York, Longman, pp. 383–417.

EHRI, L.C. (1992) 'Reconceptualizing the development of sight word reading and its relationship to recoding', in GOUGH, P., EHRI, L.C. and TREIMAN, R. (Eds) *Reading Acquisition*, Hillsdale, NJ, Erlbaum, pp. 107–43.

EHRI, L.C. (1994) 'Development of the ability of read words: Update', in RUDDELL, R., RUDDELL, M. and SINGER, H. (Eds) *Theoretical Models and Processes of Reading* (4th edition), Newark, DE, International Reading Association.

EHRI, L.C., DEFFNER, N.D. and WILCE, L.S. (1984) 'Pictorial mnemonics for phonics', *Journal of Educational Psychology*, **76**, pp. 880–93.

EHRI, L.C. and ROBBINS, C. (1992) 'Beginners need some decoding skill to read words by analogy', *Reading Research Quarterly*, **27**, pp. 12–26.

EHRI, L. and SALTMARSH, J. (1991, October) *Do beginning and disabled readers remember the letters in words they have learned to read?*, Paper presented at the NATO Advanced Study Institute on Differential Diagnoses and Treatments of Reading and Writing Disorders, Château de Bonas, France.

EHRI, L. and SWEET, J. (1991) 'Fingerpoint reading of memorized text: What enables beginners to process the print?', *Reading Research Quarterly*, **26**, pp. 442–62.

EHRI, L.C. and WILCE, L.S. (1979) 'The mnemonic value of orthography among beginning readers', *Journal of Educational Psychology*, **71**, pp. 26–40.

EHRI, L.C. and WILCE, L.S. (1980a) 'Do beginners learn to read function words better in sentences or in lists?', *Reading Research Quarterly*, **15**, pp. 451–76.

EHRI, L.C. and WILCE, L.S. (1980b) 'The influence of orthography on readers' conceptualization of the phonemic structure of words', *Applied Psycholinguistics*, **1**, pp. 371–85.

EHRI, L.C. and WILCE, L.S. (1983) 'Development of word identification speed in skilled and less skilled beginning readers', *Journal of Educational Psychology*, **75**, pp. 3–18.

EHRI, L.C and WILCE, L.S. (1985) 'Movement into reading: Is the first stage of printed word learning visual or phonetic?', *Reading Research Quarterly*, **20**, pp. 163–79.

EHRI, L.C. and WILCE, L.S. (1986) 'The influence of spellings on speech: Are alveolar flaps /d/ or /t/?', in YADEN, D. and TEMPLETON, S. (Eds) *Metalinguistic Awareness and Beginning Literacy*, Portsmouth, NH, Heinemann, pp. 101–114.

EHRI, L.C. and WILCE, L.S. (1987a) 'Cipher versus cue reading: An experiment in decoding acquisition', *Journal of Educational Psychology*, **79**, pp. 3–13.

EHRI, L.C. and WILCE, L.S. (1987b) 'Does learning to spell help beginners learn to read words?', *Reading Research Quarterly*, **22**, pp. 47–65.

EHRI, L.C. and WILLIAMS, J.P. (in press) 'Learning to read and learning to teach reading are both developmental processes', in MURRAY, F.B. and SMITH, C. (Eds) *A Knowledge Base for Teacher Education*, San Francisco, Jossey Bass.

FEITELSON, D. (1988) *Facts and Fads in Beginning Reading: A Cross-Language Perspective*, Norwood, NJ, Ablex.

GASKINS, I., DOWNER, M., ANDERSON, R., CUNNINGHAM, P., GASKINS, R., SCHOMMER, M. and The Teachers of Benchmark School (1988) 'A metacognitive approach to phonics: Using what you know to decode what you don't know', *Remedial and Special Education*, **9**, pp. 36–41.

GENTRY, R. (1981) 'Learning to spell developmentally', *Reading Teacher*, **34**, pp. 378–81.

GOELMAN, H., OBERG, A. and SMITH, F. (1984) *Awakening to Literacy*, London, Heinemann.

GOLINKOFF, R. and ROSINSKI, R. (1976) 'Decoding, semantic processing and reading comprehension skill', *Child Development*, **47**, pp. 252–8.

GOODMAN, K. (1965) 'A linguistic study of cues and miscues in reading', *Elementary English*, pp. 639–43.

GOODMAN, K. (1976) 'Reading: A psycholinguistic guessing game', in SINGER, H. and RUDDELL, R. (Eds) *Theoretical models and processes of reading* (2nd ed.), Newark, DE, International Reading Association, pp. 497–508.

GOODMAN, K. and GOODMAN, Y. (1979) 'Learning to read is natural', in RESNICK, L. and WEAVER, P. (Eds) *Theory and Practice of Early Reading Volume 1*, Hillsdale, NJ, Erlbaum, pp. 137–54.

GOSWAMI, U. (1986) 'Children's use of analogy in learning to read: A developmental study', *Journal of Experimental Child Psychology*, **42**, pp. 73–83.

GOSWAMI, U. and BRYANT, P. (1990) *Phonological Skills and Learning to Read*, Hillsdale, NJ, Erlbaum.

GOUGH, P.B., EHRI, L.C. and TREIMAN, R. (Eds) (1992) *Reading Acquisition*, Hillsdale, NJ, Erlbaum Associates.

GOUGH, P. and WALSH, S. (1991) 'Chinese, Phoenicians, and the orthographic cipher of English', in BRADY, S. and SHANKWEILER, D. (1991) *Phonological Processes in Literacy: A Tribute to Isabelle Y. Liberman*, Hillsdale, NJ, Erlbaum.

GURSKY, D. (1991) 'Whole language: A special report', *Teacher Magazine*, 2, pp. 20–47.

GUTTENTAG, R. and HAITH, M. (1978) 'Automatic processing as a function of age and reading ability', *Child Development*, **49**, pp. 707–16.

HARRIS, A.J. and JACOBSON, M.D. (1972) *Basic Elementary Reading Vocabularies*, New York, Macmillan.

HARSTE, J., BURKE, C. and WOODWARD, V. (1982) 'Children's language and world: Initial encounters with print', in LANGER, J. and SMITH-BURKE, M. (Eds) *Bridging the Gap: Reader Meets Author*, Newark, DE, International Reading Association, pp. 105–31.

HENDERSON, E. (1985) *Teaching Spelling*, Boston, MA, Houghton Mifflin.

HENRY, M.K. (1989) 'Children's word structure knowledge: Implications for decoding and spelling instruction', *Reading and Writing: An Interdisciplinary Journal*, **2**, pp. 135–52.

HOLDAWAY, D. (1979) *The Foundations of Literacy*, Sidney, Australia, Ashton Scholastic.

JOHNS, J.L. (1978) *Basic Reading Inventory*, Dubuque, Iowa, Kendall/Hunt.

JUEL, C. (1988) 'Learning to read and write: A longitudinal study of 54 children from first through fourth grades', *Journal of Educational Psychology*, **80**, pp. 437–47.

JUEL, C., GRIFFITH, P. and GOUGH, P. (1986) 'Acquisition of literacy: A longitudinal study of children in first and second grade', *Journal of Educational Psychology*, **78**, 4, pp. 243–55.

LEU, D. (1982) 'Oral reading error analysis: A critical review of research and application', *Reading Research Quarterly*, **17**, pp. 420–37.

LIBERMAN, I. and SHANKWEILER, D. (1979) 'Speech, the alphabet, and teaching to read', in RESNICK, L. and WEAVER, P. (Eds) *Theory and Practice of Early Reading Volume 2*, Hillsdale, NJ, Erlbaum, pp. 109–32.

LINDAMOOD, C. and LINDAMOOD, P. (1975) *Auditory Discrimination in Depth*, Boston, Teaching Resources Corporation.

MARSH, G., FREIDMAN, M., WELCH, V. and DESBERG, P. (1981) 'A cognitive-developmental theory of reading acquisition', in MACKINNON, G. and WALLER, T.G. (Eds) *Reading Research: Advances in Theory and Practice* (Vol. 3), New York, Academic Press, pp. 199–221.

MASON, J. (1980) 'When *do* children begin to read: An exploration of four-year-old children's letter and word reading competencies', *Reading Research Quarterly*, **15**, pp. 203–27.

MASONHEIMER, P.E., DRUM, P.A. and EHRI, L.C. (1984) 'Does environmental print identification lead children into word reading?', *Journal of Reading Behavior*, **16**, pp. 257–72.

MCGEE, L. and RICHGELS, D. (1990) *Literacy's Beginnings*, Boston, MA, Allyn and Bacon.

MORRIS, D. (1992) 'Concept of word: A pivotal understanding in the learning-to-read process', in TEMPLETON, S. and BEAR, D. (Eds) *Development of Orthographic Knowledge: The Foundations of Literacy*, Hillsdale, NJ, Erlbaum, pp. 53–77.

MORRIS, D. and PERNEY, J. (1984) 'Developmental spelling as a predictor of first grade reading achievement', *Elementary School Journal*, **84**, pp. 441–57.

PERFETTI, C. (1985) *Reading Ability*, New York, Oxford University Press.

RACK, J., SNOWLING, M. and OLSON, R. (1992) 'The nonword reading deficit in developmental dyslexia: A review', *Reading Research Quarterly*, **27**, pp. 28–53.

READ, C. (1971) 'Preschool children's knowledge of English phonology', *Harvard Educational Review*, **41**, pp. 1–34.

REITSMA, P. (1983) 'Printed word learning in beginning readers', *Journal of Experimental Child Psychology*, **75**, pp. 321–39.

ROBBINS, C. and EHRI, L. (1994) 'Reading storybooks to kindergartners helps them learn new vocabulary words', *Journal of Educational Psychology*, **86**, pp. 54–64.

ROBINSON, H., MONROE, M., ARTLEY, A.S., HUCK, C. and JENKINS, W. (1965) *Friends Old and New*, Chicago, IL, Scott, Foresman and Co, p. 190.

RUMELHART, D. (1977) 'Toward an interactive model of reading', in DORNIC, S. (Ed) *Attention and Performance VI*, Hillsdale, NJ, Erlbaum.

SCOTT, J.A. and EHRI, L.C. (1989) 'Sight word reading in prereaders: Use of logographic vs. alphabetic access routes', *Journal of Reading Behavior*, **22**, pp. 149–66.

SHARE, D., JORM, A., MACLEAN, R. and MATTHEWS, R. (1984) 'Sources of individual differences in reading acquisition', *Journal of Educational Psychology*, **76**, pp. 1309–24.

STAHL, S., OSBORN, J. and LEHR, F. (1990) *Beginning to Read: Thinking and Learning about Print by Marilyn Jager Adams: A Summary*, Urbana-Champaign, IL, Center for the Study of Reading.

STANOVICH, K.E. (1980) 'Toward an interactive-compensatory model of individual differences in the development of reading fluency', *Reading Research Quarterly*, **16**, pp. 32–71.

STANOVICH, K.E. (1986) 'Matthew effects in reading: Some consequences of individual differences in the acquisition of literacy', *Reading Research Quarterly*, **21**, pp. 360–406.

STANOVICH, K. and CUNNINGHAM, A. (1992) 'Studying the consequences of literacy within a literate society: The cognitive correlates of print exposure', *Memory and Cognition*, 20, pp. 51–68.

STANOVICH, K. and WEST, R. (1989) 'Exposure to print and orthographic processing', *Reading Research Quarterly*, **24**, pp. 402–33.

SULZBY, E. (1985) 'Children's emergent reading of favorite storybooks: A developmental study', *Reading Research Quarterly*, **20**, pp. 458–81.

TEMPLETON, S. (1992) 'Theory, nature and pedagogy of higher-order orthographic development in older students', in TEMPLETON, S. and BEAR, D. (Eds) *Development of Orthographic Knowledge: The Foundations of Literacy*, Hillsdale, NJ, Erlbaum, pp. 253–77.

TREIMAN, R. (1993) *Beginning to Spell: A Study of First-Grade Children*, New York, Oxford University Press.

TREIMAN, R., GOSWAMI, U. and BRUCK, M. (1990) 'Not all nonwords are alike: Implications for reading development and theory', *Memory and Cognition*, **18**, pp. 559–67.

VENEZKY, R. (1970) *The Structure of English Orthography*, The Hague, Netherlands, Mouton.

VENEZKY, R. and JOHNSON, D. (1973) 'Development of two-letter sound patterns in grades one through three', *Journal of Educational Psychology*, **64**, pp. 109–15.

WAGNER, R. and TORGESON, J. (1987) 'The nature of phonological processing and its causal role in the acquisition of reading skills', *Psychological Bulletin*, **101**, pp. 192–212.

WEBER, R. (1970) 'A linguistic analysis of first grade reading errors', *Reading Research Quarterly*, **5**, pp. 427–51.

WENDON, L. (1990) 'Synthesis in Letterland: Re-instating phonics in a "whole language" setting', *Early Childhood Development and Care*, **61**, pp. 139–48.

WENDON, L. (1992) *First Steps in Letterland*, Cambridge, UK, Letterland Ltd.

WIMMER, H. and HUMMER, P. (1990) 'How German-speaking first graders read and spell: Doubts on the importance of the logographic stage', *Applied Psycholinguistics*, **11**, pp. 349–68.

WYLIE, R. and DURRELL, D. (1970) 'Teaching vowels through phonograms', *Elementary English*, **47**, pp. 787–91.

*Chapter 2*

# Some Effects of Phonics Teaching on Early Reading Development

*R. Johnston, V. Connelly and J. Watson*

**Summary**

A series of studies is reported which examines the effectiveness of phonics teaching. In two studies, children learning to read by a book experience approach (in New Zealand) were compared with children whose reading program included systematic phonics teaching (in Scotland). Even though the groups were matched on word recognition ability, the first study showed that the children in the phonics program were significantly better at reading nonwords, and the second study showed that they had significantly superior reading comprehension. Further studies are also reported that show that the degree to which phonics is taught has a significant effect on reading attainment, the introduction of children to the technique of sounding and blending unfamiliar words having a markedly beneficial effect.

**Introduction**

Does the way we teach children to read have a significant impact on their progress? One school of thought is that learning to read is a natural process, like language acquisition (Goodman, 1986). If this is the case, then all we need to do is to put children into a rich and stimulating reading environment, and then they will learn to read. The argument is that children do not have formal lessons in their language in order to speak it. If reading is a natural process, then this too can be acquired without direct teaching. It follows that children do not need graded readers with a carefully controlled vocabulary which is presented repeatedly so that targeted words become familiar. Furthermore, it is argued that children should not need teaching about the way the spelling patterns of the language map on to sounds (e.g., Smith, 1985).

The reasoning seems to be that children do not have to learn that the spoken word consists of phonemes in order to learn their first language, so why should they when they are learning to read? If this is the case, then all that is needed to set children off along the road to reading competence is to make them aware of the pleasure to be had from reading and to expose them to the printed word. However, this analogy is spurious. Humans have used spoken language for a considerable length of time, and are to some extent biologically preprogrammed to acquire spoken language. Reading is a recent invention, which requires the child to understand that abstract two-dimensional visual symbols stand for words. In some languages, such as English, each word consists of multiple symbols that map on to sounds. This appears to be an advantage, as children seem to learn to read faster in alphabetic systems than ones where they have to learn logographs such as in Chinese and Japanese. Whatever script we read, reading has to be carried out using skills that we have developed through evolution for very different purposes. There are there-fore going to be individuals who would function perfectly well in a non-literate society who are found to have weaknesses in the skills required for the acquisition of literacy.

If reading were a natural, easily acquired skill, then there would not be such a large volume of research directed towards finding out why a significant proportion of school-age children do not become competent, independent readers (see Snowling, 1991, for a review). We know that some children have relative difficulties because standardized reading tests show whether a child has an age-appropriate level of skill. These reading tests vary from simple word lists which detect whether children's word-recognition skills are appro-priate for their reading age such as the British Ability Scales word-reading test (Elliott *et al.*, 1977), to tests which additionally assess how well children under-stand what they are reading (e.g., Neale, 1989). Although ultimately what is important is the level of understanding that the child has of what he/she reads, there is abundant evidence that the fundamental reading skill that must be acquired is the ability to recognize the words (Adams, 1990). It is on this foundation that comprehension of text depends. There are those, however, who think that skilled readers skip many words when reading text, the recog-nition of each word being unnecessary and time-consuming (Goodman, 1986). According to this school of thought, word recognition cannot occur fast enough to account for the speed at which the skilled adult reads. We now know that in fact words are recognized very rapidly (Perfetti, 1985) and that the skilled reader misses very few of them (Just and Carpenter, 1987). We also know that the more skilled readers are, the less dependent they are on context to decide on the meaning of an unfamiliar word (Stanovich, 1980, 1981; Perfetti, 1985). The use of context in this way is a characteristic of unskilled readers, who do this because they meet so many unfamiliar words.

Is it enough to leave children to learn unfamiliar words by trying to guess their meaning through context, or are there ways of speeding up the process by teaching them techniques which help them to relate a new word to a word in their spoken vocabulary? One approach that is often advocated is to teach children that words are composed of letters, and that letters and letter sequ-ences have sounds which combined together allow the word to be pronounced.

Although this is called a 'phonics' approach, its name is very misleading. It has as much to do with orthography, that is spelling patterns, as it has to do with sounds. It is in fact a multisensory teaching method.

A common misapprehension is that phonics is about writing, the child being encouraged to work out the sounds in words in order to be able to spell them. Bald (1993) reports that in a survey of opinions of thirty-five Surrey primary-school teachers, 30 per cent associated the technique with writing rather than spelling. This seems to be a common mistake, and a serious one. Words, with a few exceptions, have only one pronunciation but they can be spelt plausibly in many different ways. The aim of phonics teaching is to show children the regularities in English orthography in order to aid children's reading, not to turn them into phoneticians. There is also a belief that phonics only involves teaching children to use the initial sounds of words, or showing them how to sound and blend the letters of words. This ignores a very substantial part of the technique, which teaches children about vowel and consonant digraphs, rhymes, silent letters, morphemic endings and so on.

Below is an abbreviated checklist of the type of phonics program that is used in many Scottish primary schools as part of their reading program, taken from a typical phonics-teaching schedule for Primary 1–3.

1. letter sounds for the entire alphabet
2. initial sounds, e.g., *b*at, *s*it, *h*op
3. sounding and blending of three-letter consonant–vowel–consonant words, e.g., can, bet, lip, hop, bus
4. initial-consonant blends e.g., *sh*ip, *th*in, *ch*ip
5. initial-consonant digraphs, e.g., *fr*og, *sk*ip, *bl*ed, *sw*im
6. final-consonant digraphs, e.g., pa*nt*, lo*st*, so*ld*, fe*lt*
7. vowel digraphs, e.g., k*ee*p, c*oa*t, w*ai*t, s*ea*t
8. silent 'e', e.g., c*a*ke, Pete, n*i*ce, cope, t*u*be
9. soft 'c', e.g., fen*c*e, *c*ircus, *c*ycle; soft 'g', e.g., *g*iant, ca*g*e, bad*g*e, voya*g*e
10. silent letters, e.g., *k*nee, ha*l*f, lam*b*, *w*ren, whis*t*le
11. difficult endings, e.g., -less, -ness, -ous, -ious, -tious, -cious, -tion, -sion, -tial, -cial, -able, -ible

A phonics approach to reading such as this is taught in the context of learning to read text. For example, the children might initially be taught to recognize the words in their readers by sight so that they can read and understand the words in their story books. Alternatively, the children may be introduced to reading via a language-experience approach. At this stage the phonics element is limited to teaching the sounds of the letters, and drawing the children's attention to the sound of the first letter in an unfamiliar word. The next stage is to teach the children to sound the letters of unfamiliar words and to blend the sounds together. This is started between three to eight months after entering school. Following on from this, the children would be taught about consonant and vowel digraphs. This might involve asking the children to generate words with a certain sound. This would produce a list of words with similar spelling patterns, such as the following, which would be presented to the children on the blackboard so that they could see the 'word family' (each list being presented on a separate occasion):

| | | |
|---|---|---|
| s*l*ip | c*oat* | c*ake* |
| s*l*ap | b*oat* | b*ake* |
| s*l*op | g*oat* | m*ake* |

As can be seen, this approach involves showing children that there are rules in the English language for many of the spellings. For example, there are several ways in English of lengthening vowel sounds, e.g., c*oat*, c*ake*. Of course, English spelling has some irregularities and some words just have to be learnt by sight, e.g., 'yacht'. Other problems occur because sometimes the same spelling pattern has two sounds. On separate occasions the children might be taught:

| | |
|---|---|
| c*ow* | bl*ow* |
| h*ow* | sn*ow* |
| n*ow* | cr*ow* |

When faced with an unfamiliar 'ow' word, the child knows that there are two pronunciations to try, and that one of them will sound correct in context.

There are those who think that it is unnatural for children to be focusing on the letters in words in this way, especially so soon after starting to learn to read. However, there is evidence that children are aware of letters within words even before they can recognize words in conventional type. A recently completed study required 4-year-old prereaders to read the names of products which were familiar to them (Johnston, Anderson, and Holligan, submitted for publication). When presented with the names on the original wrappers, many of the children could identify 'Kit Kat', 'Coca Cola', 'Smarties' and so on, despite the fact that any clues to the nature of the product were carefully cut away. The children could not read these words in ordinary type, so recognition must have been heavily based on the distinctive lettering used. Measuring a lot of skills which might theoretically account for their ability to read these product names, such as various sorts of visual and phonological skills. The *only* predictor of product names was knowledge of the alphabet.

We can conclude from this that many preschool children are aware of the letters in words, and know that these are important cues to recognizing words. The letters were not taught to our sample in the nursery school; their knowledge had come from informal learning of the alphabet at home. It can be argued that when we teach children letter names and sounds at school, and proceed to teaching them about letter sequences and their sounds, we are developing an approach to word recognition that many of them have started to work out for themselves. However, most children by this stage do not work out for themselves that unfamiliar words can be read by sounding the letters in a systematic left to right fashion, and blending the sounds.

If many children starting school already have the idea that words are composed of letters, and that these letters have sounds, should we perhaps just leave them to get on with the process on their own? To answer this we need to know whether specific teaching of a systematic phonics programme has any advantages over leaving children to deduce spelling patterns for themselves.

There are several approaches to answering this question. Firstly we can compare children of similar backgrounds who have been taught to read by different methods. In one study Scottish 8-year-old children who had learnt by mixed methods, including phonics were compared, with 8-year-old New Zealand children who had read by a language-experience approach (Johnston and Thompson, 1989). The New Zealand children had learnt to read text by means of graded readers which are designed to develop systematically their word knowledge. They also learnt to *name* the letters of the alphabet, and were taught to decode unfamiliar words by context and by looking at the first letter of the word. The New Zealand scheme is a very well structured one, and a considerable part of the curriculum is devoted to teaching reading — much more time in fact than is spent on it in Scotland.

Thompson tested seventy children in schools near Wellington, matched as far as possible in terms of background with the forty-four children studied in Scotland. The purpose was to see what impact the different teaching methods had on how well the children could read unfamiliar words. In order to be sure the words were unfamiliar, non-words, such as 'poast' and 'hoam', which sound like words when read out, were constructed. In order to compare the children it was necessary to be sure that they were initially well matched in word-reading ability. This proved not to be the case. The Scottish children had a mean reading age of 8 years 9 months on the Scottish standardization of the Burt Word Reading Test (1974), and the New Zealand children had a mean reading age of 7 years 11 months on the Scottish norms. Thus the Scottish children were found, on average, to be ten months ahead in word-reading ability. This was not due to any differences in general verbal ability as the New Zealand children were actually ahead on a test of vocabulary knowledge. It was also confirmed as being a general phenomenon by comparing the norms on the two standardizations of the Burt Word Reading Test in Scotland and New Zealand, where the average disparity over the whole test was around six months, favouring Scottish pupils. This is striking because the New Zealand scheme is a very good one, and literacy skills are given a very high priority in the curriculum.

The purpose of the study, however, was to see how well non-words were read and the researchers did not want this to be contaminated by differences in word-recognition ability. A sample of New Zealand and Scottish children matched on word-reading ability from the larger group was therefore selected. Even with this close match, the Scottish children were 25 per cent better at reading non-words (Scottish mean = 91.7 per cent and New Zealand mean = 66.5 per cent). This means that when reading text, the Scottish children had a number of skills available for decoding unfamiliar words — they could use context, as could the New Zealand children, but they could also make a better stab at working out the pronunciation of the word from the sequence of letters.

Given that phonics is such an effective reading method, and there is considerable evidence available from many other studies to show this (see Adams, 1990, for a review), how much phonics teaching is needed? Do teachers need just to 'do' phonics now and then in an incidental fashion to set children along the road to independent reading, analysing words for themselves? Connelly (1994) has carried out a study which compared pupils at two Scottish schools which varied in the extent to which phonics was taught. The two schools had very similar catchment areas. School A and School B both used the Ginn 360 Reading Scheme and its associated workbooks. The scheme is not overtly phonic.

However, there were differences in the extent to which phonics was taught using supplementary material in the first-year classes at these two schools. School A started its phonics programme earlier, and worked through the spelling patterns at a more rapid rate than School B.

In School A, the Ginn Reading Scheme was supplemented by the more overtly phonic Link Up Reading Scheme and its associated workbooks. Soon after school entry the children were taught the sounds of the letters using individual letter cards. After three months the children were taught to sound out words and blend the sounds in order to pronounce unfamiliar words. By the end of the year they had been taught about consonant blends and vowel digraphs.

At School B the class was also taught the sounds of letters at the beginning of the year, and children were encouraged to look at the initial sound of an unfamiliar word. However, the children were taught to sound out letters and blend the sounds together only in February, after about six months at school, as opposed to three months at school A. In the last term of Primary 1 they used a Key Phonics workbook, which teaches initial letter sounds and consonant plus vowel sounds, e.g., *bag*, *got* etc. No digraphs or blends were taught until late in Primary 2. Altogether there was less emphasis on phonics teaching than at school A.

The pupils from the two schools were matched for vocabulary knowledge and were of similar age. In March, after seven months at school, the pupils at school A had a reading age on the British Ability Scales word-reading test (Elliott *et al.*, 1977) of 6 years 3 months, which was nine months ahead of their chronological age. The children at school B were doing well but were not so advanced, having a reading age of 5 years 8 months (three months ahead of chronological age). The greater progress of the children in school A was still being maintained three months later, mean reading age being 6 years 8 months compared with 6 years 2 months at school B. Even though both schools used phonics to teach reading, the degree to which it was used had a measurable impact.

The main purpose of the phonics element in these reading schemes was to show children the regularities in English spelling, and to show how sounds map on to these spelling patterns. Both schools encouraged the children to spell by working out the sounds in words, but it must be stressed that this is not the essential part of phonics. Adams (1990) has concluded, from a review of a very large literature, that children who have learned to read using a systematic phonics programme read words better and are better at spelling. What the study reported above adds to this is evidence that the *degree* to which phonics is taught has a measurable impact on reading attainment.

What aspects of phonics teaching are helpful in establishing independent reading? Is the sounding and blending of words, which is an early component of the method, a beneficial technique for children to learn? A study is currently being carried out by Watson into these issues. She is studying the impact of introducing phonics teaching on children's reading in twelve Scottish Primary 1 classes. In all of these classes the children were taught the sounds of the letters, starting straight after school entry. Most of the initial teaching, however, was aimed towards teaching the children to read words by sight, using flashcards in and out of context, with words from the children's reader. Use was made of concept key boards to alert children to the initial sounds of words, and there were visual-discrimination games.

By the third term, all of the classes had started on a more overt phonics programme which was tailored to their level of competence. Initial sounds and short vowels were systematically taught. The children were also taught to sound the letters of unfamiliar three-letter words and to blend the sounds to pronounce the words. In April, before the sounding and blending of words had been taught in all but one of the classes, most of the children were unable to read unfamiliar words which were not in their readers. On testing, they often said 'We haven't had that word'. In June, after the sounding and blending technique had been introduced in all of the classes, most of the children were prepared to attempt to read novel items. This coincided with a rapid rise in reading age between April and June. In April, the mean reading age (BAS word-reading test, Elliott *et al.*, 1977) was 5 years 1 month, and two months later it was 5 years 8 months. In the space of two months, the mean reading age of the children had increased on average by seven months.

One school, however, had worked faster through the phonics program, sounding and blending having been introduced after three months at school. These children showed a markedly superior level of performance. In April their mean reading age was 5 years 9 months (chronological age 5 years 6 months) and in June it was 6 years 2.5 months (chronological age 5 years 8 months). It seems that teaching children to sound and blend the letters of simple three letter words leads to a very significant increase in word-recognition ability. This needs to be studied further, but it seems likely that sounding and blending is critical for showing children that there is an alphabetic principle behind the written word, and that unfamiliar words can be pronounced using this method.

Another aim of Watson's study is to show just how and when phonics can be introduced as part of the reading programme. Teachers often ask how to implement a phonics programme and she hopes to be able to show a variety of ways in which this is done in a country where phonics is considered an essential part of teaching reading. Phonics rarely seems to be taught as part of the trainee teacher's course, even in Scotland. It seems to be learnt from more experienced teachers. It seems that reading books about and trying to implement phonics without seeing it done in practice is rather daunting. Some teachers also feel that it must be a very boring way to teach reading. A long time ago, phonics used to be taught in a very dull way, with children chanting the words of the word families as a whole class. There were also some dreadful phonics Readers, one of which is described by Exton and Rourke (1993), who report the truly ludicrous passage 'Let us sit by Ned on the sod. Has he not got a big cod?'. Readers like this have not been used for a very long time, and indeed Readers with an obvious phonics content are now unusual. This surely has to be due to the very positive impact of the whole-language approach to teaching reading. Nowadays, there is a wealth of attractive phonics material available, from workbooks to games, which we have seen children enjoy using. All the classes we have visited have had the children grouped according to language ability, and their phonics work is tailored toward the level suited to their instructional needs.

From talking to older teachers in Scotland, it seems that phonics these days is often being introduced later than it used to be, and the various elements are taught over a longer period. The work of Connelly and Watson suggests that it is in fact very beneficial to introduce phonics, particularly sounding and blending, early in the first year at school. Given that many preschool prereaders are very aware of the letters in words it is unlikely that paying close attention to letters early on in reading tuition is harmful. If attention is drawn to letters late on in the reading program, or not at all, this may be a handicap for some children; Feitelson (1988) points out that many Special Needs teachers comment on the difficulty they have in getting their pupils to focus on the letters in words. It may be that, in the absence of early phonics teaching, some poor readers develop a visual memory for words which is not based on detailed analysis of the component letters. This would lead them to have difficulty in using a phonics approach to reading unfamiliar words for which they have no visual memory.

In our studies of children with severe reading disorders we have found evidence that many of these children have an overwhelming bias towards a visual approach to reading, which leads to problems in reading unfamiliar items (Johnston, 1993). This suggests that programs which start phonics very early (e.g., McNee, 1990; Lloyd, 1992) may be beneficial in stopping these children following a predominantly visual-memory approach to reading. Such schemes usually involve teaching a few letters of the alphabet, followed by an immediate demonstration of how these letters can be combined into words. Lloyd (1992) points out that after teaching the letters 's, a, t, i, p, n' children can be taught the words 'tap, pan, sit, pit, pin'. Given the boost we have found that sounding and blending gives to independent reading skills, the introduction of the approach advocated by Lloyd and McNee in the first few months at school may have a very beneficial effect. According to Feitelson (1988) this method has long been the approved approach to teaching reading in Austria.

It is commonly believed that training children in phonemic analysis is an essential prerequisite for learning to read. However, we have found that incidental learning of the alphabet is closely associated with the emergence of phonemic-awareness ability in preschool prereaders (Johnston, Anderson and Holligan, submitted for publication), and that children who know no letters of the alphabet are very unlikely to be able to detect phonemes in spoken words. Furthermore, studies of phonemic-awareness training on its own are rarely successful in enhancing reading ability; the successful schemes have usually also involved training with alphabetic stimuli, e.g., Bradley and Bryant (1983), Fox and Routh (1984). A very recent study has confirmed this; Hatcher, Hulme and Ellis (1994) found that in 7-year-old poor readers, phonemic-awareness training enhanced phonemic awareness and not reading, whereas training in the association between letters and their sounds enhanced reading but not phonemic awareness. This confirms our view that phonemic awareness initially arises spontaneously in prereaders as they learn letter names and sounds, and that this awareness increases when they start formal reading instruction. However, once these phonemic-awareness skills develop they are likely to have a positive impact on learning to read. Morais, Alegria and Content (1987) have proposed a similar interactionist relationship between phonemic awareness and learning to read. This leads us to the conclusion that it is desirable to foster phonemic awareness in young children, and that this is best done by teaching them to read via a phonics approach.

One concern that teachers express about phonics is that it may enable children merely to bark at print, and that they will not understand what they read. Connelly, Johnston and Thompson (submitted for publication) have compared Scottish children who have learnt to read by a phonics-teaching method with New Zealand children who have learnt to read by a language-experience approach. Two groups of 6-year-old children who were equated on single-word reading ability (Elliott et al., 1977) were then tested on the Neale Analysis of Reading Ability (Neale, 1989), which is a text-reading test where reading accuracy, speed, and comprehension are measured. Although the groups read text with equal accuracy, the phonics-taught children were significantly better at comprehending text, being 5.2 months ahead of the language-experience-taught children.

## Messages for Teachers

Our research indicates that children need a variety of approaches to help them learn to read. They must want to read, and there must be a lot of stimulating written material available. Additionally, the reading program needs to be structured so that word-recognition skills are developed systematically. The phonics approach provides this structure and is beneficial for most novice readers, alerting them to the alphabetic nature of the English language. Of course many children will ultimately work out the spelling system for themselves, but they will acquire this knowledge much faster if they receive systematic phonics teaching. Other children have great difficulty in fathoming the alphabetic system, and may fail at reading altogether without phonics being explicitly taught.

## Conclusion

There is a great deal of evidence that a phonics program is very effective in teaching children to read. It need not be dull and uninspiring, and should most certainly be done in the context of motivating children to want to read interesting books. However, it needs to be systematic to be effective, and as far as children with severe reading problems are concerned, it may well need to be done early.

## References

ADAMS, M.J. (1990) *Beginning to Read: Thinking and Learning about Print*, Cambridge, MA, MIT.

BALD, J. (1993) '. . . and P is for Phonics', *The Times*, 20 September.

BRADLEY, L. and BRYANT, P.E. (1983) 'Categorizing sounds and learning to read — a causal connection', *Nature*, **301**, pp. 419–21.

CONNELLY, V. (1994) The influence of instructional technique on the reading strategies of beginning readers, Ph.D thesis, St Andrews University.

CONNELLY, V., JOHNSTON, R.S. and THOMPSON, G.B. (submitted for publication) 'Word reading accuracy and textual comprehension in beginning readers'.

ELLIOTT, C.D., MURRAY, D.J. and PEARSON, L.S. (1977) *The British Ability Scales*, Windsor, NFER Nelson.

EXTON, G. and O'ROURKE, P. (1993) 'Kal and real books/reading schemes', *Reading*, **27**, pp. 27–9.

FEITELSON, D. (1988) *Facts and Fads in Beginning Reading: A Cross-Language Perspective*, Norwood, New Jersey, Ablex.

FOX, B. and ROUTH, D.K. (1984) 'Phonemic analysis and synthesis as word attack skills: Revisited', *Journal of Educational Psychology*, **76**, pp. 1059–64.

GOODMAN, K.S. (1986) *What's Whole in Whole Language?*, Portsmouth, NH, Heinemann.

HATCHER, P.J., HULME, C. and ELLIS, A.W. (1994) 'Ameliorating early reading failure by integrating the teaching of reading and phonological skills: The phonological linkage hypothesis', *Child Development*, **65**, pp. 41–57.

JOHNSTON, R.S. (1993) 'Reading Disorders: Do poor readers have phonological problems?', in REID, G. (Ed) *Specific Learning Difficulties*, Edinburgh, Moray House Publications.

JOHNSTON, R.S., ANDERSON, M. and HOLLIGAN, C. (submitted for publication) 'Learning letters of the alphabet may give preschool children an insight into the phonemic structure of words'.

JOHNSTON, R.S. and THOMPSON, G.B. (1989) 'Is dependence on phonological information in children's reading a product of instructional approach', *Journal of Experimental Child Psychology*, **48**, pp. 131–45.

JUST, M.A. and CARPENTER, P.A. (1987) *The Psychology of Reading and Language Comprehension*, Boston, Allyn and Bacon.

LLOYD, S. (1992) *The Phonics Handbook*, Chigwell, Jolly Learning.

MCNEE, M. (1990) *Step By Step, A Day-By-Day Program of Intensive, Systematic Phonics, For All Ages*, East Dereham, McNee.

MORAIS, J., ALEGRIA, J. and CONTENT, A. (1987) 'The relationships between segmental analysis and alphabetic literacy: An interactive view', *Cahiers de Psychologie Cognitive*, **7**, pp. 415–38.

NEALE, M.D. (1989) *Neale Analysis of Reading Ability*, London, NFER-Nelson.

PERFETTI, C.A. (1985) *Reading Ability*, New York, Oxford University Press.

SMITH, F. (1985) *Reading Without Nonsense*, New York, Teachers College Press.

SNOWLING, M.J. (1991) 'Developmental Reading Disorders', *Journal of Child Psychology and Psychiatry*, **32**, pp. 49–77.

STANOVICH, K.E. (1980) 'Towards an interactive-compensatory model of individual differences in the development of reading fluency', *Reading Research Quarterly*, **16**, pp. 32–71.

STANOVICH, K.E. (1981) 'Attentional and automatic context effects in reading', in LESGOLD, A.M. and PERFETTI, C.A. (Eds) *Interactive Processes in Reading*, Hillsdale, Lawrence Erlbaum Associates.

VERNON, P.E. (1974) *Manual for the Burt Reading Test* (1974 Revision), London, Hodder and Stoughton.

*Chapter 3*

# Making Sense of Writing

*P. Papoulia-Tzelepi*

**Summary**

A research study which considers the stages of development of 100 Greek preschoolers in their construction and representation of the writing system is described.[1] The study attempts to reveal how Greek preschoolers conceptualize the conventions of written text as related (i) to the semantics or (ii) to the phonetics of the language. Results provide evidence of a developmental course from the rough wholes to finer and finer distinctions, to gradual discovery of the regularities of the Greek writing system. The comparison of their invented written production favours the primacy of semantic differentiation.

**Introduction**

There has been a growing international interest in the development of early writing in preschool children in the last fifteen years or so. The proof is in the number of studies; a few in the late 1960s (e.g., Gibson, 1969) and seventies (Chomsky, 1972; Lavine, 1977; Clay, 1975; Ferreiro, 1978) to quite an explosion in the 1980s and 1990s (Dyson, 1982, 1985; Ferreiro, 1986; 1990; Teberosky, 1990; Kraker, 1993; Yaden *et al.*, 1993; among many others).

Along with the growing number of research studies there is also a shift in the perspective. Whereas the early studies focused on description of the external forms of writing that children could identify or produce on their own, as they interact with the material and human environment, a great number of the more recent research reveals the underlying conceptualizations behind the recognized or produced forms of early writing by the child. Instrumental for this shift among others, is the research of Clay (1975), Ferreiro (1985, 1986), Sulzby and Teale (1985), Dyson (1988).

The examination of early writing (and reading) as a personal, active construction by the children as they interact with the social environment and the efforts of researchers to understand how this is effected, is part and parcel of a more comprehensive movement from behaviouristic to cognitive models of explaining the development of human behaviour.

Although this movement towards viewing children as active knowers and constructors of meaning in the realm of the writing system of their cultural milieu is rather recent, there is also a variety of controversial questions asked, related to the methodologies used and their underlying theories.

The Piagetian model of children's aquisition of knowledge, which examines how children's concepts are constructed, how they change over time and how they differ from adult concepts, gives a useful framework for interpreting and explaining early-literacy development (writing and reading), based on the dynamics of the concept of equilibration.

Emilia Ferreiro, a Piagetian scholar, spent many years studying writing-production activities in Mexican children in order to understand the system of ideas children build up about the nature of the writing system in their society, as they try to 'make sense' of the world around them. In search for coherence, they build up interpretation systems, 'theories', in which the information of the environment is assimilated. These 'theories' are not mirror images of the adult concepts, but personally constructed assimilation schemes through which information about print, print use, readers, writers, reading/writing is interpreted (Piaget, 1985).

When the child's scheme is repeatedly invalidated by new information, it changes to accommodate the new experience in a construction having a higher level of consistency. A new, more powerful interpretation scheme emerges, able to accommodate coherently a wider range of information. Thus the acquisition of literacy in this Piagetian framework is truly a psychogenesis with distinct levels of development, where various accomplishments follow one another in an orderly way (Ferreiro, 1986, 1990). Ferreiro (1990) presents three levels, developmentally ordered, of the acquisition of early literacy. In the *first level* children distinguish between the two basic modes of graphic representation: drawing and writing. They come to understand that in an alphabetic system writing has usually nothing to do with the nature or the appearance of the object, i.e., writing is outside the iconic domain. And whereas drawing is governed by the form of the object, writing is arbitrary and is ordered in linear (horizontal or perpendicular, according to the cultural milieu) fashion. But everything that is non-iconic is not readable. The children try to discover criteria of what is readable along the lines of quantity and quality of sign production. In order to be readable a 'writing' should have a number of signs (for Spanish children usually three) *the minimum quantity* of signs, and the signs should be varied inside the production. This is the criterion of *the internal qualitative variation.*

At *the second level* progressive control over the quantitative and qualitative variations in written production is achieved, in order to differentiate between different utterances. As learners come to understand that the same patterns of written signs cannot represent different objects, they try to differentiate their writing accordingly.

Two possible ways are open to the children, one inside the writing system and the other outside, the first concerns the linguistic domain, the second the semantic. If the first mode is adopted, the children, have already established the criteria of minimum–maximum quantity and internal qualitative variation. They then purposefully manipulate them to represent different objects, using different letters if they possess many graphic forms or changing the place of letters at the beginning, the end, or elsewhere if they do not. They try to find construction criteria inside the graphic domain by establishing relations within the formal structure of signifiers.

When the second mode is adopted the children hypothesise that the variations in numbers of letters are related to the quantifiable aspects of the referred objects. They use more letters to represent bigger, more numerous, or older objects than to represent smaller ones, or younger objects. Here the relationship is established between the structure of signifiers and structure of referents or meanings. It is in the semantic domain.

Pontecorvo and Zucchermaglio (1988) argue that, although the two ways of differentiation are alternatives and passing from one to another cannot be consider a necessary step, the second way tends to be used by older children.

Because all the children in their study use the internal variation and the minimum-quantity principles, the authors also argue that the formal differentiation is a necessary but not sufficient precondition for the external mode of differentiation. The authors propose this external differentiation as a 'deviation' and they relate it to the size of children's signs repertoire: children with a larger repertoire are more prone to the formal way of differentiation, whereas children with a smaller repertoire tend to use the external differentiation, trying to alleviate the need for formal (by signs) differentiation by looking for external points of reference. This interpretation of modes of differentiation is at variance with previous studies by Ferreiro and Gomez Palacio (1982) and Ferreiro (1985) where the primacy of semantic over phonetic representation is proposed.

Pontecorvo and Zucchermaglio (1988) conclude their study by asking for 'investigation of a larger amount of situations through which possible and different uses of external points of reference can be elicited: i.e., length of words conflicting with referents dimension; similar and non similar words pertaining to the same conceptual category; single and plurals versus collective terms etc.' (p. 382).

### Aims of the Study

In view of the above findings and controversy, the aims of this study were a) to describe what the developmental steps of Greek preschoolers are in their effort to construct the representation of the Greek writing system, and to compare the findings with those already mentioned (Ferreiro, 1990); and b) to investigate whether the differentiations of the invented writing of Greek preschoolers are influenced by linguistic or semantic factors, or by both, and in what sequence the influences appear in the children's development of literacy.

Greek preschoolers were asked to write a series of word pairs presented pictorially and orally. In the first part of the task, the children were asked to write five pairs of nouns, four of which were composed of phonetically and semantically related words. The second word of every pair was a composite or derivative, containing the first word as a first part. The first words of the pairs were mono, bi-, tri-, tetra- and polysyllabic. The words of the first pair were related semantically and partly linguistically as the second word was not overlapping with the first linguistically, it was only longer. We investigated whether children in two age groups represented a) the same syllables embedded in different words by the same characters, and b) whether they differentiate their writing according to the larger length of the second word of every pair.

This task was linguistically loaded, because not only did the phonetic overlapping lead to linguistic interpretation, but also the semantic relations between the simple and the composite word facilitate the phonetic differentiation of the composite second word.

In the second task children were asked to write six pictorially and orally presented pairs of linguistically and semantically related words, where the semantic factor was more prominent. The first pair presented two equally polysyllabic words, linguistically unrelated, the referents of which were big (newspaper) and small (toothbrush). The second pair was a small car and a big train (in Greek the related words are of inverse size). The next two pairs were one cat–three cats, two dogs–one dog and the last two were a small dog–a large dog and a large cat–a small cat. In Greek the diminutive words for the younger animals are longer than these for the adult.

Using this second task, semantically loaded, we investigated a) whether the phonetic relationship of the pairs (sameness–difference) is more prominent in the children's writing than the semantic influence of the size, the plurality or the age of the referents of the paired words.

## Method

### Subjects

Our subjects were 101 boys and girls from a number of kindergartens in and around a Greek city. They came from a variety of socio-economic strata, types of school (public–private) and kindergarten's location (urban–suburban–village). The mean age of the younger group (N. 28, Range 47–59 months) in years and months was 4: 7. The mean age of the older group (N. 73, Range 60–73 months) was 5: 5 in years and months.

### Instrument

We prepared a booklet for every child to write on with related drawings, in order to lessen the memory load of the children and also to make the task more agreeable, ensuring their motivation.

Two tasks were included in the booklet: a phonetically loaded task and a semantically loaded task. In the phonetically loaded task five pairs of words were presented along with the corresponding drawings. The first pair contained a monosylabic word (ΦΩΣ) and a phonetically and semantically related trisyllabic (ΦΑΝΑΡΙ). In the second to the fifth pair the first word (which was bisyllabic, trisyllabic, tetrasyllabic, polysyllabic in ascending order) was contained in the second as a first part of a composite or derivative word (ΣΠΙΤΙ — ΣΠΙΤΟΝΟΙΚΟΚΥΡΑ, ΤΡΑΠΕΖΙ — ΤΡΑΠΕΖΑΡΙΑ, ΠΑΡΑΘΥΡΟ — ΠΑΡΑΘΥΡΟΦΥΛΛΟ, ΕΦΗΜΕΡΙΔΑ — ΕΦΗΜΕΡΙΔΟΠΩΛΗΣ).

In the semantically loaded task six pairs of words were presented along with the corresponding drawings. The first pair contained two polysyllabic words the referents of which differ in size (ΕΦΗΜΕΡΙΔΑ newspaper — ΟΔΟΝΤΟΒΟΥΡΤΣΑ toothbrush). The second pair contained two words the length of which is in inverse relation with their respective size: a car, a train (ΑΥΤΟΚΙΝΗΤΟ — ΤΡΑΙΝΟ). The third and fourth pairs presented one cat — three cats (ΓΑΤΑ — ΓΑΤΕΣ) and two dogs — one dog (ΣΚΥΛΟΙ — ΣΚΥΛΟΣ).

The fifth and sixth pairs presented a small dog — a big dog (ΣΚΥΛΑΚΙ — ΣΚΥΛΟΣ) and a big cat — a small cat (ΓΑΤΑ — ΓΑΤΑΚΙ).

Apart from the phonetic features we manipulated the conceptual aspect in the following way. In the phonetically loaded task the conceptual features of the referents of the second word of the pair are in accordance with the phonetic lengthening of it, i.e., linguistic and conceptual features show the same direction of similarity at the beginning of the pair and differentiation at the end of the second word of the pair.

In the semantically loaded task we put the children in situations where the conceptual features of the referents are very prominent and are disonnant with the linguistic features. More or bigger or older referents are of identical phonetic length or they are shorter. Linguistic and conceptual features show to the opposite direction.

*Procedures*

Each child was tested once, in the middle of the school year (February or March) by trained graduate students and teachers working with this researcher. Each child was asked to write on the booklet next to the drawings the pairs of words which were presented orally by the researchers.

## Results

We will firstly report the results pertaining to the development of the conceptualization of children about the Greek writing system and secondly the relation between linguistically or semantically influenced differentiation in the emergent writing of Greek preschoolers.

Table 3.1: Frequency of pictoriality–non-pictoriality in younger and older kindergarteners' attempted writing

| Age | Pictorial | Non pictorial |
|---|---|---|
| Younger (N = 28) | 25% | 75% |
| Older (N = 73) | 5% | 95% |

Table 3.2: Frequency of horizontality in younger and older kindergarteners' attempted writing

| Age | Horizontal | Nonhorizontal |
|---|---|---|
| Younger (N = 28) | 84% | 15% |
| Older (N = 73) | 86% | 14% |

Table 3.3: Percentage of conventional letters in the written production of younger and older kindergarteners

| Age | 100% | 36–99% | 0–35% |
|---|---|---|---|
| Younger (N = 28) | 40% | 20% | 40% |
| Older (N = 73) | 55% | 29% | 16% |

## Development of Preschoolers' Conceptualizations of the Greek Writing System

In order to reveal the developmental nature of the changes in conceptualizations of the children concerning the structure and function of the Greek writing system, their production was examined along the lines of pictoriality–non-pictoriality, horizontality, use of letters versus non-letters and number of signs used to represent words by younger and older kindergarteners.

Table 3.1 shows the progress (statistically significant to $P < 0.01$, $x^2$ 9.72, of children to the conceptualization that writing is outside the iconic domain and thus arbitrary, being exempt from the exigencies of the referent's form.

Table 3.2 reveals that most of the young children have mastered the notion of horizontality earlier than the time of testing as 84 per cent of the younger and 86 per cent of the older children attempt to write totally horizontally, whereas the non-horizontal writers are 16 per cent and 18 per cent respectively. Consequently no significant difference is found between them.

Once children, interacting with the social environment which in modern societies is highly print-loaded, construct the representation of writing as non iconic — thus arbitrary — and directional, they move to finer distinctions. The arbitrariness of the signs starts to take the face of some identifiable, distinct, repeated signs, the letters. Is letter awareness and use (though not in their

*Table 3.4:  Number of written signs used to represent words by younger and older kindergarteners*

| Age | 1 sign | 2 signs | 3 signs | 4 + signs | 1 – 4 + | Filling the space |
|---|---|---|---|---|---|---|
| Younger (N = 28) | 8 | 8 | 9 | 63 | | 11 |
| Older (N = 73) | 1 | 2 | 11 | 57 | 24 | 4 |

*Table 3.5:  Maximum of written signs used to represent words in younger and older kindergarteners*

| Age | Range | Mean |
|---|---|---|
| Younger (N = 28) | 1–20 | 8.6 |
| Older (N = 73) | 1–28 | 8.2 |

*Table 3.6:   Variety of signs used in the whole written production: mean of a child's sign repertoire*

| Age | Range | Mean |
|---|---|---|
| Younger (N = 28) | 1–20 | 6.2 |
| Older (N = 73) | 1–43 | 12.5 |

conventional value) a developmental step in the emergent literacy of Greek children? Table 3.3 presents the percentage of letters in the written production of our younger and older subjects. There is a statistically significant difference between the groups (P < 0.10, $x^2$ 5.56) answering the question positively.

Table 3.4 presents the progression in the conceptualization that a word (or an object in the mind of the child) is represented usually by more than one or two letters. Fewer older children write a word by one, two or three signs than the younger ones, but the majority of both prefer more than three signs. This is attributed to the structure of the Greek language having a high percentage of non-monosyllabic words. This contrasts with Spanish-speaking children who prefer as minimum quantity three signs or letters (Ferreiro and Gomez Palacio, 1982). Also the younger children are more rigid in their preferences than the older ones, who, to a considerable degree, use one or several signs in various words, thus presenting a more differentiated representation of the writing system.

Although the mean of maxima used to represent a word by younger and older children does not reveal great differences (younger: mean 8.6, range 1–20 signs; older: mean 8.2, range 1–28 signs) the difference in the variety of signs of any kind used in the whole written production is very great: the mean of younger children's sign repertoire is 6.2 signs, whereas the older children's is 12.5 signs, as tables 3.5 and 3.6 present.

The above presented steps in the Greek children's acquisition of written

*Table 3.7: Towards internal variation in writing words: percentage of writing patterns*

| Age | Repertoire of less than 4 signs | | | Repertoire of 4 or more signs | | |
|---|---|---|---|---|---|---|
| | Repetition of the same sign | or | Unchanged pattern Variation | Repetition of the same sign | or | Unchanged pattern Variation |
| Younger (N = 32) | 21% | | 4% | 7% | | 36% |
| Older (N = 39) | 15% | | 6% | 9% | | 49% |

*Note*: Missing N are at pictorial level.

words representation (i.e., non-pictoriality, horizontality, arbitrariness, with emerging rules of quantity (minimum–maximum) and quality variation in signs used, constitute the accomplishments of the first level of the written system conceptualization (Ferreiro, 1990). The findings are in accordance with the already mentioned Mexican studies as well as with numerous others in different countries and orthographies (e.g., Tolchinsky Landsmann and Levin, 1985, for Hebrew; Pontecorvo and Zucchermaglio, 1988, for Italian; Grundlach, 1982, for English).

### Linguistically or Semantically Influenced Differentiations in the Attempted Writing

According to Ferreiro (1990), one of the main accomplishments of the second level is the progressive control over qualitative and quantitative modes of differentiation between pieces of writing, accounting for differences in utterances.

We described in the introduction two possible modes of differentiation and the ensuing controversy. Now we analyse the written production of thirty-eight children, seven younger, thirty-one older, in the two tasks involving phonetics and semantics respectively. Production was not analysed for quantitative differentiation outside the phonetic or semantic domains (i.e., neither is interest in whether there is random augmentation or diminution of the number of signs used in writing different words nor in the changing of signs and/or places of signs although there is abundant evidence for that).

The interest here is the emergence of a child's sensitivity towards the dual aspect of language, the phonetic form and the meaning. In children's search for criteria of differentiation the research question is which aspect is more salient for children or which one is earlier discovered, and how these criteria are orchestrated.

Thus the items of the phonetically loaded task are analysed along the lines a) of similarities in written production between phonetically similar words (i.e., looking to see if identical beginnings of the embedded words are rendered using the same signs), b) differences in written production for phonetically different words (i.e., looking to see if longer words were written with more signs) and c) sensitivity to the progressive lengthening of the words (i.e., from monosyllabic to polysyllabic words). Along the line a) were put the similarities–differentiations in the first written part of the pairs of the semantically loaded task, because they were also phonetically related, besides being conceptually manipulated.

The analysis of a, b and c (syllabic-augmentation awareness) shows a development of linguistic sensitivity from the younger to the older group. In Table 3.8 is presented the percentage of N who show an emergent awareness of the word not only as an object substitute, but also as a distinct linguistic entity with quantitative and qualitative features. Research done with Israeli children by Tolchinsky (1988) presented similar findings.

Table 3.9 presents the performance of N in the semantically loaded task. Older children are more proficient in the semantic representation of the words than younger ones are.

In order to investigate the question about the primacy of phonetic or semantic influence (or vice versa) the performance in both tasks is analysed.

In the comparison of performance in the phonetically loaded task (Table 3.8) with the performance in the semantically loaded task (Table 3.9) by Wilcoxon 'Matched-pairs Signed-ranks Test', a statistically significant difference is found in favour of the primacy of the semantic over the phonetic influence ($Z = -4.32$ 2-tailed $p < .00$). The same Wilcoxon test with the older group only, revealed the same significance in favour of the primacy of semantic influence ($Z = -4.19$ 2-tailed $p < .00$).

The influence of conceptual characteristics of referents upon the written production of preschoolers leading to the primacy of semantic differentiation, is summarised in the following order of magnitude: Plurality of objects (versus one object), size of the object, and age of the object, with plurality being by far the most influential.

## Discussion

In the invented writing of Greek preschoolers, none of whom had been taught to read/write formally, a developmental course is identified: from the rough wholes to finer and finer distinctions, to gradual discovery of the regularities of the Greek writing system. From non-pictoriality, to horizontality, to minimum–maximum quantity, to qualitative differentiation of writing for representing the different utterances (levels 1 and 2, Ferreiro, 1990) to syllabic and alphabetic principles (level 3 not presented in this study), preschoolers progress in an orderly manner in their search to make sense of literacy.

Of special interest was the level 2 children's bi-modal differentiation of *writing in response to different utterances: semantic or phonetic.* By carrying out Pontecorvo's wish for new research, data are obtained which show that the preference of the semantically influenced differentiation in writing, far from being a 'deviation', is rather a normal course of development in Greek

Table 3.8: *Phonetic differentiation of phonetically-related words in the written production of younger and older kindergarteners*

| Pairs of words | Monosyllabic /Polysyllabic derivative | Bi-/polysyllabic composite | Tri/polysyllabic derivative | Tetra/polysyllabic composite | Poly/polysyllabic composite | Difference in referent's size/same length phonetically | Difference in referent's size/inverse phonetic length | Singular/plural same size referents | Plural/ Singular | Smaller/ bigger referents. Smaller is phonetically longer | Bigger/ smaller referents. Smaller is phonetically longer | Order of syllabic augmentation awareness |
|---|---|---|---|---|---|---|---|---|---|---|---|---|
| | | Similarities of the beginning of phonetically related words: first embedded in the second | | | | | | | | | | |
| **Age** | | | | | | | | | | | | |
| Younger (N = 7) | 28 | 0 | 0 | 0 | 0 | 0 | 0 | 43 | 14 | 14 | 0 | 14 |
| Older (N= 38) | 16 | 28 | 25 | 38 | 34 | 28 | 34 | 28 | 22 | 25 | 28 | 31 |
| Σ | 18 | 23 | 21 | 31 | 28 | 23 | 28 | 31 | 21 | 23 | 23 | 28 |
| | Differentiation of phonetically different words longer words with more signs, sensitivity to lengthening of words | | | | | | Semantically loaded test items | | | | | |
| Younger (N = 7) | 43 | 43 | 29 | 29 | 14 | | | | | | | |
| Older (N = 38) | 44 | 51 | 41 | 41 | 34 | | | | | | | |
| Σ | 44 | 51 | 38 | 39 | 31 | | | | | | | |

*Table 3.9: Semantically influenced differentiation in written production of younger and older kindergarteners*

| Age | Difference in referent's size/ same length phonetically | Difference in referent's size/ inverse phonetic length | Singular-Plural/ Same size referents Same length phonetically | Plural-Singular Different size referents. Same length phonetically | Smaller-Bigger referents/smaller is phonetically longer | Bigger-Smaller referents/smaller is phonetically longer |
|---|---|---|---|---|---|---|
| Younger (N = 7) | 0 | 29 | 0 | 43 | 29 | 0 |
| Older (N = 38) | 25 | 50 | 59 | 84 | 31 | 44 |

preschoolers. This preference is documented in a number of studies, besides Ferreiro's stated elsewhere. Tolchinsky Landsmann (1988) argues that phonetic differences supported by semantic differences are represented earlier than are phonetic ones alone. The same author states that instances of congruence between the semantic relationship and the writing procedures were graphically noted at earlier ages (Tolchinsky Landsmann, 1988).

Even the letters in alphabet-book reading become (for the child) the signs for multiple referents in the real world apart from the sounds associated in their names (Yaden *et al.*, 1993). Dyson (1986) argues that young children begin using writing as a first-order symbol system referring directly to familiar people and actions about them.

A number of reasons are proposed to account for the primacy of semantic over phonetic differentiation in early invented writing. Papandropoulou and Sinclair (1974) documenting young children's difficulty in distinguishing words from their referents, attributed the phenomenon to the child's initial lack of differentiation between language and things. Markman (1976) attributed children's difficulty in distinguishing words from referents to the intangible character of words.

The above tend to underline the limited metalinguistic capacity on the part of the children, to view the word as an object of thought and scrutiny outside its communicative value. Phonological features of the word are more inaccessible, because they are abstract, intangible, whereas semantic characteristics of the referent are easily accessible as concrete and tangible. For children, feeling the necessity to differentiate their writing in response to differentiated utterances, it is only logical to take the more concrete, more easily accessible route of taking the referents' characteristics as differentiation criteria in their invented writings. Is it not the same route of mankind in trying to nail down the volatile words (Homer)?

Perhaps the primacy of the semantically influenced writing in the ontogenesis of the child's writing system representation mirrors the phylogenetic steps of humankind in the invention of writing: from cave paintings, to hieroglyphs, to syllabic, to an alphabetic rendering of oral language.

In order to document further the precedence of semantics over phonetics as a mode of differentiation and to establish time and modes of transition to the metalinguistic awareness of the phonetic entity of the utterance, further longitudinal studies are needed which avoid many of the limitations of this research, including the inequality of the younger and older group, and the rather small size of the sample.

## Messages for Teachers

The acquisition of the alphabetic principle on the part of the child, which is a cornerstone of reading capacity, is not an easy or straightforward task. It is not something received ready-made from the environment. In this study, as in many others, it is revealed that children are actively engaged in making sense of the world of print. In doing so, their conceptual steps are neither a direct mirroring of the adult conceptions nor of the conventions of the orthography. Even though children's emerging conceptions of literacy might seem peculiar to adults, they have their own logic and meaning. They represent the logic of the world of print as this world is conceived by the child at a given phase of his or her intellectual development.

The progression from one developmental step to the next is facilitated by a provocative literacy environment at home as well as in kindergarten. In such an environment facilitative instances will be presented when a pupil's current conceptual scheme is unable to accommodate the new experience. An environment, rich in literacy objects and activities will permit children to pursue their search for a fuller understanding of the world of print in the same way as adults. In this rich and supportive environment the development of their concept of literacy is encouraged. The specific developmental steps are viewed from the teacher as legitimate passages, not errors to be avoided. In cases where this transition from one step to the next is not exhibited spontaneously, the teacher could create instances to facilitate children's progression.

## Conclusion

In conclusion, one could argue that preschool children are helped to understand and master literacy, in all its complexity, if they are treated as active builders of their literacy concepts by the teachers, who, in their turn, provide a rich, non-threatening, explorable literacy environment conducive to chidren's search for meaning.

## Note

Thanks are extended to Dr D. Skouras for help in statistical analysis and to the following graduate students and teachers for helping in this research: M. Gelbassi, A. Fterniati, K. Thiveos, S. Zaharopoulou, P. Sacoveli, and G. Markakis.

## References

CHOMSKY, N. (1972) 'Stages in language development and reading exposure', *Harvard Educational Review*, **42**, pp. 1–33.

CLAY, M. (1975) *What Did I write?*, Auckland, NZ, Heinemann.

DYSON, A. (1982) 'Reading, writing and language: Young children solve the written language puzzle', *Language Arts*, **59**, pp. 829–39.

DYSON, A. (1985) 'Individual differences in emergent writing', in FARR, M. (Ed) *Advances in Writing Research, Children's Early Writing Development* (Vol. 1), Norwood, NJ, Ablex, pp. 59–126.

Dyson, A. (1986) 'Children's early interpretation of writing: Expanding research perspectives', in Yaden, D.B. and Templeton, S. (Eds) *Metalinguistic Awareness and Beginning Literacy*, Portsmouth, NH, Heinemann, pp. 201–18.

Dyson, A. (1988) 'Negotiating among multiple worlds: The space/time dimension of young children's composing', *Research in the Teaching of English*, **22**, 4, pp. 355–90.

Ferreiro, E. (1978) 'What is written in a written sentence? A developmental answer', *Journal of Education*, **160**, pp. 25–39.

Ferreiro, E. (1985) 'Literacy development: A psychogenetique perspective', in Olon, D., Torrance, N. and Hildyard, A. (Eds) *Literacy, Language and Learning*, Cambridge, Cambridge University Press, pp. 217–28.

Ferreiro, E. (1986) 'The interplay between information and assimilation in beginning literacy', in Teale, W.H. and Sulzby, E. (Eds) *Emergent Literacy: Writing and Reading*, Norwood, NJ, Ablex, pp. 15–49.

Ferreiro, E. (1990) 'Literacy development: Psychogenesis', in Goodman, Y. (Ed) *How Children Construct Literacy*, Newark, DE, International Reading Association.

Ferreiro, E. and Gomez Palacio, M. (1982) *Nuevas perspectivas sobre los procesos de lectura y escritura*, Mexico, Siglo XXXI Editores.

Gibson, E. (1969) *Principles of Perceptual Learning and Development*, New York, Appleton-Century-Crofts.

Grundlach, R.A. (1982) 'Children as writers: The beginnings of learning to write', in Nystrand, M. (Ed) *What Writers Know: The Language Process, and Structure of Written Discourse*, New York, Academic Press, pp. 129–48.

Kraker, M. (1993) 'Learning to write: Children's use of notation', *Reading Research and Instruction*, **32**, 2, pp. 55–75.

Lavine, L. (1977) 'Differentiation of letterlike forms in prereading children', *Developmental Psychology*, **13**, 2, pp. 89–94.

Markman, E. (1976) 'Children's difficulty with word referent differentiation', *Child Development*, **47**, pp. 742–9.

Papandropoulou, I. and Sinclair, H. (1974) 'What is a word? Experimental study of children's ideas on grammar', *Human Development*, **17**, pp. 241–58.

Piaget, J. (1985) *The Equilibration of Cognitive Structures: The Central Problem of Intellectual Development*, Chicago, University of Chicago Press.

Pontecorvo, C. and Zucchermaglio, C. (1988) 'Modes of differentiation in children's writing construction', *European Journal of Psychology of Education*, **3**, 4, pp. 371–84.

Sulzby, E. and Teale, W.H. (1985) Writing development in early childhood, *Educational Horizons*, **64**, pp. 8–12.

Teberosky, A. (1990) 'The language young children write: Reflections on a learning situation', in Goodman, Y. (Ed) *How Children Construct Literacy*, Newark, DE, International Reading Association.

Tolchinsky Landsmann, L. (1988) 'Form and meaning in the development of writing', *European Journal of Psychology of Education*, **8**, 4, pp. 356–70.

Tolchinsky Landsmann, L. and Levin, I. (1985) 'Writing in Preschoolers: an age-related analysis', *Applied Psycholinguistics*, **6**, pp. 319–39.

Yaden, D., Smolkin, L. and Macgillivray, L. (1993) 'A psychogenetic perspective on children's understanding about letter associations during alphabet book readings', *Journal of Reading Behavior*, **25**, 1, pp. 43–68.

*Chapter 4*

# Some Effects of Context on Reading

*R. Stainthorp*

**Summary**

This chapter reports an experiment in a series relating to the development of strategies used when reading by children aged 7 to 11 years. The children were asked to read a set of non-words in and out of pseudosentence frames. This enabled analysis of their ability to integrate bottom–up decoding skills with top–down contextual facilitation. Results indicate that although single-word reading accuracy is important, top–down strategies can modify performance. The extent to which context can be used is limited by word knowledge. However, in turn, the development of word knowledge is itself compromised when alphabetic skills are poor.

**Introduction**

This chapter begins with a discussion about the differences between 'real life' visual contexts for written words and orthographic contexts provided by the surrounding written words in texts. This is followed by a discussion of some evidence which suggests that the facilitatory effect of written context is not something that can necessarily be taken for granted as children are developing their reading skills.

*Real Life Contexts*

Most of the written words which people encounter occur in a context — but that context is not necessarily a written sentence. We see many examples of single written words in our environment: shop names, road signs, street names, product names etc. All these examples are of written language embedded within specific, meaningful situations. A good example to illustrate this would be a railway station. Signs abound in such an environmental context TICKETS, TOILETS, TELEPHONES, TAXIS. We do not need a whole sentence to facilitate such reading. 'This way to the ticket office' may be very polite but it is probably redundant. The real world physical context, our real life intentions and our accurate word-reading skills combine to enable us to see the signs as meaningful. If we enter a large station we will actively seek for something that looks like a ticket office, but probably, more potently, for a sign TICKETS. Our ability to read single words accurately enables us to pick out the sign that we actively seek from all the others.

Perera (1993) has raised the notion that this type of writing may be becoming less ubiquitous. The world is now becoming flooded with icons to augment word reading or indeed replace it. The 'No Smoking' sign has virtually been superseded with the icon ⊘. The fact that people have to learn the international symbol conventions in order to understand the sign is a separate issue. Clearly there is a general view that symbols are more likely to be universally understood. They do not have to be related to a specific language or level of literacy skill. However, sometimes it is clear that people feel unsure about the precise meaning of the signs. Many modern 'male' and 'female' icons for toilets are so stylized that it is only possible to be completely sure which is which after double checking both.

This recognition of the importance of real-life contexts for signs has greatly influenced practice in 'early-years' classrooms as evidenced by the use of 'Environmental Print' (see Hall, 1987). It is common practice to help children to build up a visual-reading vocabulary by labelling parts of the classroom — 'Crayons', 'Brushes', 'Paper' etc. The written word is thus contextualized. This practice has a dual role. Those children who have had limited experiences with books or with print in general and who have not come to a realization that the printed word can carry a message, can be given explicit meaningful teaching using labels. The children are helped to recognize that a written word can stand for a physical object. They know what crayons are and they know when they need to get them. When this happens they can use their knowledge of where the crayons are stored to map the written word onto the concrete object. It may be necessary to teach this explicitly. We cannot assume that children will learn this incidentally through their transactions in the classroom. Yes, many children will achieve this through incidental learning, but it may be best not to leave this to chance.

Of course, in reality, the process is reversed for the skilled reader. If we know what and where the ticket office is, then we do not need to look for the written sign. However, if we do *not know* the location, then we can start from the written word. Being able to read the word 'Tickets' accurately without any other context means that we can seek out the word and then find the environmental stimulus we require. If we couldn't do this we would have to seek help from others by asking for the information. Failing that, we would have to roam around until we found a structure that looked like a ticket office with people clearly buying tickets.

### Pictorial Context

Visual, figurative context is also used to help children to read in the early stages. Pictures which illustrate the text are said to provide a context which supports the word reading. It is difficult to differentiate between contextual support for word reading and the motivational support that pictures give to enable the young reader to stay on task. Protheroe (1993) has gone so far as to suggest the 'heresy' that pictures can actually distract the readers from the text. Her view receives some support from empirical study. Solman, Singh and Kehoe (1992) found that children aged 5 years 6 months learned to recognize single words more accurately when they were presented in isolation than when they were accompanied by an illustrative line drawing. They explained their results by referring to 'attentional' models of human processing which assume that, when there are competing stimuli, each one receives less processing because of limited capacity. The trade off for having the picture illustrate the written word is, therefore, that there is less focused attention on that word and so it is processed less efficiently. The net result is that it takes longer to learn the word. This may be particularly true for the young novice reader who needs to devote a considerable amount of processing capacity to the working out of unknown words. Such a finding has to be treated with caution. We have to take Alice's musings seriously:

What's the use of a book. . . . without pictures or conversations. (*Alice's Adventures in Wonderland*, Lewis Carroll)

Teachers are well aware of the enjoyment that children get from a beautifully illustrated book and this cannot be lightly dismissed. However, we may have to recognize that pictorial context may not always be a blessing; there are times when we need to be very clear that we want the children to focus on the print.

### Written Contexts

There tends to be an implicit assumption that we are automatically able to use context to facilitate learning in general and that this ability is particularly useful when reading. The effect of context on reading has often been presented as a non-controversial issue. Smith (1971) took the view that the skilled reader's method of processing text was top–down. Reading was seen as a process of using the context to generate hypotheses about text that had yet to be encountered. He felt that skilled readers needed to pay very little attention to the words because they were able to predict their likelihood from the semantic and syntactic context. Since we know there are clear differences between the skilled and the novice reader, it follows from his view that, if the characteristic of skilled reading is paying little attention to the visual aspects of the text, but using context to predict and confirm hypotheses, then these would be the skills that the novice reader would have to learn.

Certainly, there is evidence that readers are faster to identify a word when it is presented in the context of other words than when it occurs with unrelated information (Stanovich and West, 1979). Also, the amount of preceding context will affect the speed at which a word can be recognized (West and Stanovich, 1978). However, it is clear that the effect becomes less marked as children become more skilled in word reading. Older skilled readers have extensive visual-reading lexicons which enable them to recognize words quickly and accurately. They seem to be able to access the words automatically, at least at the macro-level, and so they do not need a context for recognizing the words. For skilled readers, the individual words do not present a problem, although, of course, the concepts being presented in the discourse may be intellectually challenging. Mitchell (1982) has suggested that context effects in normal adult reading are restricted to circumstances in which the normal recognition processes are held up in some way.

Stanovich (1980) has proposed an 'interactive-compensation' model of reading which is almost the reverse of the Smith psycholinguistic model. He claims that guessing, through use of context, is a characteristic of novice readers and one which disappears as the readers become skilled. He suggests that poor readers (and presumably novice readers) might have to rely on context to give clues to unknown words in order to compensate for poor or less well developed word-attack skills. These word-attack skills are the decoding skills which enable the child to work out a candidate phonology from the letters. He suggests that good readers, on the other hand, might not need to use context because (a) they have more extensive visual-reading lexicons and (b) they have the decoding skills necessary to work out any unknown words. This model implies, therefore, that use of context is a characteristic of poor reading and not a higher-order reading skill. This does not mean that good readers are not *able* to use context, simply that they do not *need* to use it. They have progressed in their reading development beyond the novice level of having to rely on context to support their limited skills. They may use the context to work out the meaning of an unknown word if, for example, it is not in their semantic system. However, in such circumstances they do not use the linguistic context only, since they are also able to use decoding skills to work out a candidate word.

This model of reading can be considered in the light of the limited capacity information-processing model of human performance mentioned above. The child who has good decoding skills can begin to build up a visual-reading vocabulary which becomes sufficiently extensive to support independent reading. This, in turn, means that the child will have greater exposure to print which leads to opportunities to build up the visual-reading lexicon even further. This extensive visual vocabulary means that the words can be accessed without taxing the system too much, so there is greater capacity available for working out unknown items and for concentrating on the meaning of the text. A child who has to use context to guess at a word has less capacity available for processing the print and so has greater difficulty in building up a visual vocabulary. This becomes cyclical. Stanovich (1986) has named this the 'Matthew Effect'.

The model does make the assumption that all children can use linguistic written context to read problematic words. This means that they are presumed to use the linguistic framework of the text that they have read so far in order to guess at the unknown word. We have to consider whether this is a reading strategy at all, particularly if the 'guessed' word bears no relation to the visual identity of the target written word. If a child is able to recognize only a very few words and only has limited decoding skills, then the context is not going to be of great help. We have to remember that the context itself has to be read successfully in order to facilitate the acceptance of a candidate phonological identification of an unknown word. Pring and Snowling (1986) have suggested that it is possible that children use context to enhance their gradually improving decoding skills as a means of teaching themselves to read.

Where written context is judged to be supporting the identification of an unknown word, the status of the word relative to the child's vocabulary is important. If a word is known in the spoken vocabulary but unknown in the visual-reading vocabulary, then the context is likely to make the target word more accessible. Decoding skills will enable the candidate phonology to be worked out and the semantic/syntactic skills will mean that this candidate phonology can be refined and modified if necessary. If the word is unknown in the visual-reading vocabulary and in the spoken vocabulary then the context has to provide a semantic/syntactic frame to enable the meaning of the word to be worked out. However, decoding skills are again clearly necessary for working out a candidate phonology, in order that it may be integrated with the meaning. This, of course, may not always be the correct phonology. Words which are encountered and learned first through written texts may be assigned a regular pronunciation when they are in fact irregular. Nevertheless, having the ability to work out a possible phonology is an important step to entering the word into the lexicon. A child who encounters new words in texts, but who has limited decoding skills, is likely to have to guess at the unknown word on the basis of the semantic and syntactic environment. However, it is a moot point as to whether such guessing can really be considered to be reading if the guess bears no relation to the visual identity of the target word (see Ehri and Wilce, 1980 and Donaldson and Reid, 1982).

### Context Effects on Non-word Reading

A recent study investigated the extent to which children would produce different pronunciations of printed non-words depending on surrounding linguistic contexts (Stainthorp, 1994). The use of non-words has sometimes been questioned on the grounds that they have no meaning. However, when investigating children's ability to decode unknown items, non-words enable researchers to control for exposure to print across a range of individual differences. Children who are good readers and well on the way to becoming experts will have had considerably greater experience with printed words than children who are still struggling. This means that comparisons between children may be invalid. Non-words are more likely to be equally unknown to children of all abilities. It is also possible to present children with unknown items which are nevertheless short and therefore orthographically less complex. Very low-frequency words tend to be also multisyllabic. The non-word is a visual stimulus which, by definition, does not have a stored visual, semantic or syntactic identity. Of course, we have to be careful when designing studies using non-words because poets and advertising agents will tend to create them and give them meaning. My dictionaries give full entries with pronunciation, syntactic status and meaning for *frabjous* and *runcible* whilst acknowledging that they are both nonsense words.

Pronunciation of non-words like TEG or FOT is fairly uncontentious. The application of letter–sound correspondence rules leads to TEG rhyming with LEG and FOT rhyming with NOT. However, because of the inconsistency of spelling-sound rules in English, it is possible to generate non-words which can reasonably be given more than one pronunciation. MIVE could be pronounced to rhyme with FIVE or to rhyme with GIVE. FIVE is a regular English word that follows the rule 'Vowel + Consonant + E', where the final marker (magic) E means that the vowel is given a 'long' pronunciation. GIVE is an exception to this rule.

In this particular study a group of sixteen, 9-year-old children were asked to read a set of twelve non-words presented singly to assess their decoding skills. These non-words were all 'ambiguous' in that they were like MIVE; they could reasonably be read aloud with at least two pronunciations. Then, ten weeks later, they were asked to read the non-words again, but this time the words had been placed in 'orthographic' contexts. Pairs of sentences had been developed which contained target real words that differed from the non-words by only the onset consonant:

Type R — I saw something fly by. It was a *moth*.
Type E — I have lost *both* my gloves.

Sentences of Type R contained a regular target word and sentences of Type E contained an exception target word. The target words were then replaced by the non-words:

Type R — I saw something fly by. It was a *foth*.
Type E — I have lost *soth* my gloves.

This procedure generated twelve regular-context pseudosentences and twelve exception-context pseudosentences.

The purposes of the study were (a) to investigate non-word reading ability and the effect that context had on accuracy *per se* and (b) to investigate the extent to which the children were able to modify their pronunciation of the non-words relative to the contexts. The children had all been given a standardized word-reading test prior to the study. This was the British Ability

Table 4.1: *Mean percentage of acceptable pronunciations of the target non-words made by the children when they were age 9 years*

|  | Non-words in isolation | Non-words in the regular contexts | Non-words in the exception contexts |
|---|---|---|---|
| Good readers (N 8) | 74 | 88 | 87 |
| Poor readers (N 8) | 57 | 54 | 75 |

Table 4.2: *Mean percentage of acceptable pronunciations of the target non-words made by the children when they were age 10 years*

| ☐ | Non-words in isolation | Non-words in the regular contexts | Non-words in the exception contexts |
|---|---|---|---|
| Good readers (N 8) | 80 | 99 | 97 |
| Poor readers (N 8) | 70 | 90 | 84 |

Scales word-reading test. On the basis of their scores they were divided into two groups of eight. One group — the good readers — all had reading ages at or above their chronological ages; the other group — the poor readers — all had reading ages below their chronological ages.

Table 4.1 shows the mean percentage of acceptable pronunciations made both in isolation and in contexts. The good readers were better at non-word reading and so it can be deduced that they had better decoding skills. However, they were also able to use the context to enhance their decoding skills. The poor readers were unable to read as many of the non-words in isolation and were less able to use the contexts to improve their performance. They were only able to improve their accuracy in the exception contexts.

The children were re-tested one year later when they were 10 years old. Table 4.2 shows the mean percentage accuracy when reading the non-words. It can be seen that the poor readers had begun to show a pattern similar to the good readers with a level of accuracy much like they had shown the previous year. When capacity to modify performance relative to the contexts was examined, the good readers showed clear context effects when they were 9 years old. The number of regular pronunciations was increased in the regular-context condition and decreased in the exception-context condition relative to the number of regular pronunciations when the non-words were read in isolation. When they were re-tested at 10 years the effects were just as marked. However, the poor readers showed no context sensitivity when they were first tested. The number of non-words read with a regular pronunciation did not change with either context. When they were re-tested the following year they did show a context effect, but by then their non-word reading in isolation had improved. Their performance at 10 years appeared to mirror the performance of the good readers when they were 9 years. This is illustrated in Figure 4.1.

Figure 4.1: Mean percentage of non-words read with a regular pronunciation singly and in the two contexts

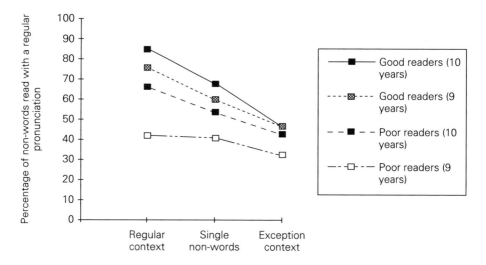

Figure 4.2: Mean percentage of non-words read with an exception pronunciation singly and in the two contexts

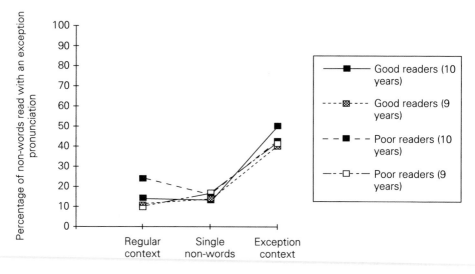

Figure 4.2 shows the percentage of non-words read with an exception pronunciation in each condition. The two groups of readers showed the same overall pattern of performance. They read very few non-words with exception pronunciations when presented with the items singly, but both groups were able to use the context to modify pronunciations when the non-words were presented in the exception contexts.

These results confirm the view that, when items are unknown, decoding skills enable the readers to work out candidate pronunciations and contexts enable these to be refined and modified. The context effects in this particular study were less marked when decoding skills were still being refined. A recent study by Rego and Bryant (1993) would support this finding. They found that ability to make use of the linguistic context when reading could be predicted by children's level of syntactic/semantic skill. This would enable the children to make a suitable guess at a word. Ability to use a decoding strategy to work out words could be predicted from the children's level of phonological awareness. Children who have good semantic/syntactic skills and who are phonologically aware are obviously at an advantage since they can draw on both aspects to help them read.

### Messages for Teachers

If the facilitatory effects of context are, in part, dependent upon children having developed some decoding skills, then we need to ensure that children are taught decoding skills to enable them to work out unknown words accurately and with independence. We should not leave the learning of letter–sound correspondences to chance. Children may need to be given the chance to practise working out the pronunciation of unknown words so that they can develop an awareness of the strategies that might be useful to them. We also need to ensure that children are given texts which are matched to their reading skills. If texts are closely matched to the children's reading development, and the child has been taught how to decode unknown words, then, applying this knowledge when working out the small minority of unknown words in such a text will mean that the child will be more likely to develop the confidence to read sufficiently widely and thus become a fluent reader.

The 'Matthew' effect alerts us to the possibility that children who have a wide range of word-attack skills are likely to read more widely. The more they read, the more their skills develop to the point of automaticity. When this happens, the only limiting factor is interest and the cognitive complexity of the ideas being presented. If, however, the children do not have any strategies for working out an unknown word, they will be limited to very simple texts which, in the end, means that they are likely to read less. The less they read, the less likely they are to develop their skills or their visual-reading vocabulary. They may often have to rely on guessing. Guessing becomes more and more difficult as texts get more complex. In the final analysis it is better to know than to guess. Word-reading accuracy is important. When the words are identified it is easier to work out the meaning.

### Conclusion

Suggesting that word-reading accuracy is important does not mean that understanding the text should be relegated to a minor role. We need to ensure that both aspects of reading are developed. If a child can read the words accurately, then there is at least a chance that understanding will be possible. If a child cannot read the words accurately then understanding is likely to be more limited. Ability to use a decoding strategy to attempt to read new, unknown words would seem to stand at the gateway to developing fluent skilled reading when learning to read an alphabetic script.

## References

DONALDSON, M. and REID, J. (1982) 'Language skills and reading: A developmental perspective', in HENDRY, A. (Ed) *Teaching Reading: The Key Issues*, London, Heinemann.

EHRI, L.C. and WILCE, L.S. (1980) 'The influence of orthography on readers' conceptualization of the phonemic strucure of words', *Applied Psycholinguistics*, **1**, pp. 371–85.

HALL, N. (1987) *The Emergence of Literacy*, Sevenoaks, Hodder and Stoughton.

MITCHELL, D. (1982) *The Process of Reading*, Chichester, John Wiley.

PERERA, K. (1993) 'Address to the Australian Reading Association', 1st International Conference, Melbourne, Australia.

PRING, L. and SNOWLING, M. (1986) 'Developmental changes in word recognition: An information processing account', *Quarterly Journal of Experimental Psychology: Human Experimental Psychology*, **38A**, pp. 395–418.

PROTHEROE, P. (1993) 'Are picture books harmful?', *New Scientist*, **1878**, pp. 44–5.

REGO, L.L.B. and BRYANT, P.E. (1993) 'The connection between phonological, syntactic and semantic skills and children's reading and spelling', *European Journal of Psychology of Education*, **VIII**, pp. 235–46.

SMITH, F. (1971) *Understanding Reading: A Psycholinguistic Analysis of Reading and Learning to Read*, New York, Holt, Rinehart and Winston.

SOLMAN, R.T., SINGH, N.N. and KEHOE, E.J. (1992) 'Pictures block the learning of sightwords', *Educational Psychology*, **12**, pp. 143–53.

STAINTHORP, R. (1994) *A longitudinal study of the development of reading strategies in 7 to 11-year-old children*, London University, unpublished Ph.D. thesis.

STANOVICH, K.E. (1980) 'Towards an interactive-compensatory model of individual differences in the development of reading fluency', *Reading Research Quarterly*, **16**, pp. 32–71.

STANOVICH, K.E. (1986) 'Matthew effects in reading: Some consequences of individual differences in the acquisition of literacy', *Reading Research Quarterly*, **21**, pp. 360–407.

STANOVICH, K.E. and WEST, R.F. (1979) 'The development of automatic word recognition skills', *Journal of Reading Behaviour*, **11**, pp. 211–19.

WEST, R.F. and STANOVICH, K.E. (1978) 'Automatic contextual facilitation in readers of three ages', *Child Development*, **49**, pp. 717–27.

# Chapter 5

# Phonemic Awareness and Balanced Reading Instruction

*A. Adamik-Jászó*

### Summary

This chapter gives a detailed description of the phonic-analytic-synthetic method of teaching reading which is widely used in Hungary. The criteria for describing a balanced beginning reading/writing program are described making reference to (i) the characteristics of the given language and orthographical system; (ii) recent research on language awareness; and (iii) the history of reading instruction. A particular heuristic reading program is discussed and presented as an interesting solution to the problem of how to balance instruction.

This chapter begins with terminological problems, and tries to describe the criteria of a balanced beginning reading/writing programme. As a theoretical basis, it uses (a) the characteristics of the given language and orthographical system, (b) the effects of aspects of psycholinguistics on child language development and the emergent literacy of the child, especially research on phonemic awareness, (c) the experience gained from the history of reading/writing instruction and, (d) philosophy; i.e., the influence of philosophical schools on education. After some necessary background information, the chapter describes the phonic-analytic-synthetic method widely used in Hungary, then introduces the reading programmes launched after 1978. It concentrates on an heuristic programme elaborated by Tolnai (1991), and the intensive/combined programme elaborated by Lovasz and Adamik (1991).

## Introduction

*Terminological Problems*

In Hungary, the methodology of teaching reading distinguishes between three approaches namely: analytic, synthetic and analytic-synthetic methods.

This distinction is different from the one often used in English speaking countries, and it is rooted in German-Austrian traditions. For example, in the *Dictionary of Reading* only the analytic and the synthetic methods are listed, the analytic-synthetic is not (Harris and Hodges, 1981). Furthermore the term global method is used for analytic or whole-word method. On a different basis, we distinguish alphabet or abc method (i.e., spelling method) and phonetic method (i.e., phonics). The former is often called the lettering method, the latter the sounding method. Naturally, these two main groups could be interwoven: the *Dictionary of Reading* speaks about synthetic and analytic phonics but similarly we can also speak about the synthetic and analytic alphabet method.

The analytic-synthetic method is a combined method but again the word 'combined' is used differently by us from how it is defined in the *Dictionary of Reading*. Our concept of a combined method is close to the definition under 'eclectic approach' which says: 'a systematic way of teaching reading that combines features of analytic, or global, and the synthetic approaches or methods.' In this definition, the emphasis is put on the word 'systematic' because the analytic-synthetic method is a balanced solution not a mixed or eclectic one in the pejorative meaning of the word (see the second meaning in the dictionary). 'Balanced' and 'mixed combined' methods are distinguished on the basis of the quality of the solution.

The criteria for a balanced analytic-synthetic method are the following. It is a combination in which the whole and its parts are of equal importance; i.e., both the words and the sound–letter correspondences. It develops the auditive and the visual skills to the same extent, but the auditive area must always have an advantage over the visual one. It develops equally the four language skills: speaking, listening, reading, and writing including orthography (this term is used instead of 'spelling'). Teaching writing occurs simultaneous with teaching reading, namely the two areas support each other. It relies on both consciousness and the intuition of pupils; i.e., it develops language awareness on the one hand, and on the other hand it uses good literature, games and drama. It also uses and develops both logical thinking and emotions. A preparatory period is always part of this approach. The programme must be balanced from the very beginning of the instruction, and must continue through several grades of the elementary school. The strength of such a programme is in its structure. In this it is similar to the Kodály method in our music education or the conductive education of the Pető Institute.

### Theoretical Basis

#### The linguistic basis

Hungarians speak Hungarian or Magyar language which belongs to the Finno-Ugric or Uralic languages such as the Finnish, the Estonian, and several other minority languages spoken in Russia. Hungarian is very different from Indo-

European languages not only generically but typologically also: it has a very rich morphology with an abudance of suffixes. Taking into consideration the variations of case, possessive, and other suffixes, a noun can have 882 forms. The conjugation system is complicated also. This agglutinative characteristic of Hungarian makes it structurally just the opposite of English. While English puts short words together Hungarian combines morphemes into long word forms. Besides the rich morphology, Hungarian has another phenomenon called stem- or root-alternation, as a result of which the long word forms change; they do not have constant forms. The pronunciation of standard Hungarian is clear; it means that the vowels are pronounced clearly in all positions, even in un-stressed syllables. According to historical traditions, Hungarian uses the Latin alphabet. The orthography — which underwent a fundamental reform in 1832 — is easy: there is a one-to-one correspondence between sounds and letters, the orthographical system has only one exception: one consonant has two letters.

All these linguistical phenomena — the long and changing word forms, the clear pronunciation, and the simple orthography — prevent a global method working really well in Hungarian reading instruction. The argument of Finnish educators is similar. Experiments to introduce a global method failed in 1862, 1870, 1947, and 1978. The phonics approach using sound-syllabication works well (during syllabication the sounds are pronounced not the names of the letters) as the main decoding strategy of the word. It is emphasized that, in this case, the keeping of our tradition is not a question of backwardness, but a question of a special language and orthography.

### The psycholinguistic basis

The interactive model of a developmental reading process could be adapted best because it is probably the only one which copes with the existing phe-nomenon of a whole–part relationship. The scheme theory has been accepted as the psychological equivalent of the linguistic field theory. The Hungarian reading programmes were always based on the oral language development of the child, and now we adapt the results gained from the research on the emergent literacy of the child. The theoretical literature on language aware-ness has already been adapted, especially the theory of Downing (1984), and the results of the Scandinavian researchers. These studies are of extreme im-portance for Hungary because they support our experience i.e., phonemic awareness is a prerequisite of reading instruction. Furthermore, *Beginning to Read* written by Adams (1990) is also crucial because it incorporates and evaluates the investigations in the field of speech perception.

### The influence of history and philosophy

The history of reading instruction is of equal importance: we can always learn from the successes and the failures of the past. It is a treasure of accumulated ex-perience, and we must remember: one of the sources of developments in meth-odology is the experience of early and current research workers and teachers.

The influence of the philosophical schools is undeniable but — to the best of my knowledge — it has not been examined in Hungary in relation to present practices in reading instruction. Naturally, historians take it into consideration, for example in the book of Mathews (1966) *Teaching to Read: Historically Considered* there is a fine analysis about the connection of the philosophy of the enlightenment and the appearance of the global method. This was the philosophy which bore the organismic theory and the syntactical principle in grammar i.e., the emphasis of the whole.

## *The communication theory*

The most important theoretical basis not only for reading instruction but for the language education in its entirety is communication theory. Hungarian education adapted the communication model of Roman Jacobson. It is interesting that the Hungarian educators emphasize the importance of the interactive theory but in this respect they do not cite the scientific literature but a famous Hungarian poet, fiction writer and translator, Desiderius Kosztolányi (1928).

> The books sleeping on the shelves of the libraries are not ready yet, they are sketchy, they do not make any sense in themselves. In order to make sense of them, you, the reader, is needed. Despite being completed masterpieces, there are only references in them, allusions, scribbles, which will awake into life in another soul. The book is always created by two persons: by the writer who wrote it, and by the reader who reads it. (Kosztolányi, 1928)

So reading is an interaction or transaction between the writer and the reader, a continously working process. Therefore it is difficult to describe it and to teach it.

## Reading Methods

In Hungary, compulsory school attendance starts at age six. There is no reading instruction at the preschool stage. The basic reading skills are to be acquired during the first year, and reading skills are practised in Grades 2, 3, and 4. There is no reading instruction in the upper grades at all. So when we speak about reading instruction we refer to the reading instruction of the elementary school, and identify it with the beginning of reading instruction.

A first-grade reading programme begins with an abc-book for the first semester in which sounds and corresponding letters are taught. It is followed in the second semester by a reader which has short stories. Pupils also practise the skills acquired during the first semester. Therefore the traditional name of the grade programme is 'ABC and Reader'. In the past the abc and the reader were bound into one volume; now they are separated into two. The 2nd, 3rd, and 4th grade readers are literature-based. These books are not kept in the school, the families buy them. Supplements, such as wallcharts, flash cards, moveable letters, worksheets, etc. are also used but workbooks and worksheets were introduced only in the early 1970s. The reason for this relative simplicity is tradition on the one hand, and our language structure and orthographical system on the other.

Phonic-Analytic-Synthetic (PAS) Method.

The classic PAS-method was introduced by Pál Gönczy in 1869, and was refined several times by other educators during the following century. The whole teaching process was based on spoken language. Therefore a very special subject was placed in the curriculum called 'Speech and Thought Exercises' (*Denk-und Sprechübungen* in German). This subject was taught in the first two grades three hours weekly. It was discontinued only in 1963, unfortunately.

The teaching of reading itself consisted of two stages: preparation and teaching. Teaching reading started with preparatory exercises i.e., a foundation for both reading and writing. The preparatory exercises lasted six weeks, and it was an oral-aural process. At the end of the preparatory period the pupils were able to analyse speech and blend sound. Having gained 'phonemic awareness', the teaching of reading could be based on sound–letter correspondences. The authors of this method definitely thought that phonemic awareness was the prerequisite of reading instruction. In addition, the pupils had special preparation for writing. They practised spatial relationships, dealt with directions and whole–part relationships, and drew simple forms and letter elements. The real teaching of reading started after this preparation. Every teaching session was divided into two parts: sound teaching and letter teaching, first the sound was taught then the corresponding letter.

The teaching process itself was analytic-synthetic. The teacher followed prescribed steps.

1. The teacher started with a story i.e., with the whole language. Since 1910, there have been pictures for stories in the abc-books.
2. After discussing the story, the teacher called the pupils' attention to a word containing the new sound which would be taught. Pupils pronounced the word, analysed it into its syllables and sounds, took the sound in question out of the word, articulated it loudly and correctly, and established its place in the order of the sounds of the word and/ or syllable. Then the sound was blended with other ones into words.
3. After this oral-aural analysis, the corresponding letter was taught. Letter recognition was practised in different ways. Then the letter was pronounced and blended with the already known letters, so oral reading was practised. Always the sound of the letter was taught and, the programmes taught pupils to pronounce the names of the letters at the end of the first year. (In Hungary, we never spell out the words in the way English speaking people do. Our decoding tool is always the sound-syllabication.)

4. Finally the written form was taken. We teach immediately the cursive forms, the pupils do not print the letters. The teacher explained the forms of the letters carefully, using the already practised letter elements. The new letter was combined with the previously learned letters i.e., the pupils wrote words, then read the written words aloud. The meaning was always explained.

The PAS-method was balanced because the pupils obtained the impression of the meaningful whole word and its relatively meaningless parts simultaneously: the 'meaning emphasis' and the 'code emphasis' were never juxtaposed in our traditional practice.

The structure of the abc-book was very carefully organized. The analysed word had always only one unknown sound/letter. Its name was a model or sample word (probably key-word in the English terminology). During the first semester the lower-case letters were taught, capitals were taught during the second semester. The structure of a page in the abc-book was as follows. At the top the picture for the story was located. Next to, or under it, was the model word illustrated by its object. Then the printed form of the letter was demonstrated. Thereafter words, sentences and short stories are used as soon as it was possible. At the bottom of the page, the written form of the letter was presented, then the written words. At the very beginning, one could read only words; the content was not really interesting, although the authors attempted to publish texts of literary value. Words were broken into syllables. In the reader i.e., in the second semester, whole words were not broken into syllables, but sound-syllabication was used in classroom practice as a decoding tool (remember the long word forms because of our rich morphology). The teachers' manual contained only general directions and model descriptions of a few lessons. There were neither directions nor exercises in the abc and reader.

Phonomimics, a kind of kinesthetic reading method invented by Róza Czukrász worked excellently in practice until 1950. To the best of my knowledge, phonomimics was used only in Hungary in mass education so it could be considered as a very Hungarian reading method which made the PAS-method easier. Phonomimics was used especially during the preparation, definitely not after the first grade. It used signs made by hand in order to aid the quick recognition of sounds, sound–letter correspondences, and the blending of the sounds.

Phonomimics was born in the spirit of child study, an educational movement at the beginning of the twentieth century. When Dewey and Parker developed the whole-word method in the USA, we in Hungary developed a kinesthetic method the essence of which was a simultaneous movement, involving activity and playfulness. Thus we chose another child-centred solution. Between 1925 and 1950 most of our abc-books were written using phonomimics; we had about forty different series, mostly coloured ones.

In 1950 the school system was nationalized and rigidly centralized. This was so for the publishing houses also. The Textbook Publisher controlled by the Communist Party served (or rather ruled) education. Only one abc and reader was approved for use: a new variation of PAS-method was elaborated without phonomimics. The phonomimics and other experimental methods were forbidden because they 'served bourgeois society' and in communist society 'learning is work not play; the children of the working classes do not have time to play in school'. In truth, the new PAS-method was not bad, but without the spirit of the denied half-century. Not the method itself, rather the reader suffered: texts were filled with political slogans, with biographies of communist leaders, communist and Soviet holidays.

It is a special phenomenon that alternative educational programmes appeared earlier than the alternative political parties so the thaw appeared in education earlier than in politics (in our usage the word 'alternative' means different i.e., different from the centralized trend). The Ministry of Education launched a new curriculum in 1978, and introduced a system of alternative reading programmes published in 1978, 1980, 1985, and 1987.

The new programmes were influenced by an experiment which started in the Budapest Pedagogical Institute in 1969 under the influence of a global-method programme written in the early 1970s for children with learning difficulties. This is the reason that in spite of their differences, these new programmes have common features as follows. The original PAS-method was changed: the preparatory exercises, the 'sound teaching–then–letter teaching' order, the sound-syllabication were cancelled. The starting point is the letter not the sound. Instead of the traditional oral reading, silent reading is emphasized from the very beginning of the instruction. Worksheet exercises were introduced. The whole process is visual rather than oral-aural. Furthermore, these programmes are fast, sometimes teaching not single letters but letter groups at the same time. Three of them use whole words or sight words but in a very different way from the general practice abroad i.e., without planned repetitions. For example, the first published one has a so-called global preparatory period, teaching thirty-eight sight words. The name of this programme is 'phonic-analytic-synthetic programme with global preparatory exercises'. The second programme entitled 'the global programme' teaches about eighty sight words at the beginning, and does not teach blending at all. The third one which is part of the language-literature-communication programme has two books: one for sight-word teaching and a second for synthetic teaching of the letters and sounds. The teacher uses the two books simultaneously, so the programme works in a similar fashion to the first one. The fourth programme, the intensive-combined programme is rather synthetic; it teaches blending carefully. On the other hand, it also uses sight-word techniques in a beginning transitional period, but does not use sound-syllabication.

The authors of these four alternative programmes incorporated some features of French and American programmes and combined them with our traditions: the results are strange mixtures — of theories and pedagogies called here mixed methods to distinguishing them from the balanced combination — observation and experience suggest that they do not work really well in practice.

It is very difficult to establish the quality of these programmes because the majority of schoolteachers use variations of their own, very often drawing the syllable boundaries into the pupils' books. Last year a new abc-book was published by a prestigious private company which reintroduced syllabication. It is interesting that the everyday practice turned against these forced programmes and developed new balanced ones which will be introduced further.

## Messages for Teachers

The recent Hungarian reading programmes are described below.

### The Heuristic Programme

The heuristic programme is a modern solution of the PAS-method. It has three important units:

1.  three series of wallcharts: the first one for vowels (lower-case letters) which 'live in books', the second one for consonants (lower-case letters) which 'live in houses', the third one for capital letters which are located in a train as initials of childrens' names;
2.  the ABC book;
3.  the Reader which is literature-based and beautifully illustrated.

The wallchart is for the analysis and synthesis of the words. Many thousands of opportunities are hidden in it waiting to be discovered by the children hence the name 'heuristic'. The ABC book is for practice blending. The Reader is introduced around the end of November so the wallcharts and the ABC book serve as preparatory tools but they could be used later, as well, for trainings.

The wallchart works as follows. First the vowels, then the consonants are taught at the very beginning of the school year. The sound is always practised with its key word: alma — a, esernyő — e; etc. Movements that recollect phonomimics are used, for example for the distinction of the short and long sounds the children swing their hands, pronouncing the consonants they snap with their two fingers: citrom — c, etc. Little songs and ditties are used also.

The meaning of the programme signs is the following:

●/2●    means that the pupils have to collect words in which the sound in question is on the second place, 3● — on the third place, etc.

▲/2    means that the pupils have to collect words in which there are two sounds in question, 3 — there are three sounds, etc.

■/2●    means that the pupils have to collect words which are structurally similar to the key word. For example, the key word is alma, its second sound is 1, so the pupils collect words in which there is an 1 on the second place: elme, ólom, alom, etc.

The wallchart provides limitless opportunities to practise the structure of the words i.e., the order of the sounds. The whole process is oral-aural. As well as the vocabulary being enlarged enormously, creativity develops. Furthermore, the pupils are engaged in an up-to-date activity: they follow programmes, and later they can write programmes to the words. In that way the work of word analysis becomes interesting.

The ABC book works as follows. It practises blending. First the consonant b is blended with every vowel using different forms. At the end of every section a big wheel is located for repetition and control, and a song is also created. Step by step more and more words are introduced in both printed and written forms. The first occurrence is broken into syllables, further the word is presented as a whole but underneath the word the syllable structure is marked.

The use of pictures in blending is considered very important, because they require the pupils to undertake oral-aural work: they must remember a certain word, to isolate its first sound, and then blend these first sounds to each other. It is a good training for developing memory and speed which are extremely important in emergent reading. The careful, interesting and beautiful illustrations break the monotony of blending and syllabication. In the meantime the whole i.e., the meaningful story, sentences, words are presented, pictures for stories are used at the beginning of every section.

Many believe that the work with the wallchart and the ABC book is an excellent preparation for reading and writing, a very good training for developing phonemic awareness. However empirical evidence on the matter is not available in Hungary. The pupils taught by this programme appear to write well and their spelling is very good. The heuristic programme has an adaptation for teaching English.

### The Intensive Combined Programme

The basic idea of an intensive combined programme is the integration of a literature base and balanced instruction. The programme has the first and second-grade parts; the authors are currently working on its third and fourth-grade materials.

What does integration mean in our interpretation? The main characteristics of these textbooks are that the activities of language arts are organized into readings. On the left pages the texts are located, on the right sides the exercises are attached to the stories. These exercises include four areas: comprehension, practice of reading techniques and correct pronunciation, grammar and orthography, and penmanship. The preparation of composition is included in the exercises, as well. In that way the language skills are practised and developed functionally, in situations connected with the whole language. Furthermore, the four areas are closely connected to each other as well. We believe that this is a natural and practical way of integrating the development of different skills. Hungarian grammar and orthography are always difficult for the pupils, therefore we make an effort to keep the important problems under review in schools i.e., we repeatedly address them.

The programme has another important characteristic. The grammatical exercises are adjusted to the requirements of the state curriculum, but they also teach the material of the next grade although not as a requirement. In that way everything is taught twice and this repetition guarantees weak pupils keep up with the others and gives an impetus to the gifted ones. We call this solution 'permanent repetition and hidden differentiation'. In addition the book gives creative exercises for the gifted pupils but these interesting exercises are not closed from the others.

In order to use the whole language approach, the programme uses mostly readings of literary value. Furthermore, the texts are organized according to a certain system. The first Reader, entitled *Letter Fair*, contains short tales and poems, often humorous ones. The *World of Children*, which is used in the second semester of the first grade, contains mostly folk and modern tales organized into sections titled: 'I can already read', 'We became six year olds', 'The family', 'School', 'Things', 'Nature', 'Spring holidays'. The aim of this grouping is to let the pupils become acquainted with reading relating to their nearer and wider environments. The themes of the second-grade book are: 'The school', 'The family', 'The town' and 'the village', 'Crafts and jobs', 'The capital: Budapest', 'The main regions of Hungary', 'The neighbouring countries', and finally 'The main regions of the world'. The book does not aim to teach geography or history, it gives only a survey using interesting stories. For example, introducing the neighbouring countries, it gives Czech, Slovakian, Rumanian, Ukrainan, etc. folktales. It also speaks about Hungarian minorities living in these neighbouring countries. The book does not stop at the neighbourhood but opens a window on Europe and the whole world. It presents Eskimo, Chinese, African, American Indian, Australian, etc. folktales. This system and content make possible the foundation of patriotic feelings and other important social values such as respect of the family, friendship, etc. On the other hand, it develops an understanding of other cultures and nations, feeling of tolerance — an attitude which is very important especially nowadays. Thus we tried to create a balance between national and international literature. Therefore the title of the second-grade book is '*Window opener*'.

The genres are varied because we wanted to create a balance between prose and poetry, fiction and non-fiction. Our goal was to develop every type of reading as literal, interpretive, critical, and creative activities. The pupils are encouraged to read not only the textbook but trade books, too. This goal is served by the 'Library Pages' which consist of recommendations for the reading of different interesting books and teach pupils the use of the library. At the end of the chapters, descriptions of children's games are provided, and at the end of the volumes there are special chapters entitled 'Holidays' with descriptions of traditional and national holidays, where old and popular customs are presented. These games can be presented providing a good opportunity to

Figure 5.1:   *Reading methods in Hungary*

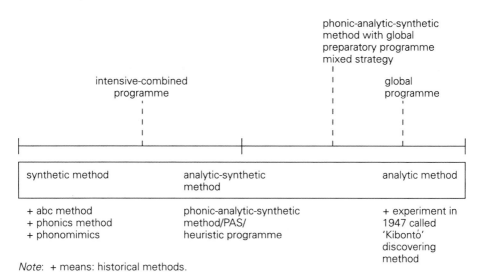

| synthetic method | analytic-synthetic method | analytic method |
|---|---|---|
| + abc method<br>+ phonics method<br>+ phonomimics | phonic-analytic-synthetic method/PAS/<br>heuristic programme | + experiment in 1947 called 'Kibonto' discovering method |

*Note*:  + means: historical methods.

create child drama. The Hungarian folklore is very rich in this respect also. The list of difficult long words and a little dictionary with word explanations are attached at the very end of the book.

### Conclusion

The present article has concentrated mostly on the beginning of reading instruction in Hungary and had a double goal:

1.  it summarized a possible theoretical basis for the methodology of teaching reading and writing; and
2.  tried to introduced the Hungarian reading and writing instruction which is very different from the one used in the English speaking countries.

Among the components of the theoretical basis, it has given an extreme importance to the experience gained from the study of the history of reading and writing instruction saying that both professional experience and the pedagogic experiment are of equal importance in informing practice. Its main philosophy is the concept of integrated and balanced instruction. It has clarified the terminology which is illustrated in Figure 5.1. The pure analytic and the pure synthetic methods are rare or have died out. Mostly combinations of methods are now used; the question is 'How effective is a balanced programme?'.

Among the failures of the communist era, the reading writing programmes had their own ideological straitjackets. Fortunately, practice is currently moving toward more flexible and balanced instruction. Our task is to create a new methodology. (In the textbook published in 1978 there were ten pages about the beginning reading writing instruction.) Apart from the problems drafted in this chapter, developing a new methodology in Hungary has a double-faced problem: to integrate insights from abroad where these hold promise, but, on the other hand, to save our traditions and the special characteristics of our reading writing instruction. This is the most difficult balance to achieve.

## References

ADAMIK-JÁSZÓ, A. (1985) 'National efforts in the teaching of the native language in Hungarian elementary schools at the end of the 19th century', *Annales Universitatis Scientiarum Budapestinensis de Rolando Eötvös Nominate*, XIV, Budapest, pp. 33–40.

ADAMIKNÉ JÁSZÓ, A. (1990) *A magyar olvasástanítás története* (History of Hungarian reading instruction), Budapest, Tankönyvkiadó.

ADAMS, M.J. (1990) *Beginning to Read: Thinking and Learning about Print*, Cambridge, Massachusetts, The MIT Press.

ANDERSON, R.C. and PEARSON, P.D. (1984) 'A schema theoretic view of basic processes in reading', in PEARSON, P.D. (Ed) *Handbook of Reading Research*, New York and London, Longman, pp. 255–91.

DOWNING, J. (Ed) (1973) *Comparative reading*, New York, MacMillan.

DOWNING, J. and VALTIN, R. (1984) *Language Awareness and Learning to Read*, New York, Springer Verlag.

ESZTERGÁLYOSNÉ FÖLDESI, K. (1993) *Az én ábécém* (My abc book), Celldömölk, Apáczai Kiadó.

GÓSY, M. (1989) *Beszédészlelés* (Speech perception), Budapest, MTA Nyeivtudományi Intézet.

HARRIS, T.L. and HODGES, R.E. (1981) *A Dictionary of Reading and Related Terms*, Newark, Delaware, IRA.

HANSEN, M. (1988) 'Project Cecilia: A language enrichment programme for 5–7 year old children', *International Research in Reading*, **5**, 1. pp. 44–46.

KATONA, N. (1991) *English Sounds and Letters*, Budapest, Tankönyvkiadó.

KEHR, C. (1879) *Geschichte der Methodik des deutschen Volksschulunterrichtes*, Vol. 2, Gotha.

KOSZTOLÁNYI, D. (1928) *Ábécé a prózáról és a regényről* (ABC on the prose and on the fiction), Budapest.

KUTINÉ SAHIN-TÓTH, K. (1992) *A maci és a betük* (The bear cub and the letters), Budapest, Fővárosi Pedagógiai Intézet.

LIE, A. (1991) 'Effect of a training programme for stimulating skills in word analysis in first-grade children', *Reading Research Quarterly*, **26**, 3, pp. 234–50.

LIGETI, R. and KUTINÉ SAHIN-TÓTH, K. (1980) *A maci olvas* (The bear cub is reading), *A maci ir* (The bear cub is writing), *A maci mesél* (The bear cub is story-telling), Budapest, Tankönyvkiadó.

LOVÁSZ, G. and ADAMIK, T. (1991) *Ablaknyitogató I–II.* (Window opener), Budapest, Tankönyvkiadó.

LOVÁSZ, G., BALOGH, B. and BARKÓ, E. (1987) *Betüvásár* (Letter Fair), *Gyermekvilág* (World of children), Budapest, Tankönyvkiadó.

LUNDBERG, I., FROST, J. and PETERSEN, O. (1988) 'Effects of an extensive programme for stimulating phonological awareness in pre-school children', *Reading Research Quarterly*, **23**, 3, pp. 253–84.

MATHEWS, M. (1966) *Teaching to Read: Historically Considered*, The University of Chicago Press.

MEIXNER, I. and JUSTNÉ KÉRY, E. (1967) *Az olvasástanítás pszichológiai alapjai* (The psychological foundations of teaching reading), Budapest, Akadémiai Kiadó.

REIN, W. (1906) *Encyklopädisches Handbuch der Pädagogik I–X.* 2nd ed., Jena.

ROMANKOVICS, A., ROMANKOVICSNÉ TÓTH, J. and MEIXNER, I. (1978) *Olvasni tanulok* (I learn to read), *Irni tanulok* (I learn to write), Olvasókönyv (First reader), Budapest, Tankönyvkiadó.

SARMAVUORI, K. (1993) *Äidinkielen opetustieteen perusteet* (Foundations of mother-tongue education), Helsinki, Yliopistopaino.

SINGER, H. and RUDDELL, R.B. (1985) *Theoretical models and processes of reading*, 3rd ed., Newark, Delaware, IRA.

TOLNAI, G. (1991) *Abécéskönyv* (ABC book), *Olvasókönyv* (First reader), Irás munkafüzet (Workbook for writing) I–II, *Feladatlapok* (Exercises), *Programfal* (Programmed wallchart), Budapest, Tankönyvkiadó.

ZSOLNAI, J. *et al.* (1985) *Szó és betü* (Word and letter), *Vázolólapok* (Workbook for preparation of writing), *Irás munkafüzet* (Workbook for writing), *Csillagjáró fehér ráró* (White horse magic), Budapest, Tankönyvkiadó.

*Chapter 6*

# Children Learn to Read by Being Taught

*M. Turner*

**Summary**

Children do not, in the main, learn to read by accident, by inspiration, contagion or osmosis, or by being encouraged in attitudes that others deem socially desirable. They learn by being taught. Reading is not a natural activity, but a set of gradually acquired component skills initially learned independently, but later integrated and automated. Comprehension and mastery of syntax can be shown to depend crucially upon phonological decoding. The 'whole language' movement may be thought, in retrospect, to have been sustained by remarkably little solid knowledge and is now distinctly irrelevant against a new background of research endeavour in a cluster of disciplines. There is no single straight path to competence in reading but there are many teaching routes which are costly in terms of child failure.

**Introduction**

There are numerous examples of research commonplaces, often technical innovations, reaching the world of education twenty years after their first appearance (Rasch testing methodology, efficiency frontier analysis). However the influence of Whole Language upon the teaching of reading in Britain and elsewhere in the 1980s has been more than a mere anachronism, whose point of origin (a 'psycholinguistic' school of thought in the late 1960s and early 1970s), has continued, like a defunct star, to radiate long after its intellectual demise.

The effects of this influence could be seen at school, LEA and eventually at national level during the later 1980s and have led to a revulsion from 'wholistic', and reinstatement of traditional, methods in the teaching of reading. Decoding of phonic and graphic structures has been discovered, for instance in the revisions of the National Curriculum order for English. This has occurred in spite of, and without compromising, the beneficial recent emphasis upon quality in children's reading materials.

The Whole Language movement may be thought to have drawn inspiration more from objectives of political reform than from any explicit methodology for the teaching of reading. Unfortunately the inspiration commonly included a repudiation of the piecemeal and provisional procedures of science. Fortunately a recovered sense of the value of the modest and partial knowledge afforded by empirical research may point the way to the future. During the last quarter of a century, the volume of research activity in reading and associated topics has increased exponentially, enhancing our understanding, not only of the learning processes in individuals and groups, but also of the ways these interact with particular instructional principles.

This chapter will attempt to indicate some of the ways in which the cognitive sciences are generating leads for teachers, both generalist and specialist, to follow, in the vacuum which has followed the demise of the 'psycholinguistic' account of reading.

### The Debacle of Whole Language

After their beginners had [had] two years of 'learning to read without being taught', the teachers were shocked to find . . . that their [Year] Two classes were full of non-readers, except for the children whose parents had ignored instructions and told their children how to read. So I found the teachers of seven-year-olds were rushing round trying to give their children phonics or Letterland or *anything*, because most of the class had only around twenty common sight words. (Yule, 1992, pp. 12–13)

That snapshot from the July 1992 issue of the United Kingdom Reading Association's journal, *Reading*, will be recognizable to anyone who has had close involvement with infant schools over the last few years. ('Emergent reading', the joke ran in 1988, had become 'emergency reading'.)

Other features in the same issue of *Reading* included a leading article by the editor, Wray, on 'structure' and an article by Carty (1992) advocating a 'conversation about spelling', in which he wrote from Canada:

During the last two years I have listened to the dilemma of elementary teachers (How should I be approaching spelling?); to the annoyance of high school teachers (How come kids can't spell anymore?); to the questioning of administrators (How come our spelling test results are declining?); and to the criticism of parents (Are they teaching spelling anymore?). (Carty, 1992, p. 17)

Such realism must have come as something of a shock to *Reading*'s regular audience.

All over the Anglophone world the costs of 'Hurricane Whole Language' are being counted. Its promoters seem to avoid being brought face to face with victims and their families. The intellectual pretensions of the programme as a whole have been courteously, if briskly, demolished (e.g., Adams, 1991). That the movement is far from dead is shown by the favoured strategies for repair: these tend to combine further non-teaching of reading with job creation. Reading recovery is not a very distinctive intervention, yet it is enormously labour-intensive and avoids the streamlining (Hatcher, Hulme and Ellis, 1994) and addition of phonics (Iversen and Tunmer, 1993) which evaluation shows enhance its efficiency. A popular computer-based speech synthesis package vigorously promoted by *The Times Educational Supplement* requires a non-teaching assistant for each child but introduces no new reading skills.

### An Irrationalist Methodology

A feature of residual interest is the explicit hostility to science and its methods to which some leaders of the whole language movement publicly commit themselves. Frank Smith has been concerned specifically to repudiate the scientific viewpoint: 'They want to study things scientifically . . . scientifically, meaning control . . . If you study learning experimentally you have got control of learning.' The elimination of science would seem a positive advantage, given some of Smith's other views ('the notion that kids will learn to read by phonics doesn't work'; 'kids learn 2,500 words every day') (Smith, 1991).

According to Kenneth Goodman, experimental research concerns itself with 'positivistic studies with control and experimental groups . . . [with] . . . tight experimental controls . . . [and] . . . manageable variables' (Goodman, 1992, p. 193). This regrettable apparatus excites his disapproval. However, freedom is within reach of all: 'As professionals, whole language teachers have moved far beyond trial and error in making their instructional decisions' (*ibid.*, p. 197).

Aylwin, reviewing Adams' *Beginning To Read*, is taken aback by 'over 500 references to research in the first ten chapters', and by the revelation that '[w]e are said to have orthographic, phonological and semantic processors in our brains . . . it all sounds like pressing a computer button to call up the language required'. He imagines that the research must be 'concerned with testing phonics in psychology lab conditions' (Aylwin, 1993, p. 30). But objectivity need not be bought so dear that idealism is compromised: 'The commitment to a vision of a better world, a democratic, social and political system is a prerequisite for objectivity in social science' (Olssen, 1993, p. 170).

If objectivity itself is contingent, why be detained by futile attempts at rigour?

> The outcomes of teaching depend upon so many variables . . . that attempts to formulate testable hypotheses about effective teaching are rarely worthwhile. This is why qualitative work within an interpretive paradigm is favoured by many educational researchers . . . [This is] one of the great achievements of educational research in recent years

... [though] for policy-makers, it is quantitative work in a positivist paradigm that is often appropriate. (Bassey, 1994)

Logical positivism, be it noted, 'dissolved as a school at the end of the 1930s' (Bullock *et al.*, 1988, p. 486); but in contemporary British education it has found its nemesis — as a catchpenny term to travesty experimental methods.

If the demands of 'normal science' are intolerable, any substitute brings relief. For Meek, 'Reading research', in particular, 'breeds its own brand of evidence. The consequent problem is that reading specialists are bound to ignore the evidence that arises spontaneously in classrooms because it isn't generalizable' (Meek, 1990, p. 151). Not one to remain at a loss in the face of such a dilemma, Meek emphasizes: 'Any significant research I have done rests on my having treated anecdotes as evidence' (Meek, 1988, p. 8).

All of this risks a worrying degree of estrangement from the principles of a democratically constituted society, with its ancient links between an independent judiciary (rules of evidence), the authority of science (academic freedom to criticize) and political pluralism (voter autonomy). With such a level of confusion among education leaders, is it any wonder that superstition should have taken hold so largely?

### The Earlier Case Against Reading Subskills

After Whole Language, important questions remain. Among these is the place of the component skills of reading, their identification and role in teaching. The following statement seems not to have been made in any spirit of facetiousness: 'Poor sequencing, for example, is taken to be implicated in reading problems despite the substantial meta-analyses of ten to fifteen years ago showing that this is not the case' (Thomas, 1993a). Now any lack of relationship between sequencing and reading ability would seem to be a rather well-kept secret. What can be the justification for such a statement, even among those who do not suppose that research is confined to 'psychology lab conditions'?

Two of three sources proposed (Thomas, 1993b) for the reference to research published in the mid to late 1970s are influential publications by Arter and Jenkins (1979) and Newcomer and Hammill (1975). Both, however, describe their work in terms of research reviews. This is not the same thing as meta-analyses. Meta-analysis, a statistical technique which surveys relatively unsubstantial, but nevertheless consistent, findings across a range of studies, is bringing to light advantages in certain treatments for strokes and breast cancer and in neglected procedures in obstetrics. The traditional review article, institutionalizing a viewpoint which becomes orthodox, may carry a cost of 25,000 preventable heart-attack deaths a year in the US (see, e.g., *Economist*, 1991). A further article, by Johnson and Pearson (1975), contains experience and opinions, but reflects empirical work only in a single passing reference to the intercorrelation of subtests in assessment batteries. This however is a common general argument. Children may be good at both swimming and riding bicycles. But this means neither that the two achievements consist in interchangeable skills, nor that there are *no* component skills in either activity.

### Precursors of Reading Skill?

The general point of Newcomer and Hammill, in their review of the literature surrounding the Illinois Test of Psycholinguistic Abilities (ITPA), is that many putative subskills are neither necessary nor sufficient for the achievement of reading. This may be accepted. Indeed a further cautionary tale may be added to that of the ITPA: the collapse of the Frostig literature on perceptual-motor 'readiness'. There was much wrong, it turned out, with both these schools of thought; yet each, though short-lived, was an honest attempt, based on theory, observation and evidence, to originate an educational tool.

Are there prerequisite general skills (sometimes called 'skills of learning') that are both necessary and sufficient for learning to read? The possibility of prerequisite skills has barely begun to be sketched out (Rabinowitz, 1990). The instructional experiments designed to 'teach intelligence' or 'prerequisite skills' have often foundered in disappointment (see Blagg, 1991).

However a single, important exception must be made: the case of phonological skills. These have been shown not only to have precursor status (antecedent position in a learning sequence) but to be causal of later reading achievement. Here the literature seems unlikely to prove fragile. Indeed, direct remedial benefits have been shown to result from phonological skill training *in conjunction with* reading teaching (Hatcher, Hulme and Ellis, op. cit.).

In general, the success of teaching general learning skills seems linked to the precision with which the skills taught relate to the curriculum to which they must be bridged. For instance reading comprehension and metacomprehension skills can be identified and taught quite successfully (for research summaries see the fourth part, and especially Chapter 29, of Carnine *et al.*, 1990).

### Remedial Teaching Rationale

The case of Diagnostic Prescriptive Remediation (DPR) or Differential Diagnosis Prescriptive Teaching (DDPT), as Arter and Jenkins call it, is less clear. The frequent absence of positive benefit for generic remedial instruction has been noted before. Arter and Jenkins rely heavily on particular 'models' (especially that of the ITPA), but reach only the modest conclusion: not proven. The modality-preference thesis, to which they devote much space, is treated with just scepticism in their review. It is often said that some children have a preference for the auditory, some for the visual, channel. Adams (1990, p. 60) quotes a survey that shows that of special-education teachers, 95 per cent were familiar with this argument and that, of those who were, 99 per cent believed such considerations to be most important, believing the modality argument to be supported by research: 'Unhappily it is not.' (Adams cites a mere nine sources from a 'long list'.) More realistic, perhaps, is the view of Engelmann, that 'The central cause of all failure in school is the teaching. When the teaching fails, the kids fail' (Engelmann, 1992, p. 79). One ought to question the relevance of much data gathered in differential individual assessments, if '. . . learning styles and individual differences have a relatively minor effect on kid performance' (*ibid.*, p. 86).

But such agreements still do not, I think, allow us to reach the conclusion that the whole diagnostic-prescriptive methodology is misconceived. Indeed, this kind of intervention can usefully be compared in its effect with the more coherent direct-instruction interventions. These more or less ignore individual cognitive differences, though not differences in attainment (Branwhite, 1983). Though weaker in effect, DPR still brings improvements.

## Decoding Can Deliver Comprehension

A doctrinaire approach to reading can flourish only in the absence of reliable knowledge. As 'wholistic' attitudes lose their hold, the empirical dimensions of reading can once again be clearly seen. The three important constructs in terms of which reading capability may be described are, briefly: accuracy, fluency and comprehension. Moreover, among the three there are mutual relations established, to an acceptable degree of robustness, in the literature. Thus, comprehension depends crucially upon fluency (a given level of fluency is necessary for working memory to rehearse sentence structure) and fluency in turn depends upon the automation of single-word recognition processes.

Decoding (phonological reconstruction of speech-sounds from letter-symbol sequences) is perhaps easiest to study and may be assisted by the use of non-words (Rack *et al.*, 1992), homophones (Johnston *et al.*, 1988) and by lists of regular and irregular words. Comprehension, by contrast, seems more intractable, though the degree to which the skills involved have been identified now permits instruction in them as needed. This process can be most successful (Oakhill and Yuill, 1991).

Nevertheless, decoding and comprehension continue to be thought of as separate. That this may be an unnecessary barrier to understanding is shown by some data which reflects the progress through the Corrective Reading Programme (Engelmann *et al.*, 1988) of a group of twenty-five first secondary year (NC Year 7) pupils at a south London comprehensive school. The success of this scheme at this school has been commented upon before (Turner, 1990a, 1990b) and these new data are available only because a subset of fourteen pupils was retested on a parallel form of the New MacMillan Reading Analysis (Vincent and de la Mare, 1985), additionally to the planned evaluation, as a result of a teacher's initiative.

*Figure 6.1: Corrective reading gains January–June 1990 for fourteen pupils Year 7 (11–12 years)*

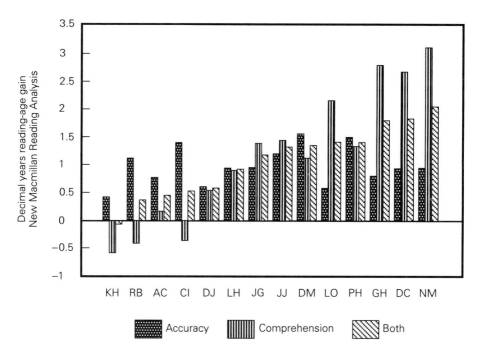

The whole group (twenty-five pupils) had showed an average gain of fourteen reading-age months over the four calendar months of the Autumn term, September–December 1989. The results of the test/retest scores for the subset of fourteen pupils are displayed in Figure 6.1, ranked from left to right in order of composite reading age (RA) gain.

Of interest, first, is the short interval between the times of testing, about four months of schooling; secondly, the intermediate stage of the testing — the large gains of the first term are in the past; and, thirdly, the possibility which exists to disaggregate the scores into accuracy (decoding) and comprehension components. These pupils were following *Decoding A*, the initial book in the series of Corrective Reading, a member of the direct-instruction family of interventions. However there is a tendency, most apparent among those making the greatest gains, to show improvement in comprehension scores at least as great as, if not greater than, their gains in accuracy. Overall these pupils progressed from RA (accuracy) 9.0 (SD 0.87) to 9.9 years (SD 1.03) and from RA (comprehension) 9.5 (SD 1.63) to 10.7 years (SD 1.36).

Undoubtedly there are pupils who fail to comprehend text because arrested at an early level of skill development with inadequate speed of decoding; others fail to comprehend because of a lack of inference and metacomprehension skills (Oakhill and Garnham, 1988). Nor are the numbers of such pupils negligible. However one obvious implication should not be overlooked: that if you teach children decoding skills, they improve in comprehension. Other recent evidence that bears the same interpretation is reported in Hatcher, Hulme and Ellis (op. cit.), where the Neale Analysis of Reading Ability (Neale, 1989), a test of passage reading with a separable comprehension measure, registers progress better than a test of sheer word-recognition ability does. This domain transference, if that is what it is, is of potential interest to all teachers of children with poor reading abilities: progress may be much more evident on measures of skills other than the ones you have been teaching.

## Messages for Teachers

The earlier (1970s) literature on instruction evaluation now seems preliminary. The present-day literature, though still provisional, represents an improvement. An important line of enquiry, less controversial today, has sought to establish the variables associated with effective teaching. Some twenty factors, of which seventeen are well documented, have been identified, among them teacher expectations, teacher clarity, questioning level, direct instruction, monitoring and pacing, feedback, praise and criticism (O'Neill, 1988). Cross-cultural studies show that in Asian schools, by contrast with north American ones, much greater emphasis is placed on certain variables (such as teacher clarity) associated with favourable learning outcomes; but in Chicago and Minneapolis teachers surveyed rated more highly variables such as 'sensitivity' and 'empathy' (Stevenson and Stigler, 1992).

### The Impact of Cognitive Psychology

An important new dimension is the linking of teaching and learning processes made possible by cognitive psychology. What conclusions seem justified from all the activity in cognitive neuroscience over the last fifteen years? The 'componential' view of intelligence retains its position as the consensus view among cognitive psychologists. It can be, and has been, applied to instruction, including reading (Beech, 1989; Frederiksen, 1982). In place of crude 'top–down' and 'bottom–up' models of reading, the direction of causality has been addressed, for instance in the case of working memory. Impaired working memory has been unambiguously implicated in reading failure; but so has the 'reading effect' in success, the tendency of reading progress itself to bring about improvements in associated subskills such as those of phonological analysis and memory. An evolving rationale for teaching component skills, therefore, is one of the most valuable contributions psychology can make to practical teaching.

In the psychometric field, which provided raw material for the reviews of a generation ago, there has been research which bears on the developmental structure of ability groups. In a comprehensive meta-analysis, Carroll (1993) has reanalysed data sets from major factor-analytic studies of virtually all cognitive skills, including reading and other language skills. This study, taking in as it does most of the psychometric literature, is of special importance. Frederiksen (1982) is cited in support of the analysis of word recognition into the following component skills: grapheme encoding, letter recognition, multiletter array facilitation, perception of multiletter units (e.g., *sh, -tion*), depth of processing, phonemic contrast and decoding (Carroll, 1993, p. 165).

Ellis and Young provide experimental evidence that 'phonological information is necessary to provide access to the internal machinery which utilizes sentence structure in the service of better text comprehension' (Ellis and Young, 1988, pp. 220–1). Syntactic parsing, in other words, depends upon 'inner speech' and hence phonological processing. Evidence from acquired reading disorders, too, supports the conclusion that translation of the written word to a phonological representation may play an important role in reading comprehension (Patterson and Marcel, 1992). The new cognitive psychology provides evidence of the relative independence ('modularity') of reading and writing skills: although not themselves inherited, they become modularized just as do natural language skills. Literacy skills are, as may be observed, fairly independent of intelligence and other general cognitive characteristics, at least in the early stages. A slightly older literature confirms the dependence of prosody, and the distribution of stresses in sentences read, upon prior knowledge of syntactic structure.

At present, the commonly accepted theory that reading is acquired in discrete developmental stages is under considerable pressure. Though children's strategies can be shown to depend very directly upon the methods used to teach them, the assumption of whole-word *Gestalt* recognition now has a great deal to answer (Seymour, 1987). Readers process letters regardless of the kind of teaching being given; and progress is greater with a flashcard approach for pupils who have a knowledge of letters. Further, Goswami (1992) has extended the earlier work, implicating phonological structures in learning to read, to spelling patterns, arguing that children learning to read use spelling–sound analogies (ring/king) in the earliest stages, though among the earliest learners an advantage accrues to individual children with some prior decoding facility (Ehri and Robbins, 1992). The tendency of 'stage models' to assume, implicitly, some developmental course of events, other than that given culturally, for instance by teaching, may be expected to fade. And it is to be hoped that an alignment of phonology and orthography in a single, first stage of learning to read will be followed by the discovery of a transfer to print of spoken morphology and comprehension skills (Elbro, 1989).

Another challenge on the theoretical front is connectionism (e.g., Seidenberg and McClelland, 1989). By means of an explicit computer model, the learning of reading by rules through exposure to a large set of short words can be achieved without explanatory recourse to a lexicon. One implication of this for teaching is that exposure to print facilitates the learning of reading.

There may be ways in which the quantity of print scanned, even by beginning or poor readers, can be increased.

The role of pictures, inflated by Whole Language even though the conditions under which pictures facilitated reading were narrowed to paired association in the early 1970s, is now known to be far more negative: picture 'cues' can actively suppress the learning of print skills (Wu and Solman, 1993).

### *Might Natural Language, Too, Be Taught?*

A widespread argument for Whole Language has been that acquiring literacy skills is analogous to the acquisition — or development — of oral language. The counter argument, essentially a Darwinian one, is soon made: '[R]eading is not a skill which spontaneously develops' (Beech, 1987, p. 188). However this leaves unexplained the question why, if a language-acquisition device provides phenotypically for the spontaneous development of speech, as many as 15 per cent of children may show clinical levels of speech impairment. Moerk (1992) addresses the acquisition of speech skills and shows that they are actually taught through regular instructional sequences. Re-analyzing Roger Brown's historic data set for 'Eve' and applying methodological innovations (Markov models, bivariate time-series analyses, cumulative records with varying intervals), Moerk has been able to show that specific morphemes, and even language-learning strategies, are the product of teaching interactions and fine-tuning of maternal feedback.

### Conclusion

The Whole Language movement may be thought, in retrospect, to have been sustained by remarkably little real knowledge and a great deal in the way of charismatic platform performance. Even the 'theories' (speculations) and 'linguistics' (the non-experimental variety) date from the late 1960s and early 1970s. These look, in the aftermath of a damaging debacle, distinctly irrelevant against a background of authentic and non-charismatic research endeavour, especially in the cognitive neurosciences. The centrality of phonological processing for both good and poor readers is recognized, as are, increasingly, the taught nature of spoken language, the nature and importance of differentiable component skills in literacy, phonological mediation in comprehension, the interlinked nature of reading and writing (spelling) processes and the importance of print experience in isolation from pictures.

The step-by-step teasing out of arguments which bear, today, on the teaching of literacy skills is very far removed from the cavalier, global statements of yesteryear. Engelmann comments:

> The curriculum (the instructional programs and the details of how kids are taught) is the difference between failure and success. The

difference is not a 'global' aspect such as 'co-operative learning' or 'discovery'. The difference has to do with what the kids are doing, how they are using what they have been taught, and most important, how they receive specific skills, facts and operations that they are to use in applied situations. (Engelmann, 1992, p. 7)

## References

ADAMS, M.J. (1990) *Beginning to Read: Thinking and Learning about Print*, Boston, MIT Press.

ADAMS, M.J. (1991) 'Why not phonics *and* whole language?', in ELLIS, W. (Ed) *All Language And The Creation Of Literacy*, Baltimore, MD, Orton Dyslexia Society.

ARTER, J. and JENKINS, J.R. (1979) 'Differential diagnosis — prescriptive teaching: A critical appraisal', *Review of Educational Research*, **49**, 4, pp. 517–55, Fall.

AUGUR, J. and BRIGGS, S. (Eds) (1992) *The Hickey Multisensory Language Course*, 2nd ed., London, Whurr.

AYLWIN, T. (1993) 'The reality of reading', *Language and Learning*, March, pp. 30–1.

BASSEY, M. (1994) 'Why Lord Skidelsky is so wrong', *Times Educational Supplement*, 21 January, p. 18.

BEECH, J.R. (1987) 'Early reading development', in BEECH, J.R. and COLLEY, A.M. (Eds) *Cognitive Approaches To Reading*, Chichester, Wiley.

BEECH, J.R. (1989) 'The componential approach to learning reading skills', in COLLEY, A.M. and BEECH, J.R. (Eds) *Acquisition And Performance Of Cognitive Skills*, Chichester, Wiley, pp. 113–36.

BLAGG, N. (1991) *Can We Teach Intelligence? A Comprehensive Evaluation of Feuerstein's Instrumental Enrichment Programme*, Hove, Sussex, Lawrence Erlbaum Associates.

BRANWHITE, A.B. (1983) 'Boosting reading skills by direct instruction', *British Journal of Educational Psychology*, **53**, pp. 291–8.

BULLOCK, A., STALLYBRASS, O. and TROMBLEY, S. (1988) *The Fontana Dictionary Of Modern Thought* (2nd ed.), Glasgow, Collins Fontana.

CARNINE, D., SILBERT, J. and KAMEENUI, E.J. (1990) *Direct Reading Instruction*, 2nd ed., Toronto, Ontario, Merrill.

CARROLL, J.B. (1993) *Human Cognitive Abilities*, Cambridge, Cambridge University Press.

CARTY, G. (1992) *Spelling: Conversations for Change*, Reading, UKRA/Blackwell, **26**, 2, July, pp. 17–22.

*Economist, The* (1991) 'Under the metascope', 18 May, pp. 119–20.

EHRI, L.C. and ROBBINS, C. (1992) 'Beginners need some decoding skill to read words by analogy', *Reading Research Quarterly*, **27**, 1, pp. 13–26.

ELBRO, C. (1989) 'Morphological awareness in dyslexia', in von EULER, C., LUNDBERG, I. and LENNERSTRAND, G. (Eds) *Brain and Reading*, London, Macmillan.

ELLIS, A.W. and YOUNG, A. (1988) *Human Cognitive Neuropsychology*, Hove, Sussex, Lawrence Erlbaum Associates.

ENGELMANN, S. (1992) *War Against Schools' Academic Child Abuse*, Portland, Oreg., Halcyon House.

ENGELMANN, S., CARNINE, L. and JOHNSON, G. (1988) *Corrective Reading Programmes*, Chicago, Science Research Associates.

FREDERIKSEN, J.R. (1982) 'A componential theory of reading skills and their interactions', in STERNBERG, R.J. (Ed) *Advances In The Psychology Of Intelligence* (Vol. 1), Hillsdale, NJ, Erlbaum, pp. 125–80.

GOODMAN, K.S. (1992) 'I didn't found whole language', *Reading Teacher*, **46**, pp. 188–99.

GOSWAMI, U. (1992) *Analogical Reasoning in Children*, Hove, Sussex, Lawrence Erlbaum Associates.

HATCHER, P., HULME, C. and ELLIS, A. (1994) 'Ameliorating early reading failure by integrating the teaching of reading and phonological skills: the phonological linkage hypothesis', *Child Development*, **65**, pp. 41–57.

IVERSEN, S. and TUNMER, W.E. (1993) 'Phonological processing skills and the Reading Recovery programme', *Journal of Educational Psychology*, **85**, pp. 112–16.

JOHNSON, D.D. and PEARSON, P.D. (1975) 'Skills management systems: A critique', *The Reading Teacher*, pp. 757–64.

JOHNSTON, R.S., RUGG, M.D. and SCOTT, T. (1988) 'Pseudohomophone effects in 8 and 11-year-old good and poor readers', *Journal of Research in Reading*, **11**, 2, pp. 110–32.

MEEK, M. (1988) *How Texts Teach What Readers Learn*, Stroud, Gloucester, Thimble Press.

MEEK, M. (1990) 'What do we know about reading that helps us teach?', in CARTER, R. (Ed) *Knowledge About Language and the Curriculum: The LINC Reader*, London, Hodder and Stoughton.

MOERK, E.L. (1992) *A First Language: Taught and Learned*, Baltimore, MD, Paul H. Brookes.

NEALE, M.D. (1989) *Neale Analysis of Reading Ability* (Revised British Edition), Windsor, Bucks, NFER-Nelson.

NEWCOMER, P.L. and HAMMILL, D.D. (1975) 'ITPA and academic achievement: a survey', *Reading Teacher*, May, pp. 731–41.

OAKHILL, J. and GARNHAM, A. (1988) *Becoming a Skilled Reader*, Oxford, Blackwell.

OAKHILL, J. and YUILL, N. (1991) 'The remediation of reading comprehension difficulties', in SNOWLING, M.J. and THOMSON, M.E. (Eds) *Dyslexia: Integrating Theory and Practice*, London, Whurr.

OLSSEN, M. (1993) 'Science and individualism in educational psychology: problems for practice and points of departure', *Educational Psychology*, **13**, 2, pp. 155–72.

O'NEILL, G.P. (1988) 'Teaching effectiveness: A review of the research', *Canadian Journal of Education*, **13**, 1, pp. 162–85.

PATTERSON, K. and MARCEL, A. (1992) 'Phonological ALEXIA or PHONOLOGICAL alexia?', in ALEGRIA, J., HOLENDER, D., MORAIS, J.J. DE and RADEAU, M. (Eds) *Analytic Approaches to Human Cognition*, North Holland, Elsevier.

RABINOWITZ, M. (1990) 'Prerequisite knowledge for learning and problem-solving', in HEDLEY, C., HOUTZ, J. and BARATTA, A. (Eds) *Cognition, Curriculum and Literacy*, Norwood, New Jersey, Ablex, pp. 47–58.

RACK, J.P., SNOWLING, M.J. and OLSON, R.K. (1992) 'The nonword reading deficit in developmental dyslexia: A review', *Reading Research Quarterly*, **27**, 1, pp. 29–53.

SEIDENBERG, M.S. and McCLELLAND, J.L. (1989) 'A distributed developmental model of word recognition and naming', *Psychological Review*, **96**, pp. 523–68.

SEYMOUR, P.H.K. (1987) 'Word recognition processes: An analysis based on format distortion effects', in BEECH, J.R. and COLLEY, A.M. (Eds) *Cognitive Approaches To Reading*, Chichester, Sussex, Wiley.

SMITH, F. (1991) 'Excerpt from a lecture at the University of East Anglia on 7 April 1991', transcribed from an audio tape made by a participant.

STEVENSON, H.W. and STIGLER, J.W. (1992) *The Learning Gap: Why Our Schools are Failing and What We Can Learn From Japanese And Chinese Education*, New York, Summit Books.

THOMAS, G. (1993a) 'Review of Augur and Briggs (1992)', *Times Educational Supplement*, 16 April.

THOMAS, G. (1993b) Personal communication.

TURNER, M. (1990a) 'Positive responses', *Times Educational Supplement*, 19 January.

TURNER, M. (1990b) 'Reading Proofs', Letter in *Times Educational Supplement*, 27 April.

VINCENT, D. and DE LA MARE, M. (1985) *New MacMillan Reading Analysis*, Windsor, Bucks, NFER-Nelson.

WU, H-M. and SOLMAN, R.T. (1993) 'Effective use of pictures as extra stimulus prompts', *British Journal of Educational Psychology*, **63**, pp. 144–60.

YULE, V. (1992) 'Learning to read without effort', *Reading*, UKRA/Blackwell, **26**, 2, July, pp. 12–17.

*Part 2*

# *Wider Concerns*

# Chapter 7

# New Moves in Early-literacy Learning in Europe

*H. Dombey*

**Summary**

All over Europe there is a spreading awareness that very young children, below the age of formal schooling, are capable of learning complex and powerful literacy lessons. This chapter draws on the work of L'Institut Européen pour le Développement des Potentialités de tous les Enfants (IEDPE), based on a report commissioned from IEDPE by the EC Commission for Human Resources.[1] Accounts are presented of successful early literacy projects carried out in different parts of Europe from which a number of lessons for teachers are drawn out.

**Introduction**

Scarcely more than a decade ago, it was widely agreed that children could not and should not learn to read before the age of six. In most of the countries of Europe this is the age fixed for the entry into 'big school' and the age at which formal literacy teaching begins. However this last decade has shown us that the acquisition of literacy is not a straightforward rite of passage into the institutional world of school, but a long and complex process that begins early, when very young children, who are far more capable than we used to believe, begin, in the world of the family and the immediate environment, to understand and express themselves through the written word. This process continues to develop and to play a significant role throughout the *longue durée* of education.

We have learnt also that becoming literate is not simply a matter of acquiring a value-free technology. Learning to read and write is now most fruitfully seen as the construction of linguistic meaning and the initiation into social practices. In the earliest stages of their entry into the written word children encounter new forms of language and new orders of meaning. As our views of literacy and literacy learning have become more complex, so we have seen the need for more complex and subtle forms of assessment. Simple tests of word recognition or the construction of simple propositional meanings do not adequately reflect what we now know of the processes involved.

In our different countries, our educational systems, our traditions, our spoken languages and our ways of writing them down vary widely. For this reason our pedagogic strategies also vary. But underneath this variety, there are fundamental similarities. The examples that follow, describe not isolated successes but the fruits of shared strategies that really respond to the needs of all children, whatever their nationalities, their languages or their socio-economic backgrounds.

## The Sheffield Project

Carried out in Sheffield, UK and directed by Dr Peter Hannon of the Department of Education at the University of Sheffield this six-month project was a case study undertaken in a disadvantaged district of Sheffield. It involved twenty children aged between 1 and 4 years. Parents and children were visited at home, and also invited to a series of group meetings in the primary school on which the project was based. The parents were encouraged to borrow children's books of good quality to read with their children, and also to point out print in their homes and in the neighbourhood.

Each home visit involved discussion about past, present and future activities, and some form of literacy activity engaged in by the visitor with the child and parent. The role of the home visitor was to:

- affirm the parent as the child's first and most influential teacher;
- support and encourage literacy activities already going on, in order to build on and extend these;
- make explicit the relevance of activities of which the parents might be unaware;
- initiate new ideas and share resources; and
- give parents information about literacy and literacy learning.

It was found that parents were willing and able to engage in a dialogue about their children's home literacy. They said that the project changed their approach to children's literacy experiences. Opportunities to acquire literacy through print in the environment appeared to be exploited more readily. There was evidence of change in the parents' recognition of their children's literacy achievement. Parents made such comments as: 'It's made me see more in children that I've never seen before. If it wasn't for the project I wouldn't have thought so clearly what children can do.'

It is now clear that parents, including those in very disadvantaged circumstances, do welcome help in promoting their children's early-literacy development. Take-up was at 80 per cent as high as it could be, given the constraints of the parents' unavoidable domestic and employment commitments. Drop-out was not a problem. The method of work tried out in the programme, including the attempt to share an emergent literacy perspective with parents, was experienced as meaningful by all concerned.

The project also appeared to have an effect on family literacy as well as on the children in the target age range: parents started using the public library themselves and felt their own literacy had been helped by using the project materials, and there was a perceptible effect on the literacy activities of school-age siblings.

## The Rome Project

This project, carried out in Rome, and directed by Professor Clotilde Pontecorvo of the Facoltà di Psicologia, Università di Roma, la Sapienza, was an experimental study involving 218 children aged from 4 to 8, from varied social backgrounds in Rome, split equally into experimental and control groups and concerned to establish continuity between nursery and primary school. Comparison was made between the two groups on children's concepts about print, the composition of texts and different forms of reading.

The children in the experimental group were involved in:

- games of making and using a variety of symbols on charts for recording class attendance, the weather etc;
- conversation and group discussion;
- activities inviting reflection on spoken language;
- stories, rhymes and poems;
- attempts at predicting the meaning of words printed on support materials;
- the production of their own spontaneous writing;
- listening to and understanding different types of text read aloud — posters, recipes, labels, reports; and
- collaborative construction of different types of text: the 'book of the child's day', various facts, invitations, recipes etc.

This approach to the written word was deliberately set in a series of maximally varied linguistic activities, and would have been unthinkable without much deliberate use of group work, in pairs or in larger groups with the teacher. The experimental group achieved at a significantly higher level, and continued to improve while the progress of the control group was most evident towards the end of the first year of primary schooling and reached a plateau after this.

## The Palencia Project

This project, carried out in Palencia, Spain, and directed by Profesora Carmen Colmenares of the Departamento de Psicologia at the Universdad de

Valladolid consisted of three case studies involving sixty four-year old children in three nursery classes, all from a low socio-economic background. The great majority of the children presented problems, such as intellectual deficit, language problems and hyperactivity, requiring the involvement of specialists such as speech therapists and psychologists.

Motivated by the idea of teaching very young children to read, the three experienced nursery teachers worked as a team. Of course the children all lived in an environment saturated with written language. But the nursery class gave them a more systematic experience. The teachers:

- collaborated with the children's parents, sharing their educational philosophy with them and impressing on them the value of reading for their children's future academic success. Although many of the parents were not in the habit of reading, they were ready to collaborate very actively with the teachers, not just over the period of the project, but well into the primary school.
- started with learning in context, presenting the business of making sense of the written word as a meaningful social activity and not something alien to the interests of the learners. This meant rejecting conventional reading schemes in favour of real story books. The teachers also made their own texts and notices about significant events and people in the children's lives.
- gave priority to what interested the learners, initially presenting the children with their own name cards, and other words of practical and personal significance. These cards were used in the form of games. Other activities included making up stories based on a few random words or copying recipes for dishes the children had been involved in making.
- took account of patterns of cognitive development, seeing the first phase of literacy learning as *global*, leading on to a second *analytical* phase during which the children started to compare the length of words or notice a particular sound in a word, and were encouraged to develop these analytical strategies. This led to the discovery of grapho-phonemic relations through word play such as changing the position of vowels. In this phase the children, including the slowest, developed metalinguistic awareness, in terms of phonology, lexis and syntax, at an astonishing rate. The third or *synthetic* phase focused on total comprehension of the text, involving other strategies such as syllabification or whole-word recognition.

Both qualitative and quantitative results emphasized that all except five of the sixty children achieved a level of reading comprehension, vocabulary and spelling above the mean for their age. Two years later only one of this small 'problematic' group was unable to read and follow the normal activities of the classroom. The rest, including the other four, completed the second primary year with better results than their classmates, not only in the area of language, but also in mathematics.

### The Brighton Project

This project was carried out in Brighton, England, by Dr Henrietta Dombey of the Department of Primary Education at the University of Brighton. This was a case study of one nursery class of twenty-six children, aged 3 and 4, from very low socio-economic backgrounds. Initially the children had little experience of stories, either read or told, and little interest in books or written text. For these reasons, the teacher in this project made story reading a central activity in her nursery class. Texts were chosen for their capacity to attract and hold the children's interest, and to be worth re-reading, and were read daily to the whole class. This is normal practice in English nursery classes, but the style of reading was not. The teacher's aim was active participation from the children, who were encouraged to:

- relate events and characters to their own experience;
- predict what would happen next;
- check their predictions by examining the pictures and listening to the text;
- make moral judgments on the events and characters; and
- 'call out' rather than wait for permission to speak.

The teacher did not set herself up as arbiter of right and wrong, but encouraged the children to use the evidence of their eyes and ears. She also placed great importance on collaboration with parents, through encouraging them to participate in the daily life of the nursery class where they witnessed her style of 'sharing' books with their children, to buy children's books at school and to share these with their children at home.

During the course of one academic year these children became very interested in books, to the extent that, rather than engage in the various enticing play activities of the nursery class, the children frequently chose to 'talk their way' through a picture book. They were also capable of relating their own versions of the stories they had heard, employing many of the features that set written language apart from speech. They had learned to produce:

- highly explicit language that was dense, full and detailed;
- coherent stories twenty or so utterances long;
- a high proportion of well-formed and structurally complete utterances; and
- complex utterances, using coordination and/or subordination.

It has long been known that familiarity with books and stories gives children a powerful motivation to learn to read. More recent research (Bussis *et al.*, 1985) has shown its importance in providing children with the syntactic and semantic cues that play a key part in early reading. Children unfamiliar with written text cannot make the educated guesses that are a necessary complement to their limited phonic knowledge.

These children had taken command of written language and learned to use it for their own purposes. Subsequently this proved to be of significant value as they learned to read, enabling them to complement their use of the visual information provided by the letters on the page with predictions based on a knowledge of the subject matter, structure and linguistic form of stories.

## The Huesca Project

This project was carried out in Huesca, Spain, directed by Dr Gloria Medrano at the Escuela Universitaria de Magisterio in Huesca, Spain. This longitudinal study, involved 150 pupils aged from 3 to 6 years in the public schools of Huesca, from medium socio-economic groupings, and thirty pupils from public schools in the surrounding countryside. It was concerned to test the hypothesis that the introduction of a 'computer corner' into nursery classes would have widespread beneficial effects.

In all the project classrooms other types of experimental materials developed in earlier projects were already in use, including a tape library and accompanying books. To these were added computer corners (sometimes placed outside the classroom) where the children could work under their own direction. The computer involved was the Commodore 64. The programmes came from various sources and included *Labyrinth I and II, Autumn* and a word-processing package. These corners gave the children the opportunity to make discoveries about written language, both individually and in cooperation with a group of their peers.

The teachers were involved in regular meetings with the coordinator's assistant and there were also meetings for parents to inform them and invite their collaboration. Teacher observation and video evidence showed that such activity encouraged:

- interaction between children and the development of communicative strategies;
- understanding of complex tasks;
- self-correction and shared correction;
- a positive attitude to mistakes;
- the development of discriminative attention and symbolic thought;
- interest in written language and appreciation of its value as an instrument of information, communication and enjoyment;
- the capacity for autonomous learning;
- making sense of written language and of the code itself; and
- the capacity to use metacognitive strategies and to communicate what they had learned.

It should be emphasized that the work with computers formed an integral part of class activity in literacy, and was supported by a variety of other activities emphasizing autonomy and making sense of meaningful texts.

All this shows that very young children, especially those from very disadvantaged backgrounds, have a great capacity for learning, and that exercising this can give them substantial pleasure.

### The Paris Project

This project, carried out in Paris, under the direction of Dr Rachel Cohen of the Département de Psychologie at the Université Paris Nord, was a case study of five *écoles maternelles* in a northern suburb of Paris, a very disadvantaged district, with children between 2 and 6 years of age. An earlier study began with the informing idea that written language, like spoken language, involves the production of messages as well as their reception and interpretation. However the motor coordination of very young children does not allow them to 'write' messages that are clear and legible to others. For this reason the children were provided with manipulable letters. But this solution was soon shown to be inadequate when it came to writing longer texts. So the team thought of using computers. This versatile instrument also offered a number of possibilities that could not be ignored.

In the first phase of the project, from 1981 to 1986, the team, composed of a group of cognitive scientists, technicians, educators and psychologists from the Centre Mondial Informatique in Paris, developed, tried out and tested programmes which allowed children productive activities and discoveries. The programmes *ALE (Apprentissage Langue Ecrite)* and *Composition* were used on a Thomson computer. These computers were introduced into the project classes, where they stimulated the following capacities:

- quality of exchanges between children: mutual aid and cooperation;
- development of oral language;
- rapid development in written language;
- richness of the imagination;
- spontaneous grapho-phonemic analysis;
- spirit of curiosity; and
- autonomy.

Focused on the particular needs of the children who came to school with no French, the second phase consisted of equipping the computers with a device using a voice synthesizer which allowed children to hear letters, words, sentences and texts typed on the computer and appearing on the screen. It was soon evident that the device was a factor in speeding up discovery and learning for all the children. The children who had come with no French learnt spoken and oral language accurately and simultaneously, in a situation of autonomous learning. This certainly did not exclude adults, but it allowed several children to cooperate, to exchange and confront ideas and implementations, and to correct themselves. Furthermore, the conception of the structure of the process of learning to read was itself changed as the following formula came into play:

$$\rceil \rightarrow \textit{write} \rightarrow \text{in order to } \textit{talk} \rightarrow \text{in order to } \textit{read} \rightarrow \text{in order to}\rceil$$

in which *listen* can be inserted at each stage.

New technologies open new perspectives of learning and development for all young children. Adults, teachers and institutional personnel do not have the right to refuse these new opportunities of success to any children.

### Messages for Teachers

All these different approaches to early literacy share important underlying ideas.

- Young children have an enormous potential for literacy learning: a potential not yet fully realized in our various educational systems.
- Early-literacy learning proceeds most productively through collaboration and interaction in which teachers treat parents as equal partners.
- The immediate participants in literacy learning — children, parents and teachers — need to feel ownership of the activities involved. They need to make their own materials, write their own stories and take published texts into their possession through relating them to their own lives.
- Children learn best when they are provided with texts of significance to them, whether these are notices of practical use or stories that engage their imagination. These should include complex texts capable of yielding more meaning and of teaching more lessons on each encounter.
- New technology can be a powerful tool in literacy learning, provided it is used in a context which has other positive features.
- Children learn most productively when they are actively engaged in forming and testing their own hypotheses, not following directions.
- Literacy learning is very complex and, like learning spoken language, cannot be achieved in a straightforwardly linear manner, beginning with small elements and proceeding incrementally to larger and larger elements. Some of the properties of the whole need to be present in the earliest stages.
- Learning to read and write — to think and make sense of the world through the written word — is a lengthy process not achieved in a few years, much less a few months.

## Conclusion

Until recently the view was widespread in Britain that the teaching of young children on the European continent was characterised by an unremittingly rigid formality, particularly where early literacy was concerned. To enlarge our understanding of early literacy and to enrich our own practice with inventive ideas that would take us and our children forward, it seemed to most of those involved, that primary education was better served by looking to the United States and other English-speaking countries than to countries on the mainland of Europe. Our persistent reluctance to master Europe's other languages reinforced this anglophonic chauvinism.

Whatever may have been the case in the past, the projects outlined in this article, and the list of lessons drawn from them, show that at the cutting edge of innovation, we now have more in common than we thought. Teachers and researchers in France, Italy and Spain share with colleagues in Britain a clear desire to give children a confident entry into the world of the written word, and make use of similarly imaginative approaches, drawing on the same kinds of theoretical understandings about children, about literacy, and about the social world in which fruitful relationships between the two can be built. Now we need to initiate a programme to ensure that we learn more about each others' successes, and build on these collaboratively to create a more literate Europe.

## Note

1. *l'Institut pour le Développement des Potentialités de tous les Enfants* (IEDPE) is an organization of teachers, teacher-trainers and researchers with an interest in early-childhood education. It was founded in 1989 by three energetic French people to bring together people and ideas from the different countries of Europe. Based in Paris, it has held a number of lively conferences in different parts of Europe, including Paris, Barcelona, Genoa and Luxembourg. In December 1992 the EC Commission on Human Resources invited IEDPE to contribute to the initiative on preventing school failure. Specifically, IEDPE was asked to present a paper based on projects directed by IEDPE members and focusing on the key factors in pre-school provision that have been shown to contribute to reducing school failure. As one of the coordinators of IEDPE's literacy group, with Margaret Meek Spencer of the University of London Institute of Education, Gloria Medrano of the University of Zaragoza and Maria Antonietta Pinto of the Università della Sapienza in Rome, I undertook to put together the section on literacy. Timing was tight and a strict word limit meant that we could include accounts of fewer projects than we would have wished.

## References

Bussis, A., Chittenden, E., Amarel, M. and Klausner, E. (1985) *Inquiry into Meaning: An Investigation of Learning to Read*, Hillsdale, NJ, Lawrence Erlbaum Associates.

CAZDEN, C. (1988) *Classroom Discourse: The Language of Teaching and Learning*, Portsmouth, NH, Heinemann.

COHEN, R. (1987) *Les Jeunes Enfants, la Découverte de l'Ecrit et l'Ordinateur*, Paris, Presses Universitaires de France.

COHEN, R. (1992) *Quand l'Ordinateur Parle . . . Utilisation de la synthèse vocale dans l'apprentissage et le perfectionnement de la langue écrite*, Paris, Presses Universitaires de France.

COHEN, R. and GILABERT, H. (1986) *Découverte et Apprentissage du Langage Ecrit avant Six Ans*, Paris, Presses Universitaires de France.

FERREIRO, E. and TEBEROSKY, A. (1979) *Los Sistemas de Escritura en el Desarollo del Niño*, Mexico, Siglo XXI Editores.

GOODMAN, Y. (1987) *Reading Miscue Inventory: Alternative Procedures*, New York, Richard Owen.

PAPERT, S. (1981) *Desafío a la Mente: Computadores y educación*, Buenos Aires, Galápago.

PONTECORVO, C., TASSINARI, G.E. and CAMAIONI, L. (1990) *Continuità Educativa dai Quattro agli Otto Anni*, Firenze, La Nuova Italia.

TIZARD, J., SCHOFIELD, W. and HEWISON, J. (1982) 'Collaboration between teachers and parents in assisting children's reading', *British Journal of Educational Psychology*, **52**.

VYGOTSKY, L.S. (1978) *Mind in Society*, Cambridge, MA, Harvard University Press.

WELLS, C.G. (1986) *The Meaning Makers: Children Learning Language and Using Language to Learn*, London, Hodder and Stoughton.

# Chapter 8

# What Do Children Know About Reading Before They Go to School?

*P. Munn*

### Summary

Learning to read is a complex process and in the early stages children's beliefs about reading may be important determinants of the process. This chapter reports on a research study in which 56 children were interviewed about reading once per term through their final year of preschool. While their behaviour in relation to books changed very little over the course of the year there was a dramatic change in their beliefs about reading. Most of the children shifted from an interpretation of reading as 'book-aided story repetition' to an understanding that reading entailed the decoding of print. This shift in their interpretation was paralleled by an understanding of the communicative function of text and by the recognition that they could not actually read. The children's excuses regarding their ability reflected the importance to their identity as readers of owning books and being able to rely on readers in their family to help them read.

'I can know what Granpa's stories are, but I don't know what your stories are. Don't know the nursery stories or your stories.'

(Diane, aged 4)

### Introduction

It important to know what children believe about reading before they go to school. The increasing emphasis as the social and 'ecological' aspects of literacy renders this knowledge particularly important (Barton, 1994). Teachers know in a general feel and sense that literacy does not begin with learning to read in school, that attitudes towards books and reading are formed very early. But how are teachers supposed to act on this knowledge? How specifically are they supposed to help children develop positive attitudes to reading in the crucial years before school? This chapter presents a detailed account of literacy beliefs found in a preschool sample and draws out the implications of these findings for effective ways of encouraging literacy in the nursery. Nursery teachers have a practical interest in the details of preschool literacy, but the beliefs that children have about reading are of interest also to primary teachers, who are often able to provide learning environments which have the potential to alter existing developmental trajectories.

Preschool literacy beliefs by their very nature are likely to have a long-term impact on children's reading habits. Literacy development (in contrast to learning to read) is not a sequential process, and neither is it a discrete event providing a transitory learning stage which transforms the pre-literate toddler into a literate schoolchild. The process of education in its broadest sense is founded on the continual development of literacy, and this in turn influences attitudes towards information and reading habits. For many areas of educational development the important question is not whether children are able to read, but whether they actually do read. Beliefs which develop in the preschool years may have implications for literacy development in this very broad sense, and for this reason be very pertinent to the management of children's reading experiences in the primary school. We know comparatively little about preschool children's beliefs about reading. Before they go to school, many children think they can read — such a belief being based on their incomplete understanding of what reading actually is. Although objectively incorrect, this belief will have quite an impact on children's subjective experiences of reading and learning to read, and is therefore of interest.

Where preschool children's knowledge of reading is concerned, there is a wealth of information about the sort of experiences that predispose children to learn to read. We know for instance, that sheer experience of books is important, because time spent at home in joint book reading predicts later speed of learning to read (Wells, 1981). Many research studies have detailed just what it is that children are learning during such experience; Snow and Ninio (1986) call this knowledge the 'contracts of literacy' — the rules which govern the activity of reading. These 'rules' are the very basic ones which stipulate that the books are 'objects of contemplation' rather than 'objects of action'; that pictures are representations of things, that words are used to interpret a picture, that pages are turned from left to right. However, books also provide a context for the development of particular kinds of language; language that through the use of rhyme and alliteration leads children into playing with language as a thing, and language that helps them to distinguish speaker reference from speaker intention.

It is apparent from what develops in the preschool period in terms of precursors to reading that the 'higher' levels of reading are developing at the same time as the 'lower' levels. The organization of joint storybook reading has been intensively studied, and a coherent picture has emerged of the way in which adult language follows a sequence in which children can contribute to a storybook interpretation even at the earliest stages. Children first begin contributing to a discussion of objects depicted in books, then to the events which are symbolized, and then to the (often psychological) precursors and consequences of these events. In this way, children understand the essential narrative structure of reading around the same time that they begin to understand the communicative functions of print — both developments taking place sometime between the ages of 3 and 5 for children who have sufficient experience of interactions around books. While children are developing an awareness of books as symbolic objects, and an understanding that print communicates in the same way as speech does, they are also developing the awareness of language that will later enable them to break words into their constituent sounds and match these sounds to their corresponding letters. In a similar sense, when children are learning to read, phonological and linguistic skills play an important part in development (Bryant, 1993).

Developments on the level of discrete abilities cannot explain the wider course of literacy development (what children go on to use reading *for*) since such developments relate to the actual process of learning to read — to the level of competence that children initially achieve. These details of what preschool children know about reading tell us little of their subjective experience of the process, and consequently predict only the relative success that the children will have when they come to learn to read. Success in learning to read will predispose children to have positive attitudes to reading in general, but in order to manage young children's experiences of reading more effectively we need a greater understanding of the subjective aspects of their experiences.

This chapter reports a study of the concepts and beliefs about reading that developed in a sample of preschool children during their final year of nursery. The children's concepts were examined on a behavioural level by recording what they did with a series of books and on a conversational level by engaging them in a conversation on the topic of reading. The aim of the study was to characterize the range of the children's responses and to chart developmental progressions in their ideas about reading. The study reported here was part of the ESRC programme on the quality of teaching and learning.

## Method

Fifty-six children from eight preschool establishments in Scotland were seen in their final year of nursery. The children were selected at random and the sample consisted of thirty-one boys and twenty-five girls. Since Scottish parents rarely favour early entry to school for their children, the age of the sample was higher than for similar English children. The mean age of the children was 46 months at the start of the study and 55 months in the June prior to school entry. The children were seen individually each term in order to investigate changes in their concepts of reading. There are two possible ways of investigating such concepts. The first is to watch a person's behaviour around a topic, the second is to listen to what that person says about the activity or object. Both approaches were adopted with these children by structuring a conversation around a small story-book (a beginning Reader with a very simple story line.). A different book in the same series (with the same character) was used each term, so that the children's responses over the year could be compared.

The children were initially requested to read the book, then had the book read to them, then were asked to retell the story. Within this format of book-reading the children were engaged in conversations about reading in as natural a way as possible, using the following questions.

- Can you read?
- Who do you know who can read?
- When will you be able to read?
- What will you have to do to be able to read?

The questions were introduced to the conversation if the topics were not brought up spontaneously.

A final question which was introduced to the conversation concerned the communicative function of text. The children were asked to 'point to where I read the story from'. All interviews were tape-recorded and then transcribed. Children's actions were recorded on a scoresheet. Codings of children's literacy behaviour and concepts were made from these transcripts and scoresheets. *Coding of responses.*

1. Understanding function of text: The children's answers to the question 'Where did I read that story from?' were coded according to whether they pointed to the pictures or to the text in response.
2. Level of narrative produced: The children's stories were coded for presence or absence of coherence — a measure which indicates the extent to which the language of the story stands alone and can be understood without the presence of the pictures in the book.
3. Beliefs about reading: Each child's conversations were coded for belief in his or her ability to read.
4. References made during conversations about reading: The children's conversations were coded for presence or absence of explanatory references in relation to reading.

## Results

### What the Children Did with the Books

All but three of the children were quite familiar with the practice of story-book reading, and showed interest in the book. They handled it correctly, and appeared familiar with the sequential, left-to-right nature of book-related behaviour. Beyond this superficial similarity of behaviour, which showed an adequate grasp of the basic contracts of literacy, there was a great deal of variation in their responses. The responses to the initial invitation to read the story fell into three categories:

1. looking at the book silently;
2. attempting to construct a narrative from the sequence of pictures; and
3. refusing to read the book — sometimes unjustified and sometimes justified by 'I can't' or 'I don't know the story'.

During the interviewer's reading of the story-book, the children usually showed interest in the short and appealing story. The children's retelling of the story fell into the same three categories as their initial responses, although their responses to the second invitation were not always the same as their responses to the first invitation. Many more of the children attempted to reconstruct a narrative on the second invitation than had done so on the first, and for about half the children who told the story twice the second narrative was more coherent than the first.

### Changes over time

There were no changes in the children's styles of response to the book-reading request; as many children 'read the pictures' or retold the story from memory at the end of the year as at the beginning. Generally speaking, the same children responded in these ways each time. There were also no changes in the quality of the children's narratives; those children who were not able to retell the story coherently in the first term did not acquire this skill during the course of the year. There was no increase in the number of children refusing to tell the story, or looking at the book silently. This finding of no progression in story-book behaviour contradicts those studies which have shown changes in children's pre-literate story-book reading (e.g., Sulzby, 1986). However it is noticeable that in samples where distinct progressions in children's early reading have been found, the context has been one of a favourite story-book, whereas in this study the children were deliberately presented with unfamiliar books. This suggests that such gains as children do make before school in story-book reading will not be evident with unfamiliar material. Further implications for the importance of affective involvement will be taken up again later.

The difference between producing a narrative or not was related to the children's individual strategies for dealing with books rather than to any progression in their behaviour. Those children who had story-telling skills did not stop using them, or even develop them during the year in the context of an unfamiliar book. Neither did those children who read silently or refused to read at the start of the year switch to a strategy of telling the story. Overall, there was considerable stability in the children's behaviour towards the books. The changes that were seen during the year were changes in the children's concepts and beliefs.

### What the Children Said About Reading

(Asterisked words are in Scottish dialect)

1. Where the children said the story came from:
   In the first term, only twelve of the children had pointed to the text as the source of the story. By the third term this number had increased to twenty-seven. Roughly half the children, then, had developed some awareness of the communicative function of print before they went to primary school.

2. Children's belief in their ability to read:
   In the first term, twenty-four of the children had asserted confidently that they could read. By the third term, this number had fallen to seven. Virtually all the children, then, had developed a sense of what reading was and had come to understand that it was something that they had yet to learn. The initial request to read the little book often provided the children with an opportunity for spontaneously voicing their thoughts about reading. It was at this point that many of the children revealed their own beliefs about reading, by justifying their refusal to read it. Some of the children were surprised, even incredulous, at the request. 'I *cannae read' was a common response, although many of the children were not so explicit about their own abilities, saying merely 'I don't know that story'.

   This latter justification refers to the mere recounting of the story of course, a distinction which emerged from more and more conversations as the year wore on. It gradually became clear that some of the children were articulating two definitions of reading. The first (and primary) definition was that of reading as recounting the story with the aid of the book. The second definition, which came into play later in the year with many of the children, was that of reading as the interpretation of text, and was the definition that was emerging from the children's growing understanding of what it was that readers did. As the children's definition of the activity of reading changed from a primary sense of retelling the pictures to a more detailed sense of understanding written words, the children's view of their own abilities inevitably had to change too. Seventeen of the children had shifted their view of themselves as readers in this way in the space of a few months. How did they manage this transition, this change in their view of themselves? The examination of the children's explanations of their reading threw light on this matter.

3. Children's explanation of their reading ability:
   In some ways, how and whether the children explained their own reading ability was of more significance than whether they did or did not believe that they could read. Such explanations of their own ability indicate that they were attending to their own mental processes and to the context of the task of reading, as the following examples show:

   > I can tell stories but I don't know how to read.

   > I can only read one book — not that one.

   Issues of ownership also entered into the children's explanations. The little girl quoted at the beginning of the chapter had made a clear distinction between those stories which were 'hers', (and which provided contexts in which she could read) and those stories which were not hers, and which provided contexts in which her inability to read became apparent.

   > I can know what Granpa's stories are, but I don't know what your stories are. Don't know the nursery stories or your stories.

This explanation was repeated by other children later on in the year:

I can read my own stories.

*Aye I can, but I can't read these stories.

I can just read Dumbo. I've got a Dumbo book. I can read that.
I can't read your little cat.

In this regard, the children were doing much the same thing as adults do when attributing reasons for ability: that is, they were citing the context rather than themselves as the cause of their failure. Some of their explanations for failure invoked people rather than specific books as contexts:

I can only read it to you if you read it first.

My Mummy usually helps me.

My Mum and Dad's got to read it and I read it to them.

It was clear, then, that for some children their changing view of themselves — the transition from reader to non-reader which was occasioned by their changing definition of reading — was explicitly managed by a set of explanations for their own ability which focused on the context of reading. The affective dimensions of these explanations were particularly striking, and deserve further mention.

4. Children's references to books or stories:
Many children appeared to be blaming the book itself for their inability to read, and spoke with warm and encouraging tones of the books they had at home.

I don't know how to read *wee books.

I can only read at my house.

It was clear that one of the things that the children's own books were giving them was a context in which they could think of themselves as readers, even though it was apparent to them that they were not 'real' readers. Some of the children confessed in a confiding manner midway through the conversation that what they were doing was not really reading and it was apparent that the two alternative definitions of reading were serving an important emotional function for these children.

5. Children's references to other readers:
Children's references to readers in their family (usually parents or grandparents, but also siblings and friends) showed that, in addition to their books, the people they were attached to provided contexts in which they could think of themselves as readers. The questions aimed at developing the conversation beyond the 'Can you read?' response further supported the importance of these affective ties in relation to children's own ideas about reading. In response to the question 'Who else can read?' the children

had invariably responded with the names of their family and friends. Only when asked directly did some of the children include the nursery staff in their list of 'people who can read'. In response to the question 'When will you be able to read?', many children had responded by referring to school entry or to a particular age. However, there were also references to family members as teachers of reading. Some were spontaneous:

I don't know how to read. Paul [brother] hasn't taught me yet.

And some related to questions about learning to read:

My Mummy will show me how to do it.

6.  Dependence, power and relationships in becoming a reader:
    The children's shift in their definition of reading, and the implication that the new definition had for their view of their own abilities, roots their identities as readers in their particular social context. Their primary definition — that reading was recounting a known story from a book — had been based on the observable and physical process of telling a story. Their new definition was based on an invisible mental process. While an understanding of what it is that one doesn't know is an essential prerequisite to learning, it is vital for children's confidence in their own learning that they are not overwhelmed by this feeling of not knowing. The contradictory rationalizations cited in the previous section provide one example of the ways children have to shield their self-esteem from knowledge of their own limitations as readers. They acknowledged that they couldn't read the words, but nevertheless maintained that there were circumstances in which they could 'read' the story.

    Dependence and relative power was the theme of other areas of conversation also. Reading was an ability attributed to older, more powerful people, and the children's conversations implicitly defined a future in which they, too, would be big, powerful, and able to read. The children's shift to an adult-like concept of reading was accompanied by an inevitable acknowledgment of their dependent status as readers. Here are two examples.

Child A:  I can't read without anybody doing it first.
          Can you read?
Child B:  No, but my sister reads all the stories for me.

Clearly, any failure in relationships of dependency or trust with adults will have implications for the delicate balance of reading concepts and self-concepts that children create before they learn to read.

## Discussion

Children's behaviour with books showed remarkably little change over the course of the year. The stories that they told, and the sophistication of these stories, did not change in any direction, suggesting that familiar contexts are necessary for the development of narrative skill.

What did change was the children's understanding of what reading involved (its relation to text) and their beliefs about their own abilities. The children's notions of text developed substantially during the year, but for many children the development of the knowledge that they could not read came in advance of any understanding of the communicative function of print. By the end of the year only half of the children had developed an understanding of the function of text. However nearly all the children had developed an understanding that they could not read. The implication is that some of the children knew only that they could not read, without knowing precisely what it was that they would have to do to learn to read. The position of these children, stands in strong contrast to children who simply have not developed sophisticated notions of reading.

Notable changes were seen in the children's beliefs about themselves as readers in the year prior to school entry. Although these changes were on the whole positive, there were a few children who had developed negative attitudes towards reading even before entering school. For most of the children, stories centred around favourite books and sharing these with family members had provided them with contexts in which they could think of themselves as readers before they began learning to read. Beliefs about the self invoke very strong emotions, and are highly likely to influence the children's first experience of being taught to read. The initial beliefs about themselves as readers that the children have are bound to affect how children view (and adjust to) the learning demands made on them in primary school. On entry to primary school children must adjust to a school-based literacy, which is sometimes defined as a solitary mental activity which may be quite different from the cooperative literacy experienced at home (Snow, *et al.*, 1991). Two implications from this study for encouraging literacy in the nursery are presented below.

### Messages for Teachers

The first implication concerns the development in the children of active and accurate concepts of the invisible mental activity that constitutes reading. The understanding that when adults tell stories from books they first scan and decode the text is not immediately obvious to small children. Sharing the activity of reading and talking about it with individual children is of great importance in helping children to make this discovery. There were two groups of children who did not develop adult-like notions. The first group simply had poorly developed reading concepts, and didn't realize the text-based nature of reading. The second group had difficulty with the notion that they were unable to read — presumably with the powerlessness which this implies. For both groups of children, shared reading activities with dependable adults would advance their understanding of reading and of their own abilities.

The second implication concerns the affective dimension of reading concepts implied in the children's references to their ownership of stories and relationships with storytellers and those who helped them to 'read'. The lack of progression seen in this sample (as opposed to others studies which used favourite story-books) suggests that repetition and affective involvement in the same book over a period of time are crucial components of preschool literacy programmes. The importance of actually owning books has been demonstrated by an intervention study (McCormick and Mason, 1986) in which children were given deliberately simple little books to take home with them.

The findings from this study point in the direction of encouraging literacy via active management of children's early experiences of literacy. Encouraging ownership of books, interactive reading sessions and family-literacy schemes are all ways of ensuring that children develop positive attitudes towards themselves as readers before they begin learning to read. The strong affective component involved in ownership and relationships may well be one of the best routes to influencing children's beliefs about reading, and about their own reading ability, at an early stage in life.

## Conclusion

Before children begin school, their concepts of reading develop in tandem with their concepts of themselves as readers. The process of becoming a learner reader requires that children maintain their self-esteem either by rationalizing their inability to read or by trusting utterly in the ability of more powerful family members. The familiarity and pleasure invoked by children's early definitions of reading as story recounting result in the use of their *own* storybooks to bolster their identity as readers. The implications for early year teachers are that literacy may be encouraged by attention to joint storybook reading and to children's concepts of themselves as readers.

## References

BARTON, D. (1994) *Literacy: An Introduction to the Ecology of Written Language*, Oxford: Basil Blackwell.

BRYANT, P. (1993) *Reading and Development in Systems of Representation in Children*, C. PRATT and A. GARTON (Eds), Wiley, Chichester.

MCCORMICK, C.E. and MASON, J.M. (1986) 'Intervention procedures for increasing preschool children's interest in and knowledge about reading', in TEALE, W.H. and SULZBY, E. (Eds) *Emergent Literacy: Writing and Reading*, Norwood, NJ, Ablex Publishing Corp.

SNOW, C. and NINIO, A. (1986) 'The contracts of literacy: What children learn from learning to read books', in TEALE, W.H. and SULZBY, E. (Eds) *Emergent Literacy: Writing and Reading*, Norwood, NJ, Ablex Publishing Corp.

SNOW, C., BAMES, W., CHANDLER, J., GOODMAN, I., and HEMPHILL, L. (1991) Unfulfilled Expectations: home and school influences on literacy.

SULZBY, E. (1986) 'Writing and reading: Signs of oral and written language organization in the young child', in TEALE, W.H. and SULZBY, E. (eds) *Emergent Literacy: Writing and Reading*, Norwood, NJ, Ablex Publishing Corp.

SULZBY, E. (1988) 'A study of children's early reading development', in PELLEGRINI, A.D. (Ed) *Psychological Bases for Early Education*, NY, Wiley.

WELLS, G. (1981) *Learning Through Interaction: The Study of Language Development*, Cambridge, Cambridge University Press.

# Chapter 9

# Teacher Decision-making in Early-literacy Teaching

*R. Fisher*

### Summary

This chapter examines the strategies adopted by two experienced reception-class teachers in the development of literacy. Two teachers were observed in their spontaneous interactions with children in relation to literacy. The teachers were also interviewed about their thoughts during these interactions. Data examined shows how teachers are operating on many levels in their interactions with children: cognitive, social and affective. The chapter looks at the multidimensionality of the classroom context and ways in which teachers adopt strategies to facilitate learning despite the changing experience from learning in the home to learning in the school setting.

### Introduction

The task faced by the teacher of early literacy is a formidable one. Society, rightly, places great emphasis on the acquisition of literacy both as a means to further learning and as a desirable attribute in itself. In England children start formal schooling just before they are 5 years old and already expectations are placed on teachers to produce results.

Researchers into the teaching of reading are constantly seeking ways of improving and assisting practice. However, much research into teaching is disseminated in such a way as to give rise to a deficit model of teaching. Many research studies conclude with advice on how teachers should change; yet, other research has shown that, in fact, teachers are slow to change. Desforges and Cockburn (1987) discuss this point in relation to mathematics education and regret the 'huge gap between aspiration and achievement' where the large amount of advice given to teachers as a result of the developing understanding of how children learn mathematics is for the most part not implemented in classrooms. (See also Desforges, 1993). Perhaps a deficit model approach is not helpful in implementing change in so complex an environment.

Doyle (1986) describes the nature of the classroom environment as consisting of many elements: multidimensionality, simultaneity, immediacy, unpredictability, publicness and history. The pace of the action in a classroom is rapid and teachers are having to make moment-to-moment decisions about what they do in response to any number of demands: from children, other adults, external influences, personal circumstances and so on. This is particularly the case in a reception class where children come from a variety of previous experience with a whole range of different expectations about behaviour, literacy, school and adults.

Many researchers highlight the difficulties children may experience on starting school where the contexts for learning are essentially different from their experiences in the home, (Tizard and Hughes, 1984; Juliebo, 1985; Wells, 1987). In the home the learning is often initiated by the child and usually takes place on a one-to-one basis with the adult who ensures the learning is within the child's frame of reference and related to previous experience. In school the child has to share the adult with up to thirty-five other children; the learning usually takes place in contexts predetermined by the teacher and can lack relevance to the child; the contexts are embedded in the here and now of the classroom rather than being placed within a network of shared experience as happens in parent–child interactions.

This chapter considers what teachers of the youngest children in school do to assist early-literacy learning and analyses this to highlight possible reasons and implications. This is not a study of methods of teaching reading but a description of the interactions that occurred between two teachers, Mrs Devlin and Mrs Harris (names changed) and the children in their classes, as observed by the researcher over several weeks during one Summer term. The intention is to describe what happened in such a way as to enable practitioners to validate and extend their own practice and researchers to identify avenues for further enquiry.

## Method

The research discussed here is part of a qualitative study into teacher decision-making in early-literacy classrooms. The study considered the practice of a small number of English reception-class teachers. The teachers' practices discussed here emphasize and take into account disparities between the learning experiences in the home and in the classroom. This part of the study was undertaken during the Summer term of 1993 in two reception classrooms in two different schools. The new children in these schools started in the term in which they were five. Therefore the classes observed had children who had been in for one or two terms and some who had just started school.

Several extended visits were made to two classrooms in two different schools during the Summer term. The teachers were observed in their interactions with the children in relation to literacy during five morning or afternoon sessions. These interactions took place within the context of five types of teacher behaviour: teacher-led class discussion; teacher reading to the class; teacher working with a group; teacher hearing readers; and teacher monitoring (i.e., overseeing children as they worked or played at given activities). At the end of each observation period the teacher was interviewed about her thoughts and intentions during the sessions. The interview schedule was flexible and various forms of open questions were used (e.g., 'What were you thinking when . . . ?). Clarification of particular points of practice and of particular incidents were similarly elicited.

Observation and the subsequent interviews showed these teachers to be operating on many levels: to settle the newest children into the class; to introduce and develop aspects of literacy and to be adopting strategies that went some way towards bridging the gap between learning in the home and learning at school. They appeared to be addressing learning on many different levels: social, affective and cognitive, at the same time as building a structure for learning which facilitates the transition from home to school.

Mrs Harris' class was in a small school in a village serving a rural community and Mrs Devlin's was in a school on an estate of mostly rented houses in a market town. The classes comprised children who were in their first year of formal schooling with the most recent starting school in the week of the first observations. The two teachers were experienced infant teachers, well thought of in their own schools and typifying a range of frequently found professional behaviours.

## Results and Discussion

Analysis of the interviews that took place after each observation showed both teachers to be operating on a variety of levels. When asked about their thoughts at a particular moment during the preceding session they would describe four identifiable areas of concern.

Firstly there was a concern for the literacy learning that they thought would ensue from a particular activity or interaction. For example, in response to a question about what she was thinking when asking certain questions at the end of a story, Mrs Devlin said

> I suppose at the very basic level the idea that the story started and then something happened and then it ended. We've had the story before and I was looking to see if they remembered the names of the characters . . .

Secondly there was a concern for the social learning of the children who had only recently started school. For example, Mrs Harris, in response to a question about a particular comment she had made about the way some children were spontaneously sharing books with each other, said

Table 9.1: Teachers' interview results over five sessions

| Type of statement response | | | |
|---|---|---|---|
| Cognitive | Affective | Social | Management |
| 96 | 46 | 35 | 36 |

That is what I was really pleased with. Because they haven't been in school very long and they come in as such individuals and the fact that they've got to this stage . . .

Thirdly there was evidence of a concern for the affective aspects of the child's development. Mrs Devlin, when describing her thoughts about a comment made to a child who had her book the wrong way up, said

We made light of that, she wasn't very confident in the first few days, tearful so that just went . . . it was pointed out and I think she was able to cope with that and I think she is the sort of child that [it] will only happen once and then tomorrow or the next time will look to see her book is the right way up because she is that type of child.

Fourthly there was a category that was initially designated as 'dilemma', but as the research developed it became clear that these dilemmas were mostly concerned with management issues such as time, number of children in the class, the different abilities of the class etc. As an example, Mrs Harris when discussing a particular group activity said

We have talked a little bit about this — this you realise was the older group — and I've got some children that I'm very aware need stretching and I'm conscious that I've given time to the new children a bit recently and I felt they needed something to really stretch them.

Numbering these elements is not intended to imply any priority. When the statements made by the teachers at interview were analysed there were found to be twice as many statements relating to cognitive aspects as any of the other three concerns (see Table 9.1). However it should be noted that, whilst the questions posed were for the most part open, the teachers knew that the subject of the research was the teaching of reading and where the researcher did ask a more focused question this led more often to a cognitive answer than either of the other three areas of concern. Therefore it is clear that these other areas of concern were also of some significance to the teachers.

The multidimensionality of the classroom referred to at the beginning of this chapter was most evident when, as was more usually the case, responses moved between concern for the child or children's literacy learning and affective and/or social learning and management dilemmas for the teacher. Mrs Harris, when describing her thoughts during a re-reading of the Big Book version of *Mrs Wishy Washy*, said

> I was trying to get them to look at the print as we go along to notice different things, drawing their attention to some letters and not over-doing it so that you lose the story . . . I don't want to spoil the story and I want to keep the momentum going. I chose that because it is tied in with the mud (a reference to a building site outside the class-room window which was of great interest to the children) and I just feel that this corporate saying of the story is very useful, a corporate way of a lot of children looking at print together — well it is so difficult fitting in reading with children separately so I do think that this is one of the ways that we can . . .

It can be seen that, alongside these teachers' concern to develop early-literacy skills, lies a concern for other aspects of the child's development. These teachers are operating on more than one level at a time in their inter-action with children. Therefore it seems that criticisms of teachers of children starting school which look at task design (Bennett and Kell, 1989) or the disparity between home and school contexts for learning (Tizard and Hughes, 1984; Juliebo, 1985; Wells, 1987) demonstrate the problems but do not give sufficient credit to the attempts made by teachers to deal with these everyday professional concerns. Analysis of what teachers do can be a more powerful model for professional development than a deficit approach.

Ease of transition from learning in the home to learning at school can be seen as one aspect where these teachers adopted strategies which went some way towards assisting the child in this transition. Evidence from this very small study suggests that teachers in reception classes can adopt strategies that com-pensate for the differences in the learning context between home and school.

The examples given below are not isolated ones but chosen from many similar ones in order to illustrate the point being made.

### *Teacher Initiation of Learning*

Wells (1987), indicates how a great deal of the learning in the home takes place within an interaction initiated by the child. Obviously with a large class and specific aspects of curriculum to cover this cannot be possible. However, the teachers in this study had strategies they employed to engage the chil-dren's interest.

For example, Mrs Harris would often use suspense as a way of gaining the children's attention. On one occasion, with the whole class on the carpet and a large closed cardboard box in front of her, she started to tell a story about what she had done after school the previous evening which led to her going to the schools' library service and choosing some new books. Another morning there was a letter pinned to the easel addressed to the class. There was much speculation about what it could contain before it was opened to reveal a letter asking for details about a favourite television programme which introduced the writing activity for the morning.

In another way many ideas were thrown into discussion in an apparently haphazard way but with the intention that for some children these might provide a springboard for further investigation. For example, at the end of a reading of *Each Peach Pear Plum*, a child asked Mrs Devlin where Robin Hood was in the picture and she replied 'I can see him, see if you can find him later'. Talking about this later she said,

> I thought maybe she would go back and look as she in fact did. It's a small book to use in the class and I wouldn't particularly want everybody clamouring around the pictures. The pictures are so clever the way they are made they are so beautifully illustrated, so the more you look the more you see.

### Frame of Reference

Not only is the learning in the home initiated by the child but the adult is able to scaffold that learning supporting the child in the next step. An important part of doing this is the ability to place the learning within the child's frame of reference. The parent is in an ideal position to do this since he or she shares the experience of the child and can refer forward or back as appropriate. This is obviously much harder for classteachers. Whilst they may know something of the children's life out of school they cannot know everything and they also cannot relate to thirty children's individual and idiosyncratic frames of reference all at the same time. However, both teachers had strategies for coping with this situation. They would often break in during story-time to ask whether children had had experience of something that was referred to in the story; for example, a bus journey where those who had not been on a bus were reminded about watching a bus going past the school.

The same thing happened on a one-to-one basis, particularly when the teacher was sharing a book with a child. When Joe met the word 'parade' in his reading book, Mrs Harris asked him if he had ever been to a parade. When he said that he had not she probed until she could find some meeting of his experience with the idea of a parade,

> Have you ever been to the carnival in . . . [names neighbouring large town]? Have you ever been to a fancy dress party? You like dressing up don't you, Joe? Well if we had a parade in the village people would dress up and . . .

She goes on to explain a parade. Afterwards Mrs Harris said,

Well I think I was trying to bring it to the child's experience, it's exploring it a little bit. It [lack of understanding] detracts from the understanding of the text . . . I was just checking it out just seeing where he was at.

Both teachers did this frequently in relation to text. They were constantly relating text to life, life to text and text to text. The first two of these interactional sequences are as referred to by Marilyn Cochrane-Smith (1984).

1.  text to life:
    When Ben was reading a story in which a dog appears, Mrs Devlin interrupted to ask him whether he had a dog at home.
2.  life to text:
    Mrs Harris was reading some poems from a new poetry book and said, 'You might guess why I'm reading this next poem, it's called Mandy Likes Mud.' The children knew immediately as there was a new classroom being built outside their window and they had been watching a digger working in the mud the day before.
3.  text to text:
    When Mrs Devlin was reading *Tidy Titch* by Pat Hutchins she first talked about the nickname Titch and related it to the names, Biff, Chip and Kipper in the *Oxford Reading Tree* books. She also drew the children's attention to the author and reminded them that they had recently had *Rosie's Walk* by the same author read to them.

*Routines or Formats*

Another key feature of learning in the home is the existence of routines that provide a basis for many interactional opportunities. Both teachers were keen to establish routines early on in the term with the new children. These appeared to have both a cognitive and social purpose. Bruner (1977) believes that for learning to take place appropriate social interactional frameworks must be provided — he refers to these as 'scaffolding'. Thus the parent provides contexts and routines that are familiar to the child, she (for it is usually the mother) is finely tuned to the capabilities and capacities of her child and helps the child to develop within the supporting framework provided.

Mrs Devlin always chose a child to be the 'leader', for the day. The 'leader' was the person who took the register to the office, stood in front of the line to go to dinner etc. This clearly had an important social function in maintaining an order within the classroom, but it was also used to illustrate a use of literacy. Each day a label was made saying who was to be the leader. At first the label was made by the class teacher but gradually the children themselves were encouraged to make their own labels. These labels were also used for reading practice at times when the children were lining up near to the sign. When the establishment of routines was discussed with Mrs Devlin, she stressed the importance of establishing these and said,

> Once they are aware of it most children enjoy it. It's security but you can see the development. This morning was the first time they had made their own notices about who is the leader. Thinking about it last night (I thought that) hopefully they will see what's going on and do that without me having to say. That will be all part of being the leader, that you make the poster to let everybody know.

And also, on another day,

> There's always a lot of hustle and bustle about who's going to be the leader, who's going to be first in line. I put that [a sign] there and throughout the day I will say many times 'Naomi is our leader today.' I do make sure we use the words that are actually written there and hopefully they will recognise the words.

### Attitudes

Children grow up in an environment where those people close to them are constantly displaying attitudes and giving opinions which become for the child an accepted way of responding. Children are not *told* to like the family dog or support Manchester United so much as absorb these attitudes as taken for granted until further experience leads them to question. Whilst many children will come to school with a positive attitude to books and reading, others may either have no really strong feelings or think of books as being to do with learning to read as an end in itself. Both teachers worked hard to establish positive attitudes to books and reading through what they said, the way they said it and the way they reacted to children's reading or treatment of books.

When introducing some new books collected from the school's library service, Mrs Harris emphasized the 'beautiful' books and talked about the 'fun' they would have reading them. Afterwards she said, 'I thought how gorgeous these books are and aren't these children lucky to have such beautiful books and I do want them to like them too.'

### Feedback

Juliebo (1985) reports that in the home constant feedback is given to encourage a sense of success. However, at school errors were often corrected without explanation. This did not seem to be the case with the two teachers observed in this study. Feedback was given in a positive way where the teachers felt it was appropriate or often errors were left without comment and something successful was chosen for comment. When asked whether they criticized children's reading or writing. Mrs Harris said,

> I try to do this more by encouragement than criticism, you have to think what's appropriate for this age group. I do criticise just occasionally and I can tell you the two it would have been this morning . . . Amy is the type of child who I'd not criticise but put it beforehand saying what I want her to concentrate on and then if she didn't deliver the goods I would say 'are you satisfied with that?

Mrs Devlin commented,

> I criticise writing rather than reading. I do criticise work that we actually record in our books if I feel it's appropriate. Matthew responds well — he will go back and have another go. It wouldn't be worth criticising at the moment Joanna or Michelle — I wouldn't use that approach with them yet.

### Appropriateness to the Individual Child

This theme of appropriateness to the individual child is one that recurs again and again. Although this was not necessarily apparent in my observations, it was striking how often in the post-observation interview the matching of response to child was mentioned. This occurred in a variety of different ways. Sometimes it was, as above, when the type of response was as deemed appropriate to the child, other times it was the content of the response. An example of this which goes some way to demonstrate the multidimensionality of the teacher's behaviour is when on one occasion, Mrs Harris, while working with the whole class on the carpet, directed a question about the letter 'r' to Andrew. This was one of a series of questions about letters in a word that were directed at children apparently at random. When asked afterwards why she had chosen Andrew for that particular question Mrs Harris replied,

> Because, although he seems bright and on the ball I've found that he doesn't actually know all the letters quite and I thought he knew the ones in his name so I thought that was one that I was going to be able to reinforce and he was going to get. But also, I had noticed he was wriggling, wasn't he, and it was a way of drawing him in, but that was why I chose that letter.

Mrs Devlin explained how she had different expectations for different children at different times. Here she is describing her expectations of two girls in a writing group,

Katie and Jennifer were very happy to go on and write on their own today, they're not terribly confident usually. Yesterday they worked very closely with me on letter shapes and looking at words and actually writing words down — so I just wanted to see what they could do by themselves. To give them a bit of confidence and they were quite pleased with what they had done in the end.

These are some selected examples of the ways in which experienced infant teachers help children learn in the new context of the classroom. This is not to say that they deliberately compensate for the context — in fact not once in the interviews did the teachers mention that this was their intention. However, as experienced teachers, sensitive to the ways children learn, they knew implicitly to employ these strategies to enable children to make a smooth transfer to school learning.

### Messages for Teachers

This chapter does not seek to imply that the difficulties outlined at the beginning are not real. They undoubtedly are. Constraints on time and curriculum coverage together with the different experience and maturity of children as they start school make the role of the reception teacher a complex and difficult one. However, by employing strategies similar to those of the parent, yet adapted to fit the different context and demands of the classroom, the teacher can help effect a smooth transition from home to school learning.

Teachers operate on many levels in their interactions with children and these are all necessary given the age and maturity of the children and the importance of reception-class learning in providing a foundation for the child's cognitive, social and affective development. It must be recognized that this study, whilst acknowledging the good practice undertaken by teachers has not considered the way in which the teachers' efforts impact upon the individual child. Much of the interaction recorded was on a one-to-one basis and, inevitably, the larger the class the less attention an individual child will receive. The dilemmas caused by the number of children and their stage of development were high in the minds of the teachers and were issues which they returned to again and again in the post-observation interviews.

### Conclusion

This chapter has attempted to highlight the practice of experienced teachers of early literacy and to analyse the ways in which this addresses the social, affective and cognitive needs of the young learner. It is hoped that there is much here that teachers can use to validate and extend their own practice. There are also issues raised that warrant further investigation to ascertain the impact of this practice on the learners themselves.

## References

BENNETT, N. and KELL, J. (1989) *A Good Start? Four-year-olds in Infant Schools*, Oxford, Basil Blackwell.

BRUNER, J. (1977) 'Early social interaction and language development', in SCHAFFER, H.R. (Ed) *Studies in Mother–Child Interaction*, London, Academic Press.

COCHRANE-SMITH, M. (1984) *The Making of a Reader*, Norwood, New Jersey, Ablex Publishing Corporation.

DESFORGES, C. and COCKBURN, A. (1987) *Understanding the Mathematics Teacher*, Lewes, Falmer Press.

DESFORGES, C. (1993) *Children as Thinkers and Learners*, the text of a lecture, London: The British Association for Early Childhood Education.

DOYLE, W. (1986) 'Classroom organisation and management', in WITTROCK, M.C. (Ed) *Handbook of Research in Teaching* (3rd ed.), New York, MacMillan.

JULIEBO, M. (1985) 'The literacy world of five young children', *Reading-Canada-Lecture*, **3**, 2, pp. 263–7.

TIZARD, B. and HUGHES, M. (1984) *Young Children Learning: Talking and Thinking at Home and at School*, London, Fontana.

WELLS, C.G. (1987) *The Meaning Makers*, London, Hodder and Stoughton.

### Children's Books

AHLBERG, J. (1989) *Each Peach, Pear, Plum*, London, Puffin.

COWLEY, J. and MESLER, J. (1985) *Mrs Wishy Washy* (Big Book version) Story Chest, Leeds, Arnold Wheaten.

HUTCHINS, P. (1968) *Rosie's Walk, The Bodley Head*, London.

(1986) *Oxford Reading Tree* (Reading Scheme) Oxford, Oxford University Press.

*Chapter 10*

# The Importance of the Teacher

*R. Campbell*

**Summary**

It is argued that the teacher (adult/parent at home or professional at school) has a most important role in helping children develop as readers. It is a role which is sometimes diminished by attention to methodologies and materials. Three areas are explored; (i) the home context with particular attention to environmental print, story reading and shared reading and opportunities for writing; (ii) classroom organization and the management of literacy events; and (iii) the teacher's role during shared readings. Transcript evidence is presented to provide a classroom-research basis.

**Introduction**

In any debate which takes place on how children learn to read the emphasis of the debate can be diverted frequently into dichotomous views about the methodologies and/or philosophies which underpin the teaching which is to take place. For example, the phonic–whole word debate has been with us for at least a quarter of a century (Chall, 1967). And more recently that debate has developed into a phonics–Whole Language debate (Goodman, 1986); expressed perhaps as phonics–real books in the UK. It is a debate in which I have been prepared to participate (Campbell, 1992). However, on this occasion I wish to concentrate instead on a feature which is common to both views. That feature is the important role of the teacher in aiding the reading development of young children. Frank Smith (1978) indicated the importance of that role very boldly — as one might expect — when he stated 'A teacher is one of the most important people in the beginning reader's life, and can make the difference between success and failure . . . teachers have a crucial role' (p. 137). That crucial role needs to be explored. Before we do so we need to consider to whom we are referring when we use the term 'teacher'.

## The Teacher

It is useful to think of the teacher as that person who facilitates, supports, guides, instructs and encourages children with literacy learning. The teacher in that sense is the parent, or other significant adult at home, and the teacher at school.

We know from a variety of studies of the key role that parents at home can play in enabling young children to develop as readers. Clark (1976) in her study of young fluent readers indicated that the children who had learnt to read before arriving at school had the advantage of 'an interested adult with time to devote to them at the stage when they were interested in reading — either to read to them, talk with them, or answer their questions' (p. 102). That view is extended because literacy is increasingly being recognized as a sociopsycholinguistic activity in which that term emphasizes the importance of the adult — child interaction as well as recognizing the thought and language processes (Teale and Sulzby, 1989). When literacy learning is viewed in that way the important role of the teacher in school is placed in the foreground, although not necessarily as a direct instructor.

However, the teacher role is important in terms of providing the print-rich environment in which literacy can be learnt (facilitator); being available to aid the child in what he or she is attempting to achieve (support); moving the learning along in particular ways when needed (guide); providing some direct teaching when the child requires information (instruct); and letting the children know when aspects of their learning are successful (encourage).

What are some of the important features at home and at school in which the parent and teacher enable the children to learn to read?

### Learning to Read at Home

We are aware of the occasional report which seems to indicate that a child has learnt to read without adult support (Torrey, 1969). However, those reports are dwarfed in comparison with the information we have on children who have learnt to read because of the literacy activities which were provided by, most usually, a parent. In particular we can consider the contact with environmental print, story reading, shared reading and opportunities for writing.

Children are surrounded, in our culture, by environmental print and it would appear that John in the Torrey (1969) study learnt to read from that print largely unaided. However, in most circumstances young children learn from that environmental print because a parent, or other adult, answers questions about the print. Or more directly the parent draws the child's attention to the print. Case studies, often by parents, demonstrate the power of adults and children talking about the environmental print at home and more widely (Laminack, 1991).

It has been argued by Wells (1986) that story reading, by parents to children during the preschool years, is associated significantly with children's subsequent literacy developments. Those story readings not only teach about books, pages, left-to-right directionality etc., they also enable children to learn about story structure, discourse patterns and language. Where such interactions are developed in a relaxed and enjoyable atmosphere, with interesting books, they will create the possiblity of a child who wants to read (Meek, 1988).

The story readings develop subsequently into shared readings on occasions. They do so because children will wish to demonstrate their familiarity with a text and a growing understanding of reading. The adult in such circumstances will need to provide time to share the book with the child and to use strategies that will support the young reader towards greater independence as a reader (Campbell, 1990).

Other studies also tell us about the importance of providing opportunities for writing. Schickedanz (1990) indicated that Adam was provided with paper with various lines and shapes. The boy used that paper to scribble, to differentiate eventually between drawing and writing, and subsequently to develop his understanding of orthography, phonemes, words, spellings etc. He did so, we could argue, because the parents had facilitated the learning by providing materials and then supported that learning by talking about the writing with the child.

## Learning to Read at School

The importance of the teacher in helping children to read at school is almost self-evident. After all the teacher will have as a first responsibility the need to organize the classroom so that literacy learning can occur and second will have to provide the day-to-day management within the classroom so that the learning is made effective. That organization will involve the development of a library corner, listening area, writing centre and play area with suitable materials to encourage literacy activities. (See for instance Hall and Abbott, 1991). It will also require an organization of the day to enable class, group and individual literacy activities to take place. Such activities, and the transitions between them, require skilful management.

The primary-school teacher, of course, has to attend to a wide range of subject demands (in England the ten National Curriculum subjects). This requirement should concentrate attention rather than deflect the teacher from the prime purpose which is to develop children's literacy. Cambourne (1988) demonstrated the emphasis that might be needed by suggesting that the first two hours of the school day should be devoted to 'language'. That emphasis reflects the view that the amount of time spent on reading and writing will relate directly to the success of literacy teaching (Harris, 1979). Good organization, management and use of time are not achieved easily; they require a skilful teacher if they are to be capitalized on to the pupils' advantage.

That organization, management and time, of course, is there to provide the basis for a range of literacy activities. The knowledgeable teacher will ensure that story reading, shared reading, hearing children read, sustained silent reading, reading–writing connections, topic work, writing for real purposes and use of the environmental and classroom print are all used as vehicles in the development of children's literacy. Furthermore, that they are achieved not just mechanistically but by a teacher who demonstrates an infectious enthusiasm for reading. The daily assessment of the children's reading and writing, whether informally or more formally on occasions such as the Standard Assessment Tasks in the National Curriculum, ensures that the teacher knows about the children's literacy development and therefore about their learning needs. Ongoing assessments occur as the teacher observes, interacts and analyses the literacy efforts of the children (Goodman, 1989).

It has been suggested that the role of the teacher is important in providing an organization, management and an effective use of time leading to a range of literacy activities. But, it is not sufficient to consider the importance of the teacher only at this macro-level. It is also necessary to evaluate the nature of the interactions between the teacher and the child in order to recognize the important features of the teacher's role at the micro-level.

Clearly it is not possible, here, to provide a micro-analysis of the teacher role during all of the literacy activities which have been suggested earlier. The following concentrates on one of them, the teacher role during shared readings.

### Aspects of the Teacher Role During Shared Readings

During shared readings teachers will take on a range of responsibilities. They might sit alongside the child while the book is being selected and this can lead to discussions about the book, the title, the author, the illustrations and perhaps some discussion of the characters in the story. These discussions might continue when the story is about to be shared and be extended to making text-to-life connections and predictions about the story.

However, once the story begins to be read the role of the teacher as a support, guide, instructor and encourager becomes emphasized and it is evident that the role requires sophisticated teaching as the teacher responds to the child's reading.

In order to clarify that view let us look at part of a shared reading between a teacher and 5-year-old Richard who was reading from Eric Carle's *The Very Hungry Caterpillar*. We will only consider the start of that interaction, although the complete reading of the story has been reported elsewhere (Campbell, 1992). In the transcripts, any *reading* of the book by either teacher or child, is indented further to the *right*. Hesitations in reading are indicated by //.

*Richard*:  I've got *The Hungry Caterpillar.*
**Teacher**:  It is *The Hungry Caterpillar,* isn't it?
Shall we read it together?

> *Richard*: Yeah.
> **Teacher**: Come on then.
>     In
> *Richard*:   In the
> **T/R** (The teacher and Richard reading alongside each other. The first named indicates who might be leading the reading.)
>     light
> *Richard*:   of the moon
>     the-the(a)
> **T/R**:   little
> *Richard*:   egg
> **Teacher**: Yes.
> *Richard*:   lay on a leaf.
> **Teacher**: Yes.
>     It lay on a leaf, didn't it?
>     Can you see the egg?
> *Richard*: Yeah Yeah.
>     Yeah but the other day I looked at the pictures and I thought it was a hole.
> **Teacher**: Did you? (Laughs)

There are several notable features of that opening to the shared reading.

1. The invitation to 'read it together', with me rather than to me, might be important, as Waterland (1998) suggested. Those words should indicate to the child that it is a collaborative activity rather than a test of the child's reading. Of course, the teacher then has to demonstrate throughout the interaction that the collaboration is real, the words are meant, and is reflected in the teacher's behaviour.

2. There was a continuous changing from the teacher leading the reading to the child reading with the teacher in support. And that is achieved because the teacher is in tune with what the child is able to do. The teacher drops into the background, mediates or supports directly according to need. In practice, this is less staccato than might at first sight seem to be the case from reading the transcript.

3. Simple miscues such as 'the' for 'a' received no teacher response because meaning was being maintained by the 5-year-old as he proceeded with his reading. This suggests, perhaps, a teacher knowledgeable about reading and about miscue analysis and therefore able to make informed responses (including non-responses) according to the nature of the miscue.

4. The end of a page provided the natural break from the reading to allow a very brief discussion of part of the story, facilitating the child's understanding of the story.

The reading then continued.

> **Teacher**: Come on then.
> **R/T**:   One

| | |
|---|---|
| *Richard*: | Summer(Sunday)<br>My mum's got *The Hungry Caterpillar* — it's — my mum's got — I've got that book like you.<br>One Summer's(Sunday) day(morning) the warm sun came out(up) and — pop!<br>Eh. |
| ***T/R***: | out |
| *Richard*: | of the egg<br>a very(came) |
| **Teacher**: | came |
| *Richard*: | came a tiny and very hungry caterpillar. |
| **Teacher**: | It did come up didn't it one morning?<br>Yes. |

5. The teacher did not mediate when Richard read: 'One summer's day the warm sun came out . . .' for the text words of 'One Sunday morning the warm sun came up . . .' But, notice how at the end of the page the teacher not only praised the reading but also modelled the correct reading to some extent with: 'It did come up didn't it one morning.' In particular the teacher included the text words of 'up' and 'morning' into the praise given to the child.

6. The teacher provided the words 'out' and 'came' where feedback and these words appeared to be needed, in order, perhaps, to maintain a flow to the reading.

7. The teacher continued to move in and out of the role as reader according to Richard's perceived needs.

Subsequently the teacher encouraged Richard to continue with the reading by asking a question.

| | |
|---|---|
| **Teacher**: | What did he start to do? |
| *Richard*: | He looked(started) |
| **Teacher**: | No. |
| *Richard*: | He starts(started) |
| **Teacher**: | Yes.<br>He started |
| *Richard*: | to look for (some) food. |
| **Teacher**: | He did.<br>He started to look for some food. |

8. The teacher used a number of different responses in order to support the reading.

- 'No' given as a soft non-punitive response — to inform the reader of a miscue;
- 'Yes' 'He started' — to confirm the reading but also to provide a model of the verb ending as it appeared in the book;

- 'He did.' 'He started to look for some food.' — to provide further confirmation, and praise for the reading, but also to provide a model of the sentence to complete the reading of the page.

The teacher then encouraged Richard to continue reading and here the rhythm of the writing and the sentence which seems to delight young children — 'But he was still hungry.' — enabled Richard to provide a more conventional reading.

**Teacher**: Yes.
*Richard*:     On Monday
               he ate through
               one apple.
               But he was still
               hungry.
**Teacher**: He was, wasn't he?
*Richard*:     On Tuesday
               he ate through
               two peppers(pears)
**Teacher**: They do look a bit like peppers.
               And they do begin with a 'p'.
               But they might be something else, do you think?
*Richard*:    pineapples — eh —
**Teacher**: Do you think they're pears?
*Richard*:    Yeah.
***T/R***:     two pears,
*Richard*:    Eh.
               but he was
               still hungry.
**Teacher**: He was still hungry, wasn't he?

9. The teacher mediated the miscue of 'peppers' for 'pears' by emphasizing the phonemic aspect of the miscue. 'They do look a bit like peppers. And they do begin with a 'p'.'

10. Subsequently the teacher provided a more substantial scaffold by asking 'Do you think they're pears?'

If we look more closely at some of the examples from the shared reading and present them in a slightly different format in order to concentrate upon the miscue of the reader and the teacher response to that miscue (rather than including all the details from the interaction) then we can detect a number of different responses serving a variety of purposes.

1. Miscues which retain the essential meaning of the story may receive a *non-response* from the teacher. That non-mediation from the teacher keeps the reader involved with the story and emphasizes meaning in the shared reading.

*Richard:*       In the light of the moon
                 the(a) little egg lay on a leaf.
**Teacher:**  —

2. The teacher might want to respond to those miscues which detract from the meaning of the text. One useful strategy for the teacher to use is to mediate and read part of the sentence that leads up to the miscued word. And, importantly, to do so with a rising intonation that invites the child back as the reader. (As the teacher did later in this shared reading).

That *word cueing* strategy is a simple one but it does create a minimal disruption to the reading; it informs the reader of the need to reconsider a word, but it does so by maintaining the focus upon the text. Children do appear to be helped by this teacher strategy.

*Richard:*       one cupcake and
                 one slice of salami(watermelon).
**Teacher:**  one slice
*Richard:*       one slice of watermelon.

3. At other times the teacher might simply inform the reader that the prediction had not worked and to do so by using the *soft 'no'* that is non-punitive but informative (Smith, 1971). Again the use of that simple strategy worked albeit that Richard just corrected the verb without also getting the verb ending accurate following the teacher response.

*Richard:*       He looked(started)
**Teacher:**  No.
*Richard:*       He starts(started)
**Teacher:**  Yes.
                 He started

4. Occasionally the teacher might just *provide the word* for the reader, most probably in order to maintain the flow of reading from the child.

*Richard:*       out of the egg
                 a very(came)
**Teacher:**  came
*Richard:*       came a tiny and very hungry caterpillar.
However the teacher would want to avoid using that particular strategy too often as it does not require the child to process the text and it might make the reader over reliant upon the teacher. In a shared reading on another occasion it was evident that another pupil, Jason, had become over reliant upon his teacher — or he had decided to encourage his teacher to do the reading for him (Campbell, 1988).
*Jason:*       He can //

| Teacher: | make |
| Jason: | make // |
| Teacher: | Black |
| Jason: | Black // |
| Teacher: | Pony |
| Jason: | Pony // |
| Teacher: | run |
| Jason: | run // |
| Teacher: | fast. |
| Jason: | fast. |

Jason was using, apparently, a hesitation (//) in his reading in order to get the teacher to read the text. As teachers we would probably wish to avoid such episodes. After all, the purpose of the shared reading interaction, while maintaining the interest and enjoyment of the reader, is to encourage the child towards independent and silent reading, rather than remaining reliant upon the teacher.

5. Although *non-response, word cueing, a soft 'no'* and *providing the word* might predominate as the teacher responds to the reader's miscues, because they should keep the child involved with the text, other strategies would also be used on occasions. These would include drawing the reader's attention to the *letters and associated sounds* in a word. There was a simple example of this in Richard's shared reading.

| Richard: | he ate through |
| | two peppers(pears) |
| Teacher: | They do look a bit like peppers. |
| | And they do begin with a 'p'. (letter sound) |
| | But they might be something else, do you think? |
| Richard: | pineapples — eh — |

Reminding the child to use the graphophonic cue system will be part of the guidance that the teacher provides.

## Messages for Teachers

The teacher will use a variety of responses to a child's miscues according to perceived needs of that child. However, the teacher will also be guided by a number of principles which provide the rationale for those responses. The teacher will attempt to keep the child involved with the story by providing a minimal interruption to the reading (e.g., *non-response, word cueing* and *provide the word*). In that way the child is encouraged to remain as an active learner in the process of reading (Donaldson, 1989). Furthermore, the teacher will want to use strategies (e.g., *word cueing*) that not only help the child with the reading immediately but also might suggest strategies for the future when reading independently.

The importance of the role of the teacher is further underlined if we look again, briefly, at one section of Richard's reading.

**Teacher**: What did he start to do?
*Richard*: He looked(started)
**Teacher**: No.
*Richard*: He starts(started)
**Teacher**: Yes.
He started
*Richard*: to look for (some) food.
**Teacher**: He did.
He started to look for some food.

The question to be asked is whether Richard miscued with 'looked' for 'started' or whether he was answering the question 'What did he start to do?' The answer to that question is difficult to establish but it is possible that the teacher encouraged Richard to produce what appeared to be a miscue but in reality was not.

That negative example (and the example from Jason's shared reading) does not detract from the view of the importance of the teacher. Indeed, arguably it strengthens the view that the teacher's role is of considerable importance in helping children learn to read. That importance is not only in the initial organization and management of the classroom and time for literacy activities, it is also in the fine detail of teacher behaviour during those literacy interactions.

## Conclusion

This chapter finishes where it started with a bold quote from Frank Smith, who stated 'Methods can never ensure that children learn to read. Children must learn from people.' (p. 34). Those people, mostly parents at home and teachers in school, have an important role to play in the development of children's literacy. And it is a role which is sometimes diminished in attention to methodologies, apparatus and materials. But it should not be. The importance of the knowledgeable, skilful and enthusiastic teacher in helping children to learn to read needs to remain a central focus of inquiry.

## References

CAMBOURNE, B. (1988) *The Whole Story: Natural Learning and the Acquisition of Literacy in the Classroom*, Auckland, Ashton Scholastic.

CAMPBELL, R. (1988) *Hearing Children Read*, London, Routledge.

CAMPBELL, R. (1990) *Reading Together*, Buckingham, Open University Press.

CAMPBELL, R. (1992) *Reading Real Books*, Buckingham, Open University Press.

CHALL, J. (1967) *Learning to Read: The Great Debate*, New York, McGraw-Hill.

CLARK, M.M. (1976) *Young Fluent Readers*, London, Heinemann Educational.

DONALDSON, M. (1989) *Sense and Sensibility*, Reading, Reading and Language Information Centre, University of Reading School of Education.

GOODMAN, K. (1986) *What's Whole in Whole Language?* Portsmouth, NH, Heinemann Educational.

GOODMAN, Y. (1989) 'Evaluation of students', in GOODMAN, K., GOODMAN, Y. and HOOD, W. (Eds) *The Whole Language Evaluation Book*, Portsmouth, NH, Heinemann Educational.

HALL, N. and ABBOTT, L. (1991) *Play in the Primary School*, London, Hodder and Stoughton.

HARRIS, A.J. (1979) 'The effective teacher of reading, revisited', *The Reading Teacher*, **33**, 2.

LAMINACK, L. (1991) *Learning with Zachary*, Richmond Hill, Ontario, Scholastic Publications.

MEEK, M. (1988) *How Texts Teach What Readers Learn*, Stroud, Thimble Press.

SCHICKEDANZ, J.A. (1990) *Adam's Righting Revolutions: One child's literacy development from infancy through Grade One*, Portsmouth, NH, Heinemann.

SMITH, F. (1971) *Understanding Reading*, New York, Holt, Rinehart and Winston.

SMITH, F. (1978) *Reading*, Cambridge, Cambridge University Press.

SMITH, F. (1992) *Reading Today*, **10**, 2.

TEALE, W.H. and SULZBY, E. (1989) 'Emergent literacy: New perspectives', in STRICKLAND, D.S. and MORROW, L.M. (Eds) *Emerging Literacy: Young Children Learn to Read and Write*, Newark, Delaware, International Reading Association.

TORREY, J.W. (1969) 'Learning to read without a teacher: A case study', *Elementary English*, **46**, pp. 550–6.

WATERLAND, L. (1988) *Read with Me: An Apprenticeship Approach to Reading*, Stroud, Thimble Press.

WELLS, G. (1986) *The Meaning Makers: Children Learning Language and Using Language to Learn*, London, Hodder and Stoughton.

*Chapter 11*

# Stance, Meaning and Voluntary Reading

*M. Hunter-Carsch*

**Summary**

This chapter advances the view that the reading process is essentially enactive, interactive, creative and involves recreation of meaning. The levels of meaning to which the reader has access are shown to be affected by experience, 'stance', motivation, the value attached to the text and the nature of the text. This view is drawn from several frames of reference including (i) philosophical perspectives employing logical analysis of reading development, (ii) cross-cultural considerations and (iii) observational research in schools and libraries exploring reading development, voluntary reading and student teachers' views at the beginning of their course of training.

**Introduction**

In recent media debates about the alleged falling of standards of children's reading, it has largely been assumed that there is a shared understanding amongst professionals and between professionals and the laity, about what counts as being able to read, and what is meant by 'reading standards'.

Conflict reported in the media has focused on particular methods of teaching reading. These are approaches referred to generally as the 'traditional method' which includes an emphasis on teaching phonic skills (*part* of reading) and uses graded vocabulary texts (reading schemes) for practising reading, versus the approach which is referred to in the UK as 'real books'. The latter is associated with an emphasis on 'reading for meaning' of the *whole* story. In the UK this has come to be termed variously as the 'story method', the 'story approach', or relatedly, the 'apprenticeship approach'. Each of these variations differs in some aspects of practice, but tends to share the common emphasis on 'meaning'.

In the USA the debate centres on traditional ('basal' reading schemes) versus the 'Whole Language' approach. The stakes are high as publishers frequently obtain substantial orders as a result of state-policy decisions to employ particular schemes.

Until the very recent and well publicized attention to research into the place of phonological awareness in learning to read, (e.g., Goswami and Bryant, 1990; Goswami, 1993) this essentially false polarization of 'phonics' and 'real books' approaches to teaching reading was facilitating a shift of attention from the methodological issues and the underlying issues concerning theoretical perspectives, to the personalizing and manipulation of images of 'kinds of teachers'. In the extreme, these led to the image of 'the old fashioned teacher' (considered by supporters of phonics and schemes to be 'reliable and thorough') and the 'trendy books' approach (considered to be 'careless and lacking in rigour') (see also Morris, 1993).

Despite, or perhaps even because of the current swing in fashion in England and Wales towards regarding the teaching of phonics in a somewhat more favourable light, it is pertinent to note that the results of selective and unsystematic media presentations of 'the debate' included not only distortions but also the loss of opportunities to share knowledge which had been published over a considerable period of time. Sources of highly relevant information include government publications such as the Bullock Report (DES, 1975), recent HMI reports and discussions by eminent researchers. One such researcher wrote eloquently on the subject, advising 'Sense and Sensibility in the Teaching of Literacy' (Donaldson, 1989). That paper anticipated the most recent wave of reductionist thinking and warned about the dangers of false polarizations on the subject.

Given the attention it deserves, Donaldson's paper might be employed to undo some of the damage caused by populistic perspectives which have had a divisive and destructive impact on both professional discourse and on the laity who are becoming increasingly involved with the decision-making processes, (e.g., participation on school governing bodies whose responsibilities include becoming sufficiently well informed to assist in matters affecting the curriculum).

Until there is agreement about what constitutes 'reading', it is unlikely that any valid comparisons can be made of standards of reading, over time, in different locations, with different populations. The problem of comparing reading standards of different groups or of the same group over time, is compounded if different methods of measurement are employed.

The problem is further compounded when attempts are made to explain seeming differences as being largely attributable to a single cause, in this instance, the teaching method (Lake, 1991; 1992).

Politically and economically, not to mention ethically, the implications for teacher education are profound. It is an issue that we cannot afford to neglect.

## A Matter of Stance and Meaning

The idea of 'stance', in this context, is intended to differentiate between diverse frames of reference which separate different disciplines variously employed in education and curricular perspectives (e.g., history, linguistics, philosophy, psychology, sociology). The use of the term 'stance' thus seeks to avoid the seeming permanence and missionary overtones sometimes associated with 'positions', 'arguments' or 'methods'. While retaining the slight distance normally attributed to detached observation, 'stance' can be taken to respect interdisciplinary perspectives and to maintain flexibility. It can be taken to include those perspectives from the arts which make possible the artist's facility in adjusting focus from far–distance to close–up and the agility of imagery of the choreographer who can simultaneously 'inhabit' the movement patterns of the individual dancer and envisage the dynamic patterns of the entire *corps de ballet* throughout a dance sequence on stage.

The benefits of including these perspectives in discussions about reading relate to the need for the reading process to be considered with reference to all texts and contexts, not solely the reading of the printed text, as potential means of communication. This is important in the essentially multidisciplinary underpinning of the primary-school teacher's grasp of child development and the management and organization of the curriculum to facilitate that development.

The flexibility required to appreciate the existence and nature of different stances and to engage with different stances involves also the response to different kinds of texts (e.g., two-dimensional pictures representing three-dimensional objects in art and illustrations in printed texts; also records of sequences of movements in dance as represented by different forms of notation such as Laban's notation or the Benesh notation).

The idea of stance, as it relates to this particular issue of understanding the nature of reading, is particularly pertinent for teacher educators whose work entails encouraging student teachers to be ready

- to engage with the child learner's intended direction of movement (as surely in the teaching of reading as in the teaching of dance); and
- to anticipate where teacher intervention is required in order to 'move the child on' with confidence and competence, to the next step in learning.

It is in this interaction between the learner, teacher and text that there exists the opportunity for understanding the vital relationship between 'learning to read' and 'teaching reading'.

An attempt to answer the central question, 'What do we mean by reading?' would need to take into account not only perceptions of the reading process from the stance of the learner as well as the teacher and other theoreticians but also the issues implicit in the following underlying questions: Who decides what counts as reading? What is involved in the reading process? What is the 'text' that is being read?

These questions could be considered from any of a range of stances. Related matters include the need to clarify whether definitions of reading are proposed in terms that are either *absolute* (specifying the criteria which must be met in order to consider a response to be classed as showing evidence of 'being able to read'), or *relative* (describing ability to read in terms which are qualified (e.g., 'very able', 'able', 'less able', 'unable' and which may imply a continuum of reading ability within a specified population or sample of pupils).

The questions which arise involve:

- how to describe the behaviour of a person who is not able to read a particular text and whether such a person should be described as 'unable to read' (generalizing from the particular). (The matter cannot be resolved without reference to the text in question, i.e., what is being read.);
- the time taken or allowed for reading and what constitutes the evidence of 'being able to read' (orally or silently?); and
- whether reading is viewed as a 'static' ability (once a certain performance level has been reached) or whether it is conceptualized as 'dynamic', possibly taking into account matters of breadth and depth of understanding, quality of performance and degrees of fluency.

It would require a substantially longer chapter to do justice to any one of these questions. The purpose at present is simply to establish recognition of the need to take all of these factors into account in attempting an answer to the central question: What counts as being able to read?

## Who Decides What Counts As Reading?

### Designers and Users of Reading Tests

If we turn to reading tests to find out what counts as reading, we are likely to become involved in a similar problem to that faced by the critics of intelligence tests who dismiss the requirement to define 'intelligence' by describing it as 'what intelligence tests test'. It is necessary to examine precisely what it is that lies behind the central concept. 'Reading', like 'intelligence', is a complex concept. It would be regrettable if, in the face of these complexities, any attempt were to be made to dismiss the increasing knowledge which is now available on both subjects in favour of what is popularly considered to be 'common sense'. Indeed it is likely to be of central importance in appreciating what is uniquely 'human', to be able to understand the idea of 'reading' in terms of the relationship between 'reading', 'language', 'thinking', 'communication' and what we refer to globally as 'intelligence'.

Gorman and Fernandes (1992) note that 'it is not always realized that any test of reading embodies a particular definition or view of the reading process'. They cite three characteristic views of reading evident in reading tests, namely:

Reading essentially involves:
(1)   decoding print into sound;
(2)   making sense of the grammar of sentences; and
(3)   making sense of coherent and complex texts (understanding the purpose of a piece of writing and the intentions of the person who wrote it). (Gorman and Fernandes, 1992)

It might therefore be suggested that one answer to the question, 'What counts as reading?' might be that the reading behaviour should be analysed on the basis of each and all of these views of reading. It might also be pertinent to differentiate between the three views cited by Gorman and Fernandes and the tripartite definition of reading provided by the Bullock Report, *A Language for Life*, which is as follows:

(a)   A response to graphic signals in terms of the words they represent,
(b)   A response to text in terms of the meanings the author intended to set down,
(c)   A response to the author's meanings in terms of all the relevant previous experience and present judgements of the reader. (DES, 1975)

Gorman and Fernandes' classification (1) is very similar to the Bullock definition (a). However, their subsequent differentiation of views into (2) and (3) draws attention to surface features of texts and to increments in the size of the unit of analysis from 'decoding . . . *graphemes* (implied) into sound' to *the sentence* in view (2) and then, to *the whole text* in view (3). This choice of terminology emphasizes the features of text rather than the role of the reader's experience (see Bullock (c)) or the writer's intended meaning, despite the mention in their view (3) of the intended 'purpose of the piece of writing'. Thus it is not clear to what extent the idea of reading as 'interactive' with individuals as models or as part of the communicative function of writing and reading played a part in any of the tests which were analysed.

The following sections draw upon the findings of a number of studies, some not published or still in progress, in order to explore the relevant views of reading held by (a) student teachers, (b) children, (c) researchers and experienced teachers and derived from (d) analysis and discussion of reading in the National Curriculum.

*Student Teachers' Views*

A sample of 179 student teachers' views on what they considered counts as being able to read were collected by anonymous questionnaire during the first week of the 1992–3 Leicester University Post-Graduate Certificate of Education, a one-year initial training course for teaching in primary schools. The question was asked after a period of one week's observation in schools but prior to any coursework on the teaching of reading.

The open-ended question involved the invitation to answer briefly, 'What, in your view, counts as being able to read?'. The space provided for the answer included three lines on which to write. Some students chose to make space for more than six lines of written answer.

The analysis of the answers was carried out initially on the basis of the following three categories, the second and third of which differ from the Bullock categories and the Gorman and Fernandes categories:

Category 1:   including reference to letter–sound correspondence,
Category 2:   including reference to word recognition,
Category 3:   including reference to meaning.

The aim in attempting this first level of analysis was to discern the frequency of mention of the idea of (1) 'cracking the orthographic code' as distinct from the idea of 'reading for meaning' (3). The middle category, (2), was included with the intention of providing a unit of analysis between letters and sentences or whole passages (whether 'words' were mentioned in terms of being 'built up from sound' or simply, 'recognized').

Examples of responses are:

* Example 1   being aware of what sounds grouped letters represent and being able to attempt to build up unknown words. This response was classified as (1) and not (3).
* Example 2   to recognize enough words to be able to understand the content of the book. This was classified as (2) and (3).
* Example 3   being able to look at a page of print and understand what message it relays. This was classified as (3).
* Example 4   A further example indicates the way in which some responses included all three categories: 'knowing the letters of the alphabet. Being able to form letters into words. Being able to pronounce those words and understanding what they mean and how the meanings of words depend on the context in which they are used.' This was classified as (1), (2) and (3).

The results reveal that reference was made to *all three categories* by 36.3 per cent (sixty-five) of the respondents. *Word reading* was mentioned by 91.6 per cent (164) and reference was made to *meaning* by 81.9 per cent (145). There was thus a substantially greater incidence of reference to 'meaning', than solely to 'decoding' (81 per cent/59.2 per cent).

Figure 11.1 illustrates the relative distribution of responses to categories (1) and (3). It indicates that 17.9 per cent (thirty-two of the sample of 179 students' answers) concerned *only* letter–sound correspondence (i.e., fell into only category (1)), but 41.3 per cent (seventy-four responses) concerned *both* meaning and letter–sound correspondence (i.e., included (1) and (3)). Thus

*Figure 11.1:  Initial student teachers' views of what counts as being able to read (views at beginning of training course) (N = 179)*

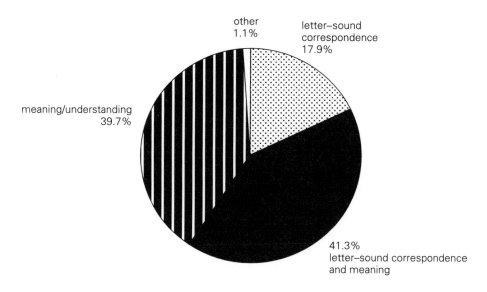

59.2 per cent of the answers *included* reference to letter–sound correspondence (one hundred and six responses).

Responses which concerned *only* 'meaning' (i.e., fell into only category (3)) amounted to 39.7 per cent (seventy-one responses) however 41.3 per cent (seventy-four responses) fell into *both* categories (1) and (3).

Although more than half the responses (59.2 per cent) mentioned letter–sound correspondence, the remaining 40.8 per cent of the responses did not.

This raised the questions of whether and how to explore further the views of the 40.8 per cent of student teachers who did not spontaneously mention letter–sound correspondence in their answers to the question, 'What counts as being able to read?'. It also prompted concern that the training course should take this 'baseline' into account and include a means of checking and heightening awareness of the role played by 'within word' factors in the process of learning to read and its relationship to making sense of the whole words in context, i.e. the process by which children become 'able to read'. The initial survey briefly reported above has led to further research employing a test–retest design aimed to explore the impact of the course on the relevant perceptions of the student teachers in the 1993–4 cohort.

*Children's Views*

In an action-research project exploring and evaluating the setting-up and running of 'Family Reading Groups' (FRG) it became evident that children's confidence and competence in reading was promoted in the FRG context (Beverton, Hunter-Carsch, Obrist and Stuart, 1993). This context incidentally provided opportunities for observing voluntary reading. Developments in learning to read were effectively taking place without explicit 'teaching' by a teacher in a classroom context (see also 'Young Fluent Readers', Clark, 1985). In the Family Reading Groups it was evident that 'choosing to read' played a large part in what children count as 'being able to read'. The findings of the study include evidence to support the value of FRGs as a means of promoting voluntary reading through children sharing their enthusiasm about books which they enjoyed and selecting more books by the same author.

The writer's discussion with children while working in 'Partnership School programmes' with PGCE students reveals that even young children view reading in a socially perceptive manner, depending on whether they consider the questioner to be a teacher or 'another person/not a teacher'. Classroom-reading experience colours their perceptions of what counts as reading. For example, in the context of an exploratory study of the use of the Science Research Associates (SRA) Direct Instruction System for Teaching Arithmetic and Reading Programme (DISTAR), the writer observed that, in the absence of their teacher, children were able to enact a reading lesson with evident awareness of what was expected from both the teacher and pupil in lessons on the word-blending aspects of learning to read. Also, in classes where the DISTAR programme was not in use but other structured approaches to teaching reading were employed, children could generally explain, with some clarity what they considered to be 'reading' and 'learning to read'. However, in classrooms where the reading 'lessons' were less obviously signalled as a 'subject' or specific time was not clearly allocated for work on reading whether carried out individually, in groups or as a class, children's views of reading tended to be related to their personal experience of 'reading to the teacher' or reading books (and other materials, e.g. comics) at home.

Further study is required in order to explore systematically, with a larger sample of children, the impact of explicit and structured discussions about their views of what counts as reading. An impression has been gained on the basis of informal discussions with junior-age children (7–12-year-olds), that the discussions appear to have a positive impact on the children's subsequent reading behaviour, particularly with reference to extending the children's interests in what reading *does* for them (and to them) as well as what reading *is*.

## What Is Involved in the Reading Process?

*Researchers' and Experienced Teachers' Views*

The reading process has been variously represented in the extensive literature on the subject (e.g., Beard, 1993). Bettelheim and Zelan (1982) and also Meek

(1982, 1991) are proponents of the view that reading is important not only as a means of retrieval of information from print but as an 'active encounter of one mind and one imagination with another' and, for the readers, as a means of 'becoming more than themselves/becoming what they want to be'.

The literature on the teaching of reading employs several different models of the reading process (Ruddell, Rudell and Singer, 1994). Some models are derived from clinical studies addressing the relationship between the visual and auditory aspects of processing of the orthographic system (e.g., Stuart, 1992). However, it is not always made evident which theoretical model underpins proposed classroom practices. The writers do not consistently make the necessary distinction between models of the reading process and models for the teaching of reading. This was an issue of central concern in the challenge facing the writers of the Kingman Report (DES, 1988). The need persists for a ·metalanguage for professional use.

Models for the teaching of reading are frequently portrayed as involving two complementary directions of development which are termed broadly 'top–down' and 'bottom–up', referring respectively to the need to 'get together' a grasp of the meaning as a whole and the orthographic system employed to encode and for decoding the letters and words. The direction (top–down or bottom–up) refers to the starting point for teaching and the relative emphasis and direction in which the teaching approach proceeds: starting from the top, (the whole text or global meaning), or bottom, the (details, letter sounds).

Jansen's model (1985) subtly emphasizes the dynamics of both directions and takes into account three 'fields', sounds and letters; vocabulary (words); and *word order* and meaning, which he notes are, in practice, mingled. He states that 'a developmental theory of teaching reading where any one of the three fields may be used as a starting point is needed'. This model is set out in Figure 11.2. In essence, it schematically underlines the complex interactions between various aspects of language and experience that, over time, change as the individual's reading skills develop.

In order to understand the reading process, it may be necessary also to study its relationship to the writing process (encoding and decoding). This was explored in a collaborative research project involving all the teachers in a small inner-city multi-ethnic school in Leicester with the aim of developing a school language policy (Hunter-Carsch, 1984a). The findings of the study included the postulation of three essential stages in the social-interactive process of reading development.

- experiencing books as part of an enjoyable and trusting relationship with adults;
- sharing different kinds of story experience with wider groups, i.e., beyond one adult and one child or very small group of children; and
- appreciating and sharing meaning through personal reading and writing.

*Figure 11.2:   Jansen's model*

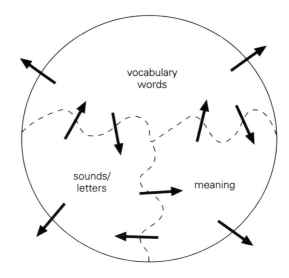

*Source*: M. Clark, 1985

'What counts as reading', thus, might be regarded as differing at each stage of the developmental process, unless a specification is made of a point taken as 'getting through all three stages' and in that sense demonstrating the behaviour of a voluntary reader for a range of purposes.

Further light may be thrown on the reading process by exploring it in terms of the logical sequence of levels in reading as in the model of reading presented by Barrow (1982) in the context of a discussion of three questions: Is reading worthwhile? How can it be evaluated? Can levels of reading be distinguished?

In answer to the third question Barrow outlined five discrete levels, as follows:

Level 1:   handling the symbols
Level 2:   handling the surface meaning
Level 3:   grasping the grammar
Level 4:   contextual understanding
Level 5:   understanding how the author has achieved the effects conveyed in his or her art.

A more recent study, the Language in the National Curriculum (LINC) project, adopted an 'anthropological' stance (Carter, 1992). Carter described reading in term of what readers do . . . as:

1. a behaviour or set of behaviours which are culturally determined;
2. a process of bringing world and generic knowledge to the text; and
3. a psycholinguistic process based on expectations and predictions of syntactic, semantic and graphophonic cues in writing. It also describes reading in terms of the role of text in creating possible meanings: They are constructed artefacts created in particular contexts, and *it is in the meeting of the reader and writer in the text that meanings are made.* (Carter, 1992)

LINC's 'cross-cultural model' may be related to Cortazzi's (1992) illustration of what counts as being able to read in Turkey (reading scriptures in Arabic in an Islamic context). The following five levels of reading are found within a generally shared appreciation of two purposes for reading. One is for material knowledge; the other for spiritual knowledge. The levels derive from the traditional mode of learning to read the Koran (for spiritual knowledge). In each instance 'reading' goes beyond 'decoding' or 'deciphering' the printed page to indicate relevance to life, to provide a guide for desirable conduct for expectations of others or, e.g., a distinction between different levels of relationships:

Level 1: recite (poetry/rhythm emphasized as valued shared knowledge)
Level 2: intone (to elicit correct culturally patterned affective response in the reader and the audience)
Level 3: learn and understand the meaning (through interaction with those who have the knowledge)
Level 4: total recall of 'the word' (i.e., emphasis on tradition through precision)
Level 5: read and explain it to others (having attained the appropriate level of knowledge for 'permission' to interpret for others)

It may take extensive study, of several years even, to move from one stage to the next.

For Muslim children in the UK, learning to read in the community and in school may represent two different experiences with differing sets of perceptions about what counts as being able to read and the relationship of reading to understanding.

The differences may become the more striking in this age of 'The New Literacy' (Willinsky, 1990): A diverse movement has arisen to make reading and writing more personally meaningful and to make the processes of the formation of literacy more powerful (Apple, in Willinsky, 1990).

The problems, conceptualized in a mainly Western cultural frame of reference, concern the 'relevance' of the reading and writing carried out in the classroom. Their resolution is sought in terms of connecting literacy to the life of the school and community, recognising literacy as a social process (not an isolated set of skills) which involves increasing the student's control over text and meaning, in the course of which their relationship with the teacher changes. Willinsky identifies a relative shift in the locus of control (from teacher and text, to learner and text) which he considers constitutes one of the issues with reference to perceptions of patterns of teaching and learning and how the curriculum is mediated. (Apple, M.W. in Willinsky, 1990: Px1)

There is a need to understand not only the relationship between learning to read and learning to write (literacy), but also the relationship of literacy learning to thinking, knowing, comprehending and appreciating. It is in this sense that the concept of 'reading for meaning' should be further explored as it is a basic concept within the professional publications including national guidelines for English 5–16 in England and Wales and also the Scottish Working Papers on English Language 5–14 (SED, 1990). The knowledge gained from the National Writing Project's exploration of 'emergent writing' might be related to 'emergent understanding through reading'.

## Reading in the National Guidelines

The student teacher faces the dual problem of discovering a metalanguage for professional discourse about teaching reading and developing a conceptual map which relates how children learn to plan and develop their reading ability, to the content of the curriculum (what they must learn), and how best to teach reading. National guidelines constitute an essential part of this knowledge base. The conceptual clarity with which they are designed thus becomes a crucial factor affecting the individual teacher's effectiveness and the development of realistic and efficient policies for schools, classes and the individual pupil. It is useful to compare the national guidelines in England, Scotland and Ireland.

The 'pioneering' guidelines for English in the National Curriculum in England and Wales (May, 1989) and the subsequent Guidelines (No. 2, March, 1990) undertook a substantial task in attempting to provide a ten-level developmental outline of the Attainment Targets and Programmes of Study (non-statutory guidelines) for each of three profile components, Speaking and Listening (AT1), Reading (AT2) and Writing (AT3–5). The introduction and background notes did not provide a rationale for the approach to learning and teaching. The absence of a rationale has perhaps contributed to conceptual confusion which persists in the National Curriculum Council Consultation Report (NCC, 1993).

The Consultation Report is shorter, tighter in format and is organized in terms of providing the Programmes of Study prior to the Statements of Attainment, which are presented in three strands in Reading (AT2). These strands are, 'Initial Reading Skills', 'Comprehension and Information Handling' and 'Responses to Literature'.

The logical parallel development of all three strands is not, in fact, provided since the 'Initial Reading Skills' strand ceases after level 3 and there is no progression, for example, to 'higher-order' skills. The three strands are not conceptually discrete nor is their relationship to each other made evident. Part of this conceptual confusion may derive from the implicit model, which is dominated by a focus on listing 'components of reading' rather than considering how the components combine to lead to increasingly efficient and effective reading for a range of purposes. The organizational problem derives from an underlying lack of clarity (or agreement) about 'what reading is'.

The National Guidelines for Curriculum and Assessment in Scotland (English Language 5–14, (SED, 1991)) avoid this conceptual problem by shifting the emphasis from 'what reading *is*' to 'what reading *does* for the reader'. The curriculum is conceptualized in terms of enabling the learners to develop the relevant capabilities so that they progress in terms of independence and efficiency in employing reading for a range of purposes. The rationale for the curriculum explicitly relates the purposes for reading to the wider connections between language and education, noting that 'language is at the heart of children's learning' and that schools should provide 'structured and stimulating opportunities (for children) to use language with increasing precision in contexts appropriate to the needs of individuals . . . opportunities for *communicating, thinking, feeling* and *making.*' (SED, 1991, p. 3).

It is thus clear, for teachers, that in teaching reading they are likely to be addressing one or more of the purposes for reading. The purposes are listed as follows:

> To obtain information and respond appropriately;
> To appreciate feelings of others;
> To reflect upon ideas, experiences and opinions;
> To gain imaginative and aesthetic pleasure. (SED, 1991, p. 4)

It is also clear that children's reading development can be facilitated (taught), observed and recorded (tested) with reference to 'reading outcomes' which are described in terms of 'strands' ('aspect of learning which pupils experience') most of which have 'Attainment Targets' attached to them and are generally described in terms of a progression through five levels (A–E). The strands are:

> Reading for information;
> Reading for enjoyment;
> Reading to reflect on the writers' ideas and craft;
> Awareness of genre (type of text);
> Reading aloud;
> Knowledge about language. (SED, 1991, p. 16)

The underlying emphasis on 'What reading *does* for the reader' naturally leads the teacher to an emphasis on encouraging the learner readers to do these things for themselves. It makes evident the relationship between teaching and learning. It thus provides information which is more accessible, because of its conceptual integrity, than the more diffuse information presented in the format of the DES (1989, 1990), NCC (1993) and SCAA (1994) documents. These run the risk of becoming fragmented foci on measuring the increments in isolated skill development rather than monitoring integrate development along a path towards greater independence and efficiency in achieving a range of purposes.

The Northern Ireland Curriculum for English (1990) includes Programmes of Study and Attainment Targets (in that order). There is no introductory rationale overall, but each of the Programmes of Study (talking and listening; reading; writing, and cross-curricular themes) is introduced in a way which provides an organic unity through the focus on establishing a supportive attitude within a context which encourages learning (establishing 'a classroom atmosphere in which pupils feel relaxed, accepted and affirmed and in which their ideas are welcomed, encouraged and listened to'). (NI Curriculum, p. 2.)

The first sentences of the Programme of Study for reading (at Key Stage 1) emphasize 'a stimulating environment of print' and 'enjoyment'. This is in contrast to the tone of the first sentences of the Programme of Study for AT2: Reading in England (Consultation Report, 1993):

> Pupils should learn to read with fluency, accuracy and understanding. Thus they should be taught the alphabet, phonic skills, the basic conventions of words and print and effective techniques for decoding, understanding and responding. (NCC, 1993, p. 35)

Priorities in developing the relationship of 'understanding' and 'responding' to 'decoding' are apparently left for the teacher to decide. This is, perhaps, easier for experienced teachers. For beginner teachers in particular, it may be helpful to have a few signposts towards drawing their own conceptual map. From the writer's experience the following 'key words' present themselves as potential signposts (They form a few further basic 'Rs' . . . ): Reading requires *retrieval* of memory, *reasoning* and *resources*.

In Figure 11.3, selected features of AT2 reading have been extracted from the DES (1990) guidelines for teachers in England and Wales and these have been related to further 'key words' which provide a hierarchy of reminders (to *motivate*; connect with *memory*; focus on *meaning*;/purpose and *communication* to others) for planning and engaging in the teaching and learning interaction. The 'tools' are listed on the left side of the chart and the overriding factors that influence the learner's ability to recreate meaning from the printed word are listed along the right side. (This is not intended to represent a 'right-brain/left-brain shift' diagram as such, but it does serve to indicate the role played by both 'perceptual' and 'linguistic' factors.) (For further information on the observed normal developmental 'shift' at about 7–8 years and its relationship to Perceptual-Linguistic classification of dyslexia (Bakker, 1993).

Reading requires motivation. It is essentially enactive. It engages the reader's

*Figure 11.3: Guidelines and emphases*

| | Features of the DES 1990 guidelines for AT2; outcomes for pupils: | The writer's emphases for the teaching–learning interaction: | |
|---|---|---|---|
| | 1. • evidence of *interest* (e.g., level 1c) • sustained *concentration* | Motivation (engaging children's attention/curiosity and sharing what is in the text with them) | Context / Code |
| | 2. • relating *experience*/knowledge to the text (e.g., 2d, 2e, 2f, 4b, 4c) • *imagining*/projecting self into situation (e.g., 2e, 4b) | Memory and Meaning (facilitating children's 'decoding' via Transformations and relating Phonics 44 to 'emergent understanding') | Text |
| | 3. • accessing resources/ *information* (e.g., 1d, 2f, 3f, 4d, 5d) | Communication (developing children's ability to relate reading, listening, speaking, writing, doing and thinking (use DARTs) to promote their communication) | Purpose |

*Left margin label:* Using sight words, phonic cues, understanding text and structure [e.g., 2a, b, c, e, 3e, 5e, 6e]

*Notes:* — (writer's italic emphasis)
— Transformation: see Kemp (1989)
— Phonics 44: see Morris (1984 and 1993)
— DART; Directed Activities Related to Text (Lunzer, and Gardner, 1984)

mind. It requires the activation of imagery to match symbol and referent whether picture, letter, word or sequence of words in pursuit of meaning. In so doing it draws upon experience not only of a range of texts and of the communications they hold but also of the readers' life experiences and their capacity to connect their 'being' with 'becoming'. In this they effect an extension to 'beyond themselves' in order to 'become themselves'. It can be regarded as an active and creative process of attempting to *create* meaning and, as the reader becomes more sophisticated and more able to deal with a range of texts, where relevant, to *recreate* through some form of mental imagery what it is assumed is the writer's meaning. This may 'feed' the reader and potentially empower the reader to become a more capable, informed speaker, listener and writer, thus affecting, reciprocally, their further reading ability.

Healthy, 'normal' children appear to be insatiable natural readers of pictures, television and people's expressions. They appear to internalize models (images) of what is involved in being able to read and to 'pretend-read books' from very early years. They seem to discern from their models something of the quality of permanence of stories which are printed. They seem to 'know' (have learned) that the printed words always say the same thing. This kind of 'knowledge' appears to be derived from social interaction rather than from explicit teaching.

It can, however, be developed quite explicitly in the course of working on 'transformations' (Kemp, 1989), employing a teaching strategy for writing (encoding) the child's words (sentences) in reporting on an event or expressing an idea and then studying the sentences together to develop the meaning by moving the words and/or adding words. Using the child's own words as a starting point for 'learning words' (word recognition) is highly motivating (see also McKay, Schaub and Thompson, 1979), and facilitates the connections between understanding what skills are required to deal with letters and words, and making sense of words in sentences. Using the child's illustrations and drawings in order to discuss the nature of their understanding of what they have read also provides a window on the process of reading to make meaning (MacMartin, 1989, 1992). It is important to know what influences children's motivation in terms of the images they find readily memorable both from 'reading television' and reading books and, in this sense, what constitutes their reading diet (Harcourt and Hartland, 1992; Bird's Eye Survey, 1993; Utley, 1993).

Reference is made elsewhere in this chapter to the cultural context in which children's expectations of printed texts and their attitudes to reading are formed. The above observations are made particularly with reference to young children in a predominatly white, mixed lower to middle social class and mainly Christian context.

## Reading for Meaning: Levels of Understanding

In connection with 'reading for meaning' it is useful to consider the efficacy of the terminology employed in describing and differentiating between levels of understanding.

Figure 11.4 presents different 'layers of thinking'. The German terms are etymologically more closely related than the English translations. The most sophisticated, topmost layer, 'transcendental reasoning', implies a stance which is sufficiently 'decentred' to be able to extend understanding beyond a particular cultural context (Graves, 1983; Jackson, 1989).

It is beyond the scope of this chapter to delineate the model more fully in order to explain the concepts underpinning the distinction between 'subjective reasoning' and 'objective reasoning'. A more detailed discussion would require reference to be made to the work of Horkheimer (1947) and to illustrate the potential contribution reading can make to the attaining of the capability of engaging in 'objective reasoning'.

The need to establish a shared vocabulary for describing as well as differentiating between levels of reading and levels of meaning is particularly important in matters which concern the testing of reading achievement and reading ability, matters pertinent to the debates on reading standards. Inevitably the terms which are employed for the purpose convey images which relate to the perceived nature of the reading process.

*Figure 11.4:   Levels of experience and modes of experiencing as strata of cognition*

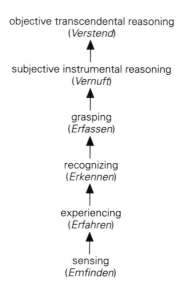

objective transcendental reasoning
(*Verstend*)

subjective instrumental reasoning
(*Vernuft*)

grasping
(*Erfassen*)

recognizing
(*Erkennen*)

experiencing
(*Erfahren*)

sensing
(*Emfinden*)

Part of the desired shared vocabulary would need to include reference to, and some understanding of, the role played by mental imagery in the process of reading for different purposes (and, implicitly, reading in a way which draws upon experience in order to engage with different levels of meaning).

An awareness on the teacher's part, of how the learner perceives the reading task and what kinds of mental imagery are being brought into play is likely to assist the teacher in exploring with the learner the extent to which the learner is, at that moment, able to engage with particular 'levels of meaning'. An appreciation of the nature of individual differences in modes of experiencing is likely to be of significance for the teaching of school children (or indeed adults) whether in classes, groups or individually (MacMartin, 1989, 1992.)

*The Role of Imagery in Reading As 'Recreation of Meaning'*

The importance of considering children's preferred avenues for learning is beautifully illustrated in the published correspondence between Helen McLullich, a teacher who is an able visualizer, and Sue Palmer, a teacher who considers herself to be a non-visualizer (in Hunter-Carsch, 1990).

How children think about what they are learning to do in the course of reading is likely to involve them in employing some form of imagery. Relatively little is known about the ways in which imagery is employed in reading symbols and in what is broadly referred to as 'reading for meaning'.

Recent work on motor imagery and motor processes related to training in sports, suggests that it is possible to become a more able athlete by mental practice (e.g., concentrating on imagining and 'going through' the movements required to make a jump). While there is a need for precision in the definition of what is meant by, for example, internal visual imagery and kinesthetic imagery and how best to define 'internal talk', it appears that 'mental practice can affect processes of skill learning which are normally seen as dependent on overt motor performance, given that the 'medium' of the still does not require further exploratory activity' (Vogt, 1992).

When such findings are taken along with the increasing body of research in visual and auditory imagery since the 1970s (e.g., Segal, 1971; White *et al.*, 1977; Merry, 1978; Riding and Calvey, 1980) and in 'teaching children how to learn' (e.g., Cruickshank, 1963; Stott, 1971; Feuerstein's methods in Sharron, 1989) the implications for understanding both the reading process and how to teach reading become particularly evident when learning to read is related to learning to write.

From the early 1960s it has been recognized that a selective emphasis in teaching reading by only one method, whether it favours visual learning or auditory learning, is likely to deny adequate opportunity for learning to some children. To avoid 'reading failure' de Hirsch, Jansky and Langford (1966) advocated employing both 'look and say' and 'phonic' approaches.

At that time, the fashion was to promote 'multi-sensory approaches' to 'teaching beginning reading', particularly for children with reading difficulties. There appears to have been relatively little understanding, however, of the impact of differing sequences of stimuli within the proposed VAKT 'battery' (visual, auditory, kinesthetic, tactile) as applied in mainstream classes. The lack of clarity still persists with reference to what are called 'mixed methods' of teaching reading.

There is thus a need for making connections between the findings of recent published research suggesting the importance of phonological awareness (e.g., Bryant and Bradley, 1989; Goswami and Bryant, 1990) and research which illustrates the ways in which classroom-teaching methods can employ a range of strategies for developing children's use of imagery for learning (thinking and remembering) about how to read and increasing their understanding of what they read.

## *What Is the Text That Is Being Read?*

In the context of delivering in-service education, the writer has carried out an informal study of the reactions of experienced teachers to being asked to read various texts. Their responses may serve to illustrate the extent of individual differences in interpretation, association, imagery and expectations. Groups of up to 200 teachers on various courses and conferences relating to the teaching of literacy and children's reading difficulties, were invited to read a range of texts including 'pictures' projected onto a screen by overhead projector. The customary reactions were of both interest and willingness to respond.

The first stimulus text was a photograph of a sculpture in classical mode portraying a woman and child. The child stood close to the woman, at her knee, looking up into her face. There was a book on her knee.

Responses included 'interpretation' which might be classified broadly as follows:

- attempts to grasp the whole picture and to 'explain it generally' in terms of the content, e.g., 'a mother reading to a child', or 'a child and adult sharing a book';
- reflection of global feelings of 'like' or 'dislike' of the content e.g., 'I don't like it', or 'that's lovely!'; and
- 'identification' possibly with one or other of the sculpted figures resulting in responses such as, 'He doesn't like reading, you can see that!' or 'He's reading her face, not the book!'.

The second text which was employed in the exploration of teachers' 'reading ability' was composed of a set of symbols which were evidently unfamiliar to most of the audience (dance movements in Laban and Benesh notation).

Reactions shown in response to this text by the same groups of teachers, all of whom might be considered to be 'able readers', were typified by silence or by puzzlement and requests for 'clues'. This text aimed to remind readers of the fact that there are different symbol systems for representing/encoding meanings.

With another sample of text which included musical notation, there were, in general, more frequently positive reactions in the sense of indications of recognition of the fact that the text consisted of musical notation. In the case of a minority, there was a fairly speedy recognition of the symbols and an attempt to model the message by playing on an imaginery piano, or the humming of the melodies represented in the text. On the whole, however, there was little evidence of widespread shared ability to read musical notation, and there was a general sense of uncertainty as to whether this kind of reading ability was expected of a group of teachers. This experience in the UK might be contrasted with the likely situation in China in which all student teachers of kindergarten children must learn to read music and play at least one instrument (discussion with Dr M. Cortazzi on his return from a study visit to China, 1992).

The above examples may serve to illustrate the need for teachers of reading to be aware of their own assumptions about what constitutes reading in the wider sense of reading not only the printed word but 'reading' art, music, dance, people's expressions (social interaction) and television. This is not to deny the importance of being able to read the sound–symbol system, but to locate it as one in a constellation of systems for representing symbols which represent referents.

## Messages for Teachers

The exploration of issues underlying the central question, 'What counts as being able to read?' has led to the following concluding statement of six points concerning the writer's view of reading as 'recreation of meaning'.

The points are interrelated. They concern the social interactive nature of the reading process and its relationship to matters of stance, motivation and materials to be read (context and text).

1. 'Being able to read' involves more than being proficient in applying a number of 'component reading skills' such as phoneme–grapheme correspondence, word blending or word recognition. The whole of reading is greater than the sum of its parts. For the reader, it involves being able to 'get the parts together' in such a way as to be able to do more than make sense through 'recreating meaning'. It also involves the reader in a process of listening to the thoughts as in an enactive attempt to 'speak' and internally to 'hear' and check the sense of the emerging meaning. (This is not to be confused with 'subvocalization' or with the idea of 'reading the words'.)

2. In this way reading involves the heightening of awareness of experience and extension of experience in the process of implementing the intention to seek meaning.

It goes beyond the recognition of the surface features of printed text to the wider engagement of interest in associating symbols with referents and the process of participating in the social interactive process through which there arises the awareness and increasir g understanding of reading as 'meaningful' and 'valuable'. In this sense it involves sharing the culturally patterned recognition in 'literate societies' that value is attributed to the printed text and 'survival value' thus related to ability to cope with printed texts.

3. The development and use of reading ability in such societies is closely intertwined with the development of identity and feelings of self-worth. It is part of the complex communication pattern which provides for the identity and specific forms of motivation of a given society. It constitutes a means by which external experiences can be 'filtered' either for integration or rejection as the self concept dynamically develops.

4. The learner readers' attitudes to reading and their personal mental imagery employed in the course of interaction with those who are their models and with the text itself are both affected by, and have a resultant impact on, their reading development.

The child's progress as a voluntary reader is likely to be promoted if associations with the experience (cognitive and affective) are positively weighted. If, for whatever reasons, their experience is neutral or relatively negatively weighted (i.e., they do not engage sufficiently in the process of becoming an enactive 'imager') their progress as voluntary readers capable of sustained interest in reading the text may be affected negatively. This is exemplified in the 'cycle of depression' experienced by some children with reading difficulties who find reading hard, thus don't read, thus can't read without practice, thus won't read. It is a variant of 'learned helplessness'. Its recognition is a prerequisite of its amelioration.

For the learner reader, the difficulty in the process of 'cracking the code' in a way which brings rewards frequently enough and sufficiently positively in terms of engaging affect (including 'meaning'), is ameliorated by the extent to which the home and classroom contexts and social group with which the child is associated, provide sufficiently positive models. Becoming a reader involves not merely a sufficiently 'print rich' environment, but the experience of hearing others read, being read to and sharing incidental as well as explicit reading experience. It is a dynamic matter of the extent to which the people in the child's immediate environment (perhaps including people on television) attract, share and 'inspire' the child's attention and interest in print, that interacts with the extent to which the child meets and engages in the communication. It involves also the absence of competing distractions which may be tempting by virtue of their requirement of a relatively smaller investment of energy and even time.

5. Becoming able to read and voluntarily reading is thus affected by the dynamics of the social interactive dimensions of early-reading experience and the cultural milieu.

The child's expectations of what reading is about are culturally influenced. What counts as being able to read, is a matter which needs to be understood in terms of the particular cultural context.

6. There is, relatedly, the potential of reading as a means of transcending the particular cultural context.

## Conclusion

A learner reader's view of what counts as being able to read will be affected by the society's attribution of particular value to particular kinds of reading and to reading for particular purposes (e.g., for total recall of text of religious or poetical works, or for information, for critical thinking or for pleasure). The readers' relevant expectations will thus affect their reading ability. It is thus important in attempting to answer the central question, that it is understood in terms of the particular cultural context.

## References

ADAMS, M.J. (1990) *Beginning to Read*, Cambridge, MA, Massachusetts Institute of Technology Press.

APPLE, J. (1990), in WILLINSKY, J. *The New Literacy*, London, Routledge.

BAKKER, D.J. (1993) 'Dyslexia and the Ecology of the Brain', in HORNSBY, B. (Ed) *Literacy 2000*, London, Hornsby International Centre, pp. 1–6.

BARROW, R. (1982) Unpublished Lecture, Leicester University, MA Ed. Studies, Reading Course.

BEARD, R. (1987) *Developing Reading 3–13*, Sevenoaks, Hodder and Stoughton.

BEARD, R. (Ed) (1993) *Teaching Literacy: Balancing Perspectives,* Sevenoaks, Hodder and Stoughton.

BEECH, J. (1985) *Learning to Read: A Cognitive Approach to Reading and Poor Reading*, London, Croom Helm.

BENTON, A.L. and PEARL, D. (1978) *Dyslexia: An Appraisal of Current Knowledge*, New York, Oxford University Press.

BEQUIRAJ, M. (1970) Discussion with Dr H. Carsch, a former colleague of Professor Bequiraj, with whom 'The Model' had been discussed and who provided the translation and with a former student of Professor Moor who considered that Moor's representation of the 'levels of understanding' while presented in lecture in a different format, was essentially similar to that of Professor Bequiraj.

BETTELHEIM, B. and ZELAN, K. (1989) *On Learning to Read: The Child's Fascination with Meaning*, London, Thames and Hudson.

BEVERTON, S., HUNTER-CARSCH, M., OBRIST, C. and STUART, A. (1993) *Family Reading Groups Guide*, Widnes, United Kingdom Reading Association.

BIRDS EYE SURVEY (1993) *The Birds Eye View of Getting into Kids' Good Books*, Walton-on-Thames, Birds Eye Wall's Limited.

BROOKS, G., GORMAN, T., KENDALL, L. and TATE, A. (1992) *What Teachers in Training are Taught about Reading*, Slough, NFER.

BRYANT, P. (1994) 'Children's reading and writing', *The Psychologist*, **7**, 2, p. 61.

BRYANT, P. and BRADLEY, L. (1985) *Children's Reading Problems*, Oxford, Basil Blackwell.

CARTER, R. (1992) *The Language in the National Curriculum Project* (materials), LEA, Leicestershire.

CATO, V., FERNANDES, C., GORMAN, T., KISPAL, A. and WHITE, J. (1992) *The Teaching of Initial Literacy: How Do Teachers Do It?*, Slough, NFER.

CATO, V. and WHETTON, C. (1991) *An Enquiry into LEA Evidence on Standards of Reading of Seven Year Old Children*, Slough, NFER.

CHAPMAN, L.J. (1987) *Reading 5–11*, Milton Keynes, Open University Press.

CLARK, M.M. (1976) *Young Fluent Readers*, London, Heinemann Educational Books.

CLARK, M.M. (1979) *Reading Difficulties in Schools*, London, Heinemann Educational Books.

CLARK, M.M. (1985) *New Horizons in the Teaching of Reading*, London, Falmer Press.

CORTAZZI, M. (1992) Unpublished materials discussed with the writer.

CRUICKSHANK, W. (1963) *A Teaching Method for the Brain Injured, Hyperactive Child*, Syracuse, Syracuse University Press.

DENI (Department of Education, Northern Ireland) (1990) *English Programmes of Study and Attainment Targets*, Belfast, HMSO.

DEPARTMENT OF EDUCATION AND SCIENCE (1975) *A Language for Life* (Bullock Report), London, HMSO.

DEPARTMENT OF EDUCATION AND SCIENCE (1988) *Report to the Committee of Inquiry into the Teaching of English Language* (The Kingman Report), London, HMSO.

DEPARTMENT OF EDUCATION AND SCIENCE AND THE WELSH OFFICE (1989) *English in the National Curriculum*, London, HMSO.

DEPARTMENT OF EDUCATION AND SCIENCE AND THE WELSH OFFICE (1990) *English in the National Curriculum*, London, HMSO.

DEPARTMENT OF EDUCATION NORTHERN IRELAND, ENGLISH (1990) Programmes of Study and *Attainment Targets*, Belfast, HMSO.

DONALDSON, M. (1989) *Sense and Sensibility: Some Thoughts on the Teaching of Literacy*, Occasional Paper No. 3, Reading, Reading and Language Information Centre, University of Reading.

DONALDSON, M. and REID, J. (1982) *Reading Difficulties, Theory and Practice*, London, Ward Lock.

DOWNING, J. (1979) *Reading and Reasoning*, London, Chambers.

DOWNING, J. and LEONG, C.K. (1982) *Psychology of Reading*, New York, Macmillan.

ELLIS, A.W. (1984) *Reading, Writing and Dyslexia: A Cognitive Analysis*, Hillsdale, NJ, Lawrence Erlbaum.

FEUERSTEIN, R. (1989) in SHARRON, H. *Changing Childrens' Minds*, New York, Souvenir Press.

GARROD, S. (1993) 'Better read', *Times Higher Education Supplement*, 4 June, p. 15.

GOODMAN, K.S. (1967) 'Reading: A psycholinguistic guessing game', *Journal of the Reading Specialist*, **6**, pp. 126–35.

GORMAN, T. and FERNANDES, C. (1992) *Reading in Recession*, Slough, NFER.

GOSWAMI, U. (1993) *Analogical Reasoning in Children*, Hillsdale, NJ, Lawrence Erlbaum.

GOSWAMI, U. and BRYANT, P.E. (1990) *Phonological Skills and Learning to Read*, Hillsdale, NJ, Lawrence Erlbaum.

GRAVES, D. (1983) *Writing: Children and Teachers at Work*, London, Heinneman.

HARCOURT, K.W. and HARTLAND, S.M. (1992) *Discovering Readers*, The Joint Newspapers in Education Research, Project 1992, Tunbridge Wells.

DE HIRSCH, K., JANSKY, J. and LANGFORD, W. (1966) *Predicting Reading Failure*, New York, Harper and Row.

HMI (1992) *The Teaching and Learning of Reading in Primary Schools*, Department of Education and Science, HMSO.

HULME, G. and SNOWLING, M. (1994) *Reading Development and Dyslexia*, London, Whurr.

HORKHEIMER, M. (1947) *The Eclipse of Reason*, Oxford, Oxford University Press.

HUNTER CARSCH, C.M. (1984a) *Talking with Books*, Occasional Publication University of Leicester.

HUNTER-CARSCH, C.M. (1984b) The Distar Project: A Study of approaches to Structured teaching of children with reading difficulties unpublished study supported by Science Research Associates and Leicestershire Local Education Authority.

HUNTER-CARSCH, C.M. (1985) *The Role of Talking in Developing Reading: the Talking with Books Project*, Spoken English, **18**, 1, pp. 3–9.

HUNTER-CARSCH, C.M. (1990) 'Learning strategies for pupils with literacy difficulties: Motivation, meaning and imagery', in PUMFREY, P.D. and ELLIOTT, C.D. (Eds) *Children's Difficulties in Reading, Spelling and Writing*, London, Falmer Press.

JACKSON, W. (1989) *The Foundation of Writing Project*, Edinburgh, Moray House College of Education.

JANSEN, M. (1985) 'Language concepts: Play or work? Serious or fun? Basics or creativity?' in CLARK, M. (Ed) *New Direction in the Study of Reading*, Lewes, Falmer Press, pp. 168–75.

KEMP, M. (1989) *Watching Children Read and Write: Observational Records for Children with Special Needs*, Melbourne, Australia, Thomas Nelson.

LAKE, M. (1991) 'Surveying all the factors: Reading research', *Language and Learning*, **6**, pp. 8–13.

LAKE, M. (1992) 'Commentary in open dialogue — reading standards: Peer review', *British Psychological Society Education Section Review*, **16**, 1, pp. 14–15.

LEONG, C.K. (1987) *Children with Specific Reading Difficulties*, Amsterdam, Swets and Zeitlinger.

LUNZER, E. and GARDNER, K. (1984) *Learning from the Written Word*, Edinburgh, Oliver and Boyd.

MACKAY, D., SCHAUB, P. and THOMPSON, B. (1979) *Breakthrough to Literacy* (Teacher's Manual), 2nd ed., London, Longmans for Schools Council.

MACMARTIN, M. (1989) 'Factors affecting reading comprehension in primary pupils', in HUNTER-CARSCH, M. *The Art of Reading*, Oxford, Blackwell.

MACMARTIN, M. (1992) 'Factors affecting reading comprehension in primary pupils', Open University, unpublished Ph.D thesis.

MEEK, M. (1982) *Learning to Read*, London, Bodley Head.

MEEK, M. (1991) Invited guest lecture at Leicester University, School of Education.

MELNICK, M. and MERRITT, J. (1972) *Reading, Yesterday, Today and Tomorrow*, Milton Keynes, Open University Press.

MERRY, R. (1978) *Imagery and Children's Strategies in Reading, Comprehension and French Vocabulary Learning*, Birmingham, Aston University.

MOON, C. and RABAN, B. (1975) *A Question of Reading*, London, Ward Lock Education.

MORRIS, J. (1984) 'Phonics 44 for initial literacy in English', *Reading*, **8**, 1, pp. 13–23.

MORRIS, J. (1990) in HUNTER-CARSCH, M., BEVERTON, S. and DENNIS, D., *Primary English in the National Curriculum*, Oxford, Basic Blackwell, pp. 109–19.

MORRIS, J. (1993) 'Phonicsphobia', in HORNSBY, B. *Literacy 2000*, London, The Hornsby International Centre.

MOYLE, D. (1970) *The Teaching of Reading*, London, Ward Lock.

NATIONAL CURRICULUM COUNCIL (NCC) (1993) *National Curriculum Council Consultation Report on English in the National Curriculum*, York, National Curriculum Council.

PUMFREY, P. (1991) *Improving Children's Reading in the Junior School: Challenges and Responses*, London, Cassell.

RAYNOR, K., GARROD, S. and PERFETTI, C. (1992) 'Discourse influences during parsing are delayed', *Cognition*, **45**, pp. 109–39.

RIDING, R.J. and CALVEY, I. (1980) 'The assessment of verbal-imagery learning styles and their effect on the recall of concrete and abstract prose passages by eleven year old children', paper in correspondence.

RUDDELL, R.B., RUDDELL, M.R. and SINGER, H. (1994) (Eds) *Theoretical Models and Processes of Reading* (4th. ed.), Newark, Delaware, International Reading Association.

SCHONELL, F.J. (1942) *Backwardness in the Basic Subjects*, Edinburgh, Oliver and Boyd.

SCHONELL, F.J. and GOODACRE, E. (1974) *The Psychology and Teaching of Reading* (5th ed.), Edinburgh, Oliver and Boyd.

SCOTTISH EDUCATION DEPARTMENT (SED) (1990) *English Language 5–14*. SEGAL, S.T. (Ed) (1971) *Imagery: Current Cognitive Approaches*, New York, Academic Press.

SHARRON, H. (1989) *Changing Children's Minds*, New York, Souvenir Press.

SMITH, F. (1978) *Understanding Reading*, New York, Holt, Reinehart and Winston.

STOTT, D. (1971) *Flying Start Materials, Learning to Learn*, Kits, Edinburgh, Holmes McDougall.

STUART, M. (1990) 'Factors influencing word recognition in pre-reading children', *British Journal of Psychology*, **81**, 2, pp. 135–46.

STUART, M. (1992) 'A Dual Model of Reading', Paper presented at St Martin's College, Lancaster, September, International Reading Conference.

TURNER, M. (1990) *Sponsored Reading Failure*, Warlingham, Education Unit, Warlingham Park School, Surrey.

UTLEY, A. (1993) 'Busy minds in front of the small screen', *Times Higher Education Supplement*, 22 October, p. 48.

VERNON, M.D. (1957) *Backwardness in Reading*, Cambridge, Cambridge University Press.

VERNON, M.D. (1971) *Reading and its Difficulties*, Cambridge, Cambridge University Press.

VOGT, S. (1992) 'Mental practice in the learning of motor actions: effects on sequencing eye-coordination and movement consistency', in ANNETTE, J. (Ed) *British Psychological Society International Workshop on Imagery and Motor Processes*, Leicester University, pp. 23–35.

WHITE, K.D., ASHTON, R. and BROWN, R.H.D. (1977) 'The measurement of imagery vividness — nominative data and their relationship to sex, age and modality differences', *British Journal of Psychology*, **68**, pp. 203–11.

WILLINSKY, J. (1990) *The New Literacy: Redefining Reading and Writing in Schools*, London, Routledge p. ix (Editor's Introduction).

*Chapter 12*

# A Conceptual Basis for a Literacy Curriculum

*M. Reed, A. Webster and M. Beveridge*

## Summary

Recently teachers have been described as lacking a full and organized understanding of how children acquire literacy. Proposals have been made by the DfE which give greater prominence to more structured, skill-based primary-school teaching. It is claimed, that this will raise standards and better prepare children to meet the demands they will face as they move into secondary education. This chapter presents a study which analyses teachers' 'conceptual maps' of literacy teaching. The analysis is based on a four-quadrant model of the practice of teaching. Using a questionnaire format, important similarities and contrasts were found between the methods of primary and secondary teachers. The study reveals that teachers have complex models of literacy and do not adhere to simplistic unidimensional methods.

## Introduction

The teaching of literacy continues to be a focus of controversy and to attract media attention. Despite criticism of the data, recent evidence of 'falling standards' has been used to argue the case for a radical reform of the methods adopted to teach English to pupils, so as to place greater emphasis on formal 'back to basics' approaches. Revision of the Statutory Order for English in the National Curriculum, together with the published discussion papers and correspondence between the School Curriculum and Assessment Authority (SCAA) and the Department For Education (DfE), indicate a move to a narrower and more prescriptive curriculum. Also, teachers are thought to lack a coherent and consistent 'conceptual map' of literacy development.

Against this background of political revisionism, polemic and professional confrontation, we propose here a new framework for describing different approaches to the teaching and learning of literacy, which is capable of codifying a wide range of beliefs and practices. Using a questionnaire derived from this framework, data are presented from a survey of teachers' basic tenets of how reading and writing are best fostered in curricular practice and, in particular, contrasts between primary and secondary teachers are highlighted. Evidence reveals important theoretical differences between the architects of the National Curriculum for English and the practitioners who must implement it. Results of this enquiry indicate that teachers possess complex, often consensual, yet sometimes contrasting, conceptions of the teaching of reading and writing.

The conceptual map of literacy and the curriculum we offer, the model of interaction and mediation we propose, and the questionnaire we have constructed, result from the preliminary stages of research carried out between 1991 and 1993. Here, we are concerned with what teachers conceptualize as their intended practice, not what they do in the classroom. Although our classificatory framework for understanding the interactive nature of literacy encounters is, we believe, original in design; it is based on recent developments (see, for example: Bruner, 1986; De Castell, Luke and Egan, 1986; Wood, 1988; Moll, 1990; Green, 1993).

## Context for the Research

This chapter reports the initial findings of a research project which is currently developing school-based methods of mapping the literacy curriculum in collaboration with teachers, by identifying the range and scope of pupils' uses of literacy within different subject domains.

Our own concerns are that the forms of literacy, including reading, writing and some oral activities, are studied in relation to the needs of children to think, problem-solve and learn within each subject area. We do not believe that literacy should be considered as a set of taught skills which must be acquired before or outside the general curriculum. Such a view implies that literacy is only a vehicle or medium for more serious subject study: a requirement or precondition, rather than the business of all teachers whatever their subject specialism. Similarly, we cannot separate the acquisition of literacy from our knowledge of effective teaching and learning. Our own research agenda has begun to address what is, for us, the central question of the relationship between the growth in children's understanding and use of literacy, and what is required of them within each learning context.

Current research has also begun to look at ways in which children come to know and use reading and writing as constituted by the wide variety of forms and functions they serve in different learning contexts. This view of literacy has enormous implications for schools. It shapes perceptions of who should take responsibility for teaching literacy, how achievements can be assessed and how pupils with learning difficulties should be treated; and it has important implications for how learning environments can be modified. These relationships between what children learn and the quality of the learning process require new models. As indicated earlier, in the course of the chapter we shall be outlining a conceptual framework for considering the teaching and development of literacy. This framework has been derived from theoretical accounts of effective teaching and from close observations of teachers in their classrooms. Data will be presented to show whether the model fits the perceptions which teachers themselves hold about their own work, its value and direction.

### The 'Standards are Falling' Debate

It would be a serious indictment of schools if children read and write less well and less often than they did a decade ago. However, a number of studies in the last twenty-five years have suggested an apparent decline in reading achievements across particular age groups. For example, the National Foundation for Educational Research (NFER) Report *The Trend of Reading Standards* (Start and Wells, 1972) compared evidence from national surveys initiated in 1948 and summarized in 1966. Results were derived from two tests 'of silent reading . . . of the incomplete sentence type': the Watts-Vernon and the National Survey Form Six (DES, 1975, p. 16). Closely following this publication, a committee of enquiry was set up under the chairmanship of Sir Alan Bullock. Its brief was to consider all aspects of the teaching of English in schools, including reading, writing, spelling and oracy.

The Bullock enquiry encountered difficulties in finding an acceptable definition of literacy upon which everyone agreed. It also faced problems in interpreting results from different tests carried out in different regions of the United Kingdom in order to arrive at an estimate of national trends. Moreover, the evidence from the type of tests used reveals the concern of psychologists to devise uniform markers of reading *progress*, not reading *process*. As the authors of the Bullock Report assert:

> We do not regard these tests as adequate measures of reading ability . . . their *doubtful validity* is now apparent. (DES, 1975, p. 16)

What these measures do reveal is a predominant view, shared by many psychologists and some educational researchers of the time, that literacy can be 'narrowly conceived' in terms of a limited selection of pupil responses to fragmented units of text presented without the normal supports to meaning found in learning environments.

Whether such data, derived from a restricted view of the reading process and gathered in test settings outside the normal classroom context, can be relied upon to demonstrate either a 'standard' for a far broader and more complex understanding of literacy in use, or any reliable indication of a decline in standards, remains a highly contested point of difference. It is our belief that *in vitro* evidence of this type cannot and should not be given priority or prominence in any debate concerning general standards of reading or literacy. A narrow regime of clinical testing may be less expensive and more politically expedient than the painstaking task of providing qualitative evidence of pupils' developments of literacy and learning in schooled contexts, but it provides no watertight case for either a standard or its decline. As Margaret Meek made plain in response to the Bullock Report:

> We believe that all teachers should be aware of what kind of knowledge and what degree of insight are relevant to the understanding of the reading process . . . To be truly effective, we need to untangle the features of the process by means of descriptive protocols and longitudinal studies, from observations of the reader's interactions with the environment, his relations with his teacher and the materials, as well as from the concomitant activities of writing and talk. Then, the very individuality of the process, known to every infant teacher and forgotten by every successful adult, will offer us the possibility of significant generalisations. (Meek and McKenzie, 1975, p. 8)

Notwithstanding these serious question marks over the status of the evidence available, the Bullock Report did allege a general decline in reading performance in children from the age of 7 years onwards relative to the same age groups in previous decades. It ascribed the causes of reading failure to factors in the child's home background, 'where conversation is limited and books unknown . . .', to children's 'limited natural abilities', to the displacement of reading by watching TV, and to badly trained teachers and poorly organized remedial teaching. The Report suggested that 'literacy is a corporate responsibility' in which every teacher shares (DES, 1975, pp. 516–17). 333 specific recommendations were made to schools, many of which were accepted at the time, yet 'have remained without specific action . . . Literacy still seems to belong nowhere', certainly not in the whole-school policies envisaged (Beveridge, 1991, p. 60).

Perhaps the most important source of information about standards of pupil achievement, drawn on, for example, in the report on primary schools (Alexander *et al.*, 1992) is the data collected by the Assessment of Performance Unit (APU). This was set up in 1974 to promote the devising of methods of monitoring attainments of school children and to identify the incidence of underachievement (Rosen, 1982). The APU undertook five annual surveys between 1978 and 1984 involving some 2 per cent of 10-year-olds nationally in English, maths and science testing, whilst a second phase of testing in English took place in 1988.

The original intentions behind the APU's brief remain controversial, particularly with reference to the monitoring of language. The concerns surrounding the validity of the methodology of the NFER's evidence (Start and Wells, 1972) on reading progress were met by the promotion of new forms of testing. That the APU was established in order to measure underachievement in language development (and more generally across what is now considered the 'core' curriculum) in the year before the Bullock Report's publication, reflects some pre-emptive action to shore up the arguments for falling standards in the knowledge that the published evidence was unconvincing. Although it was not the initial, publicized intention of the APU to report on a decline in standards of literate, numerate and scientific understanding, its publications have been quoted invariably in such a context. Furthermore, although the APU's 'battery' of tests recognize in part the context of the classroom, they concentrate on features of pupils' language performance through textual analysis, not on the pedagogical qualities of interaction between teachers and pupils (APU, 1988). In his critique of the APU's Primary Survey Report, *Language Perform-ance in Schools*, Rosen argued that the perspective on the language development of children remained divorced from the living, social context of children's literate intentions:

> No reputable researcher would take seriously the proposal that lan-guage development could be studied by using the results of an annual series of tests. When we bear in mind that the development of lan-guage beyond the early years (almost unknown territory) is compli-cated by functional variety, cultural diversity and literacy, we know that kind of proposal would be dismissed as an absurd irrelevance. A serious study of language development would require at the very least numerous detailed and longitudinal case studies of the language of children being used for genuine purposes. (Rosen, 1982, p. 18)

Leaving aside the methodological disquiet which is central to our own critique of the standards' debate, the APU data showed that, on the measures devised for testing reading and writing, national standards appeared to have shifted very little overall in this age group of 10-year-olds (APU, 1988; Alexander *et al.*, 1992, pp. 32–3). Evidence of a decline in reading standards amongst 7-year-olds was at the heart of the controversy which arose when the results of tests administered in the 1980s by nine anonymous local education authorities were published by Turner (1990). In his view, changes in methods of teaching reading account for pupil failure in recent years. He argues that reading is not a natural activity, but a set of gradually acquired component skills which must be taught. Consequently, in Turner's view, declining standards can be blamed on teachers moving away from more traditional, structured approaches involving reading schemes and 'phonics', in favour of informal 'apprenticeship' models and the use of 'real books'. (See Chapter 6).

As a consequence of these disclosures, in the Autumn of 1990 the Schools Examinations and Assessment Council (SEAC) commissioned a survey of the evidence on reading standards of 7-year-olds held by LEAs. This survey, carried out by the NFER, considered information from ninety-five LEAs out of a total of 116 in England and Wales. In only twenty-six of the LEA returns was it possible to make a judgment about possible declining standards. In three instances no change was indicated, one showed no consistent pattern at all, whilst three other LEAs reported a rise. Of the nineteen where a decline could be interpreted, this mainly occurred in the 1980s and was offset by a more recent rise. The NFER report concluded that it was impossible to make an accurate judgment regarding the national trends in reading standards for 7-year-olds from this data (Cato and Whetton, 1991). Some evidence from further NFER research, based on a reading test conducted with Year 3 pupils (7 to 8-year-olds) in 1987 and compared with the performance of a similar group in 1991, suggested a statistically significant fall (Alexander *et al.*, 1992, pp. 36–7). However, both the LEA evidence and the NFER's test rely on 'proxy' evidence of reading performance (reported measures of reading achievement through externally contrived testing), not observations carried out longitudinally in normal classroom contexts.

Her Majesty's Inspectorate (HMI), reporting in 1990 and 1991 on *The Teaching and Learning of Reading* in primary and secondary schools, and again in 1992 for primary schools, find no evidence to support Turner's claims (DES, 1990, 1992). In fact, inspection of many thousands of schools showed that almost 85 per cent of primary teachers used 'a blend of methods to teach initial reading skills', always including a phonics approach, and over 95 per cent used published reading schemes. High-quality teaching of reading was evident in two out of five classes and poor-quality teaching in one out of five (DES, 1992, p. 5). Of all the evidence presented in the debate over 'falling standards' HMI state emphatically that in their observations of the teaching of reading in actual classroom contexts (over 3000 primary schools visited every year) they have not gained 'a picture of falling standards' (DES, 1990, p. 3). Nor do they reveal a shift in teaching practice, methods or resources which might account for changes in standards.

Results from the first administration of National Curriculum assessments in 1991 showed that 61 per cent of Year 2 (7-year-old) pupils attained level 2 in English, with 17 per cent gaining level 3. A negative interpretation of these findings might suggest that one in five pupils remained functionally illiterate at the age of 7, which would seem to add critical substance to an emergent panic over national standards of literacy and its teaching. However, one could interpret these results more objectively by recognizing that the 22 per cent of pupils who attained level 1 were in the process of acquiring the basic features of literacy, which is markedly different from 'functional illiteracy'. Since this was the first run of National Curriculum assessments, with teachers new to the procedures, many local variations in resources and training, and the possibility of wide discrepancies in how the Statements of Attainments are interpreted, it is difficult to draw any firm conclusions from these results. As the current 'English Orders' are to remain in place, we may in the future be able to make comparisons for successive cohorts of children against the same initial baselines for early-literacy development. One of the immediate consequences of hostile reporting of the 1991 results and the political scapegoating of teachers of Key Stage 1 pupils has been a reluctance in the profession to administer the tests since 1991, so longitudinal comparisons are fraught with complications (see Volume 2, Chapter 9).

It is not our intention to debate further the issue of falling standards, since we wish to promote a more circumspect and detached perspective. More relevant to enhancing teaching and learning is a focus on the processes of literacy required by the immediate teaching context. What does literacy learning look like in the classroom? How can more effective teaching be facilitated without narrowing our perspective and understanding to incidents of individual failure? Underlying such questions is a methodological insistence that learning is understood in the 'context of situation' (Malinowski, 1923, in Maybin, 1994, p. 6) and that 'the situation is the environment in which the text comes to life' (Halliday, 1978, in Maybin, 1994, p. 24).

## The Nature of Literacy Encounters

In this section we outline our own conceptual map of the nature of literacy encounters. It underpins our proposals for a new way of identifying, analysing and interpreting teachers' own 'frameworks' for engaging with the literacy development of pupils.

Literacy learning, of which learning to read is an important part, is always more than the aggregate of what is read and written by any given learner, or of the achievement that can be demonstrated through portfolios, records, closed tests and levels on a normative scale (Reed and Beveridge, 1993, p. 191). Both learning to see language and to relate to its symbolic and syntactic forms and, furthermore, learning to use language's meaning systems and adapt its potential into literate expression, are characterized by certain qualities of thought, talk, reading and writing. Understanding and applying such learning is the priority of all teaching encounters, within and beyond school. The curriculum draws endlessly on this literate 'cognitive estate'.

A more commonly-held conceptualization of literacy claims that it lies at the base of learning as a set of skills which quickly merges into an underlying competence to learn 'other subjects'. From this it follows that literacy skills are basic, mechanical understandings which can be taught and learnt in isolation. Reading is 'cracking the code', writing is 'applying the code'. The 'code' remains static and uniform: it can be tested, quantified, standardized in 'common sense' and 'basic' ways.

Such a basic view of literacy and its development is both unhelpful and wrong. It is not possible to separate out a set of discrete skills which characterizes literacy and remains unchanged throughout a person's education. It is, however, expedient to suggest that literacy learning is basic and that its skills are simple, ordinary or mechanical behaviours. By the same token, it is frequently held that literacy takes place during English lessons and is synonymous with one's national language. We are so used to a school curriculum organized and represented in these terms that there is a danger of substituting this convenience in the place of the complex social and psychological reality of literacy learning.

Children acquire the ways and means of literacy through learning encounters. This may read as a tautology. In fact, it demonstrates how literacy is integral to learning. Our literate development is both sequential and accretive: the layering of experience upon and within experience, until literacy becomes the habitual environment of understanding. Or, as Jerome Bruner puts it, a 'tool for thinking', which not only enables children to take part in the schooled curriculum but also changes how individuals think and learn (Webster and Wood, 1989).

Literacy is the mainstay of schooled understanding and, in many respects, constitutes the major objective of schooling. This is why it is both simplistic and dangerous to suggest that literacy can be considered outside the curriculum. Just as it is impossible to conceive of a situation in school which has not been shaped or marked in some significant manner by literate understanding, so it is impossible to consider that interaction, encounter and interchange between teachers and pupils in classrooms have no bearing on the development of literacy. Without literacy the educational bus goes nowhere: without learning encounters the literate drive is never engaged. Stated simply: literacy *is* the curriculum and must be examined in all those mundane encounters which characterize school experience.

Since literacy is indeed basic to learning across the curriculum, it is hard to understand why it does not remain the pre-eminent focus of learning in all the subjects which come to constitute the school curriculum. In the general readiness to measure and compare achievement, rather than to describe the processes and qualities inherent to all learning, the predominant conceptual basis for literacy seems destined to remain that of a 'body of knowledge' or set of skills.

HMI, in their reports on the teaching and learning of reading in primary schools mentioned above, make explicit a belief that, on the evidence and observations undertaken, 'quality of teaching' is the most important factor in determining pupils' standards of attainment through reading:

> The most effective teachers regarded the children's success in reading as the key objective that required thorough planning and entailed the careful organisation and management of classwork, groupwork and the teaching of individuals. (DES, 1990, p. 5)

In our view, a neglected but highly significant aspect of literacy development concerns the quality and nature of children's learning encounters across the subject curriculum in both primary and secondary schools.

### Teachers' Conceptual Maps

Within a year of the implementation of the National Curriculum's English Order (DES, 1990), the National Curriculum Council had commissioned an evaluation from Warwick University 'designed to investigate aspects of the subject's implementation in schools'. One of the three 'problems' in implementation to be gauged by the project team concerned 'the question of teacher knowledge and understanding' (Raban *et al.*, 1993, para. 10). A questionnaire survey of the practices of teaching reading in institutions of initial teacher training had been commissioned by the DES from the NFER two months before the start of the Warwick research (CATE, 1992). Although the prescription of a specific method of teaching reading is carefully disclaimed, as it will be in all the subsequent calls for revision to the English Order, the discourse centres repeatedly on the teaching of 'phonics'. In attempting to measure the time spent on this method of teaching initial reading, attention is drawn to the conceptual basis from which teachers operate. An increasing parallel is drawn between a basic teaching method and the ideological demand for a return to 'basics'. As a case is built for the revision of the English Order, widely expressed concern for general standards of literacy across the curriculum is focused on the issue of teaching children basic skills (NCC, 1992).

After internal reporting from the commissioned researchers at Warwick to the NCC, the proposals for the revision of the English Order were published and presented to the Department For Education in April 1993. Under the heading 'Teaching Children to Read' a disturbing reference to the then unpublished Warwick research is made:

> Responses to the consultation confirmed that teachers did not possess a 'conceptual map of reading development' . . . There is, in particular, no consensus about the phonic skills which pupils require. (DfE, 1993, p. 4)

Curiously, a close reading of the final report of the Warwick team, published in November 1993, nearly seven months after the proposals to revise the Order and well beyond the end of the consultation period, reveals no such statement.

'Evaluation of the Implementation of English in the National Curriculum at Key Stages 1, 2 and 3 (1991–3)' is full of frameworks and useful reconstructions of phonological development, spelling, knowledge about language, and more advanced reading skills (Raban *et al.*, 1993). The researchers had to fashion and reconstruct a conceptual basis and observational framework for literacy because of the eclectic nature of the English Order and its lack of a clear conceptual structure. It is the architects of the curriculum, not its practitioners, who have failed to provide the map that teachers seem to lack.

There is, of course, much to commend a mapping process which situates literacy learning in the context of classroom interaction. However, very little of the evidence in the public domain, to which we have referred in some detail, conceptualizes literacy development in terms of the interactive context in which it is learnt and schooled. The question of whether teachers do, or do not, possess a conceptual basis for the teaching of literacy is one which we have investigated across the primary–secondary school divide. It is our belief that teachers need far more encouragement to recognize the potential for literacy development across the school curriculum. Sustained examination of current institutional practices in their normal context might reveal more of the critical practices which develop literacy effectively across the curriculum. We have sought to provide a model for such an examination, in order to assist schools in beginning to audit their practice and realize change.

### A Four-quadrant Model of Teaching Through Adult–Child Proximation

In order to generate the model on which our questionnaire is constructed, we needed to break away from the trend to identify literacy as a subject on the school curriculum:

> Once we recognize that the ways in which people come to understand and practise reading and writing are strongly shaped by the exemplars, values, processes and requirements operating in the social contexts within which they engage print, it becomes clear that the curriculum is a most important site of literacy formation; and further, that as a site of literacy formation, curriculum includes all areas and subjects of formal school learning and the connections (or lack of connection) between them. (Lankshear, 1993, p. 155)

It is perhaps a stride away from the argument that the school curriculum is a major, social context of literacy to the suggestion that literacy is the curriculum, yet it is a step most teachers in our experience will take. Beyond the concern that understanding literacy has not been a feature of their professional development or in any lasting sense an experience in initial teacher training, lies a recognition of the potential territories of teaching and learning which remain to be explored in practice. To begin to talk about a pupil's understanding and one's relationship with a child's literate production is to begin a process of sharing: it allows stronger relationships between the teacher and the taught, since it is the teacher who must learn how to follow more when the pupil takes the lead. When teachers find that literacies can be understood as ways of thinking and records of thought, then the differences between subjects become less immutable.

Above all we want to understand literacy in terms of mediation, of the roles played by teacher and pupil in creating what Vygotsky called the Zone of Proximal Development (ZPD):

> The zone of proximal development defines those functions that have not yet matured but are in the process of maturation, functions that will mature tomorrow but are currently in an embryonic state. These functions could be termed the 'buds' or 'flowers' of development rather than the fruits of development. The actual developmental level

characterizes mental development retrospectively, while the zone of proximal development characterizes mental development prospectively. (Vygotsky, 1978, pp. 86–7)

From this description we understand the importance of that type of interaction between an adult and a child, or between peers, in which mental development occurs through mediation and proximation, or sharing and closeness. We also recognize the importance of examining achievement 'prospectively' *in* the learning encounter, rather than *after* it.

A model of the practice of teaching was devised to study systematically teachers' underlying conceptions of literacy. The model can incorporate aspects of assessment, resource management, adult intervention and classroom organization. Since it is such an important methodological issue, we should make it clear that what teachers say they do, or think, is not necessarily the same as what they actually do. We have designed the questionnaire as an initial framework by which teachers can reveal some of the characteristics of their own conceptual maps of teaching literacy. The domains constructed in our model of proximation are not apparent to the questionnaire respondent, nor were they revealed until systematic observation of literacy encounters in actual classrooms had been completed. This observation of practice, rather than of conception, constitutes the second phase of our research, which we will report separately.

The model was used to generate eighty statements in four sets, corresponding to one of four quadrants. The statements were intended for use on a fixed item questionnaire format with different teacher groups. Teachers who took part in the research would be asked to identify in each of the twenty sets one of the four statements which they felt most closely represented their own views in relation to the specific aspect of the teaching, assessment, function or development of literacy. The underlying model was not revealed to the teachers before or during completion of the questionnaire.

Two orthogonal dimensions provide the framework of the model. The vertical axis is concerned with the level of mediation, control, structure or management exercised by the teacher. The horizontal axis is concerned with the level of initiative, engagement, collaboration and active involvement enjoyed by the child in the learning process. Our major concern has been to develop an effective framework for description, rather than for judgment. Hence, we have no a priori assumptions regarding which quadrants are 'best'. Indeed, we would expect teachers to locate some of what they do at different times, and for different purposes, in a range of the quadrants.

Quadrant A is characterized by high adult structure and didactic teaching without negotiation in which the child takes the role of passive participant. Literacy teaching in this domain would be viewed as a set of skills to be handed over. Typical learning would happen through prescribed steps, rule-driven, decontextualized, and treated as an assembly line of subtasks and skills fitted together. Assessment is likely to be based on skills as objectives. An

Figure 12.1:   Adult–child proximation through literacy learning

HIGH
Adult
Mediation

A        Abstracted Literacy                                     Critical literacy        D

- Rote learning through prescribed steps: adult-structured with frequent reinforcement; decontextualized learning with little negotiation; repetitious, rule-based teaching.

- Attention is centred on memorizing the surface conventions and contents of textual systems to the exclusion of 'meaning-laden' contexts.

- Image of learner as a passive, empty vessel.

- Model of literacy as a set of skills to be handed over.

- Collaboration and dialogue within reading and writing events: negotiation, discussion, review, weighing the evidence and drawing conclusions.

- Attention is drawn to 'acts of mind', 'ways of telling', and the forms, functions, and 'secrets' of textual understanding.

- Image of learner as an active partner.

- Model of literacy as a dialogue in the making.

LOW          linear curriculum                      spiral curriculum       HIGH
Child ◄─────────────────────────────────────────► Child
Initiative                             Immersed literacy    Initiative
        Marginal literacy

- Limited enjoyment of, and exposure to, textual forms and uses; lack of modelling in context; disparagement of literate purpose.

- Assumption that pupils do not have the capacity, motivation, or need, for literate understanding beyond the superficial.

- Image of learner as an observer in need of containment or entertainment.

- Model of literacy relates to the interested few.

- Exposure to and experience of real books; topic-led creative writing centred on personal or expressive modes of thought.

- Assumption that pupils 'read when ready' and are self-motivated in determining the objectives of literate enquiry.

- Image of learner as a lone voyager.

- Model of literacy as a garden of delights.

B        hollow curriculum                        seamless curriculum        C

LOW
Adult
Mediation

example which would typify this quadrant is a remedial reading programme based on highly controlled exposure to sight vocabulary or phonic rules taught separately from the context of a text. This quadrant was used to generate statements such as: 'Presentation skills are best practised as a specific exercise, e.g., cursive writing within tramlines.' Because it is high in teacher management, Quadrant A is described as teacher-driven.

In contrast, Quadrant B is characterized by lack of explicit theory, adult or child initiative, and a limited amount of management, direction, modelling, exposure or enjoyment. Literacy in this quadrant is a peripheral activity for all but the select few. Assessment takes the form of monitoring rather than being the basis for planning or weighing what children have learned. An unstructured library period where pupils are simply supervised in a library resource area without any specific objectives for being there other than for those who can get on independently with their own reading would be an example of Quadrant B. This quadrant was used to drive statements such as: 'The alphabet should be gradually absorbed without direct teaching.' Because it is low in teacher management, pupil initiative or negotiation, Quadrant B is described as resource-driven, non-interactive, open learning.

Quadrant C is described as 'immersed literacy' because it depends on an image of the child as self-motivated to explore books, whilst the adult's role is to provide a wealth of resources and materials to furnish a rich and stimulating environment. The child takes the initiative and is encouraged to pursue an interest with little guidance, structure or management. Assessment is concerned almost exclusively with the qualities of the child's unique performance. This quadrant draws on child-centred models of teaching and learning and the view that children are basically the architects of their own understanding. It is consistent with many interpretations of Piaget's work in relation to education. Quadrant C was used to generate questionnaire statements such as: 'The teacher's task is to immerse children in a wide range of written forms and genres.' Because it is low in teacher management or collaboration, this quadrant is described as child-driven.

Finally, Quadrant D ascribes active roles to both adult and child in the learning partnership. Tasks are negotiated with pupils. Adults behave contingently, recognizing the child's initiative but stepping in to make suggestions, encourage, guide, remind, and offer assistance; thereby helping the child to plan, use appropriate resources and stay on task. Having attempted a problem, the adult reviews with the child how and why a task was tackled, what has been learnt and what can be carried forward to the next task. Assessment is reflective, process-orientated and formative, identifying key issues for the next teaching steps.

Quadrant D was used to generate questionnaire statements such as: 'Spelling strategies are discussed as an integral part of the composing, editing and publication process.' This quadrant is consistent with Vygotskian descriptions of developmental processes and effective teaching or learning.

In our many discussions of this conceptual framework with teachers, we have been asked whether Quadrant D represents an 'ideal' relationship between teacher and taught, which may, in the day-to-day practicalities of classroom life, be achieved only briefly for a few pupils in selected areas of the curriculum. A difficult Year 10 group of pupils, for example, where management of behaviour and classroom atmosphere is high priority, may constrain the teacher to adopt more didactic styles of setting tasks and motivating pupils.

Our response to teachers posing this question is that we are concerned both with how teachers would like to work and what they do in practice: their belief systems and their behaviours. We are aware that we are probing, to some extent, the gap between prescription and reality. However, as stated earlier, we are trying to build a framework for *describing*, not *judging*, what teachers do.

The full questionnaire requires twenty responses to questions concerning favoured teaching methods in different areas of literacy. These are:

- print skills (alphabet, letter sounds, phonic blends);
- vocabulary (sight vocabulary, vocabulary development);
- reading (assessment, text selection, reading content, discussions of problems);
- writing (spelling, function, presentation, letter formation, letter patterning); and
- literacy curriculum (relation to learning, who is responsible, creative components, relation to children with reading problems, curriculum construction, role of pupils' interest).

Many of the questionnaire's items reflect the language and focus of attention to be found in the English Order of the National Curriculum (DES, 1990) and in the current proposals by the School Curriculum and Assessment Authority.


## Method

In the pilot phase of the research twenty teachers were asked to work in pairs to reallocate the eighty questionnaire statements to the quadrants which generated them. Using a procedure devised by Fleiss (1971) for measuring the nominal scale agreement among many raters, a figure of $p = 0.87$ was calculated, which incorporated a correction factor for the extent of the agreement by chance alone. This can be interpreted as approaching 90 per cent agreement amongst twenty raters that statements in the questionnaire fitted the model. Given this reasonable coherence of the questions in the context of the model, the finalized questionnaire was then given to a larger number of different teachers.

The research was carried out in the Bristol area using a sample of primary and secondary schools serving multiethnic communities and a wide range of housing types. In order to focus the research on contrasts between primary and secondary schools, questionnaire data were analysed from fifty primary teachers of Year 6 (10 to 11-year-olds) and fifty secondary teachers of Year 7 (11 to 12-year-olds), including English, science and humanities specialists. Each Year 6 teacher represented a single primary school, whilst ten teachers of Year 7 represented one secondary school. The sample therefore covers fifty primary schools and five secondary schools. All of the sample schools are maintained by the local education authority of Avon.

### Results

*Table 12.1: Teachers' concepts of literacy*

|            | A   | B   | C   | D   |
|------------|-----|-----|-----|-----|
| Primary    | 1.7 | 3.8 | 4.6 | 9.9 |
| Secondary  | 2.1 | 4.2 | 4.2 | 9.5 |

*Note*: Figures represent the mean questionnaire responses out of 20 in 4 quadrants.

The sample showed a high degree of consistency (Table 12.1). It should be remembered that, at the time of completing the questionnaire, the nature of the underlying model was neither mentioned nor revealed. Even so, the largest share of questionnaire responses was allocated to Quadrant D by all teachers. This reveals a high tendency to stress the importance of teaching literacy through contingent negotiation. Around 50 per cent of overall responses from both primary and secondary teachers identified Quadrant D.

The remaining 50 per cent of responses, while emphasizing child-centred factors (Quadrant C) also suggested use of more prescriptive, rule- or resource-based approaches. For example, 42 per cent of primary teachers said they would use graded reading schemes; 66 per cent felt that time should be given to practise letter shapes and handwriting; 62 per cent noted children's enjoyment of activities based around rhyming or spelling patterns. However, 82 per cent of primary teachers said they would not attempt to correct or rehearse spelling outside of the process of children composing, editing and presenting a piece of writing for a specific audience.

As suggested earlier, the data also reveal interesting differences between primary and secondary teachers in a number of areas. Primary teachers are more likely to select graded reading materials for pupils (chi square: 8.0, df: 3, p<0.001). Most primary teachers would teach spelling strategies within the context of composition. Whilst many secondary teachers take the view that faulty spelling should be corrected and rehearsed out of context (chi square: 11.1, df: 3, p<0.02). On the other hand, primary teachers do give specific time to the practising of handwriting skills outside the context of writing for a genuine audience (chi square: 13.2, df: 3, p<0.01).

Primary teachers also give greater recognition to the value of enjoyable activities which draw attention to the rhyming and spelling structures of words (chi square: 8.6, df: 3, p<0.05). Primary teachers are much more likely to consider literacy as an integral part of teacher–pupil dialogues, whereas some secondary teachers see literacy as only indirectly related to their subject teaching, or the responsibility of the English department (chi square: 8.5, df: 3, p<0.05).

*Table 12.2:  Differences in primary and secondary teachers' concepts of literacy*

|  | **A** | **B** | **C** | **D** |
|---|---|---|---|---|
| **Primary** | 1.7 | 3.8 | 4.6 | 9.9 |
| **Secondary** | | | | |
| English | 0.8 | 2.5 | 3.9 | 12.8 |
| Humanities | 1.8 | 4.9 | 4.5 | 8.8 |
| Science | 3.7 | 5.2 | 4.3 | 6.9 |
| **All Sec.** | 2.1 | 4.2 | 4.2 | 9.5 |

*Note*: Figures represent mean questionnaire responses by secondary-subject specialists compared with primary generalists.

Overall both primary and secondary teachers were, in the main, propo-nents of a negotiated literacy curriculum. However, teachers cannot be simply categorized as falling into (or failing at) one philosophy versus another (such as real books versus structured reading schemes). Some of what teachers say they do is concerned with practising skills, some with enjoyment and experience. At other times teachers have in mind processes such as composi-tion. For the main part teachers are concerned with the complexities of inter-active literacy contexts. An important conclusion is that teachers *do* have an organized understanding of literacy development in children but it is not a simplistic conceptual map based on unitary methods, resources or skills, nor is it eclectic in the sense that methods are selected out of the context of par-ticular learning opportunities.

Although we have identified a broad consensus of opinion in the primary and secondary samples (with some differences in emphasis), variation within the subject specialisms of the secondary teachers is worth noting (see Table 12.2).

Despite the relatively small numbers of different subject teachers involved in the study, analysis of variance revealed some significant differences. The rate of questionnaire responses falling into Quadrant D, which we have de-scribed as learning-driven, is higher amongst English specialists than any other group, including primary teachers. Quadrant D response rates are, however, lowest amongst science teachers (1-way Anova, $F (3, 96) = 11.2$; $p<0.0005$). The response rate for Quadrant A, which we have described as 'teacher-driven' is highest amongst science teachers ($F (3, 96) = 6.4$; $p<0.001$).

What these findings demonstrate is that many secondary teachers have a map of literacy development which covers very similar conceptual domains to primary teachers. Points of difference do, however, arise between subject specialists in some aspects of their approach to literacy. For example, science teachers are more likely to suggest that help with literacy is provided outside their subject area ($F (3, 69) = 5.9$; $p<0.001$).

Teachers were given the opportunity to comment freely about any aspects of literacy highlighted in the questionnaire. This revealed qualitative evidence, particularly from primary teachers, of a flexibility in approach and of tailoring strategies, resources and tasks to meet the needs of individuals, rather than applying a single method to all children. Some secondary teachers were prompted to write about their relative inexperience in teaching literacy, the lack of training and opportunities for professional development, and gaps in understanding:

> As a secondary school teacher . . . I have had no specific training or development in literacy . . . Maybe it has been assumed I do not need these skills or that I would acquire them as I went along . . . I do not feel very confident in taking young people through the process of learning to read and . . . have received no professional support in this. (A teacher of humanities)

### Messages for Teachers

1. In all the evidence which has been presented to the British public concerning a supposed decline in standards of literacy, there are numerous instances of assessments of reading performance, in particular, which are based on no compatible baseline 'standard' and which do not situate reading in its actual schooled context.

2. Assessments made *in vitro*, which are not situated in the context of children's learning, do not in themselves support the allegation that standards of literacy are falling; nor are they reliable indicators of learning to read.

3. Evidence concerning reading cannot, and must not, be taken to represent literacy development, which is a far more complex and, as yet, under-described process of learning and, in part, schooling.

4. It is frequently the most negative interpretations of the patchy evidence available that are used to fuel the argument for curricular reform, particularly in the subject of English.

5. Literacy learning is part and parcel of learning across the curriculum and should not be designated through expedience to the subject area of English.

6. The qualities of literacy learning are best described in terms of 'quality of teaching'; therefore, through observation of the quality and type of interaction between all teachers and all pupils, regardless of curricular domain.

7. The development of literacy for learning, and a recognition of the literacy curriculum, does not inform the implementation and revision of the National Curriculum for all subject areas in any constructive sense.

8. A conceptual framework is offered, demonstrating four types of 'proximal' literacy (abstracted, marginal, immersed and critical), which arise through interaction between a teacher and a learner.

9. Teachers' conceptualization of literacy learning is shown to be complex and broad, and reliant on no single method or favoured practice.

10. Areas of consensus and variance in the conceptualization of literacy are shown between primary and secondary teachers. The greatest variance seems to exist between subject specialists in secondary schools.

11. Greater attention needs to be paid to observation of the quality and effectiveness of teaching and learning styles in the development of literacy across the curriculum. Important institutional and professional development will take place if this process of 'mapping the literacy curriculum' is explored through methods of research which are sensitive to the social and cognitive dynamics of actual teaching and learning situations.

## Conclusion

In this chapter, we have explored a number of issues to do with current conceptualizations of literacy in response to what some have perceived as declining standards through changing teaching methods. We have explained the tenuous and limited nature of these perceptions, which do not present literacy encounters in their everyday situation, and frequently ignore the context of the broad curriculum.

A new model for understanding literacy development, which is concerned with the enhancement of teaching and learning encounters, has been proposed. This requires teachers and researchers to examine teaching and learning contexts with a more appropriate focus on mediation and collaboration. Our framework for describing the conceptual basis of the literacy curriculum, with respect for the social dynamics of classrooms, has allowed us to report an initial enquiry into teachers' conceptual understandings of literacy in practice. It will be recalled that the Department for Education has sought to restructure the curriculum on the basis that teachers lack any coherent conceptual map of reading development in particular.

This investigation has not revealed simple or contradictory conceptual maps of literacy teaching amongst the primary and secondary teachers who took part. Importantly, teachers are not in the main driven by particular resources or methods, but are rather more concerned with the process of learning. Teachers' views on literacy are complex, paying attention to a range of factors such as the place of reading schemes, phonic patterns, practising handwriting and developing strategies for proficient spelling. These 'maps', despite their common tendencies, defy simplistic description as belonging to one pedagogical approach.

There are many similarities, but also some major differences, between subject specialists in the secondary sector. Though the samples were small, significant differences were still found; for example, between science specialists and other groups concerning the role of the teacher in managing and prescribing learning, and the responsibility of the teacher for promoting literacy.

It seems unlikely, given this evidence, that more effective teaching of literacy, or, the 'raising of standards', will arise from a narrowing of the curriculum to particular formal or prescribed methods, to particular resources or through subject-specific teaching. This study suggests that some of the professional development needs of teachers should be focused on how literacy at secondary level can be embedded within the curriculum, with a sharing of responsibilities for literacy across subject boundaries. Above all, it suggests that, given understanding and encouragement, both primary and secondary-school teachers are well capable of developing the conceptual basis for literacy across the curriculum and of sharing and exploring its practices. The prospect of assisting in that development remains an intriguing possibility for further work.

## References

ALEXANDER, R., ROSE, J. and WOODHEAD, C. (1992) *Organisation and Classroom Practice in Primary Schools: A Discussion Paper*, DES, pp. 32–3, 36–7.

ASSESSMENT OF PERFORMANCE UNIT (APU) (1988) *Language Performance in Schools: Review of APU Language Monitoring 1979–1983*, DES, London, HMSO.

BEVERIDGE, M.C. (1991) 'Literacy and learning in secondary schools: Problems of texts and teaching', in WEBSTER, A. (Ed) 'Language and language-related difficulties', *Educational and Child Psychology*, **8**, 3, p. 60.

BRUNER, J. (1986) *Actual Minds, Possible Worlds*, Cambridge, MA, Harvard University Press.

CATO, V. and WHETTON, C. (1991) *An Enquiry into LEA Evidence on Standards of Reading of Seven-Year-Old Children*, Windsor, NFER.

COUNCIL FOR THE ACCREDITATION OF TEACHER EDUCATION (CATE) (1992) *Training Teachers to Teach Reading: A Review*, Elizabeth House, London, CATE.

DE CASTELL, S., LUKE, A. and EGAN, K. (Eds) (1986) *Literacy, Society, and Schooling: A Reader*, Cambridge, Cambridge University Press.

DEPARTMENT OF EDUCATION AND SCIENCE (DES) (1975) *A Language for Life*, London, HMSO, pp. 16, 516–17.

DEPARTMENT OF EDUCATION AND SCIENCE (DES) (1990) *The National Curriculum for English 2*, London, HMSO.

DEPARTMENT OF EDUCATION AND SCIENCE (DES) (1990) *The Teaching and Learning of Reading in Primary Schools: A Report by HMI*, London, HMSO (Ref.: 10/91/NS), pp. 3, 5.

DEPARTMENT OF EDUCATION AND SCIENCE (DES) (1992) *The Teaching and Learning of Reading in Primary Schools 1991*, London, HMSO (Ref.: 42/92/NS), p. 5.

DEPARTMENT FOR EDUCATION (DFE) AND THE WELSH OFFICE (April 1993) *English for ages 5 to 16 (1993): Proposals of the Secretary of State for Education and the Secretary of State for Wales*, London, HMSO, p. 4.

FLEISS, J.L. (1971) 'Measuring nominal scale agreement among many factors', *Psychological Bulletin*, **76**, pp. 378–82.

GREEN, B. (Ed) (1993) *The Insistence of the Letter: Literacy Studies and Curriculum Theorizing*, London, Falmer Press.

HALLIDAY, M.A.K. (1978) 'Language as social semiotic', in MAYBIN, J. (Ed) (1994) *Language and Literacy in Social Practice*, Clevedon, Multilingual Matters in association with The Open University, p. 24.

LANKSHEAR, C. (1993) 'Curriculum as literacy: Reading and writing in 'New Times', in GREEN, B. (Ed) *The Insistence of the Letter: Literacy Studies and Curriculum Theorizing*, London, Falmer Press, p. 155.

MALINOWSKI, B. (1923) 'The problem of meaning in primitive languages', in MAYBIN, J. (Ed) (1994) *Language and Literacy in Social Practice*, Clevedon, Multilingual Matters in association with The Open University, p. 6.

MEEK, M. and McKENZIE, M.G. (1975) 'Learning to read and the reading process', in ROSEN, H. (Ed) *Language and Literacy in our Schools: Some Appraisals of the Bullock Report*, Studies in Education, 1, University of London Institute of Education, p. 8.

MOLL, L.C. (Ed) (1990) *Vygotsky and Education: Instructional Implications and Applications of Sociohistorical Psychology*, Cambridge, Cambridge University Press.

NATIONAL CURRICULUM COUNCIL (NCC) (1992) *National Curriculum English: The Case for Revising the Order — Advice to the Secretary of State for Education*, NCC.

RABAN, B., CLARK, U. and McINTYRE, J. (1993) 'Evaluation of English in the National Curriculum at Key Stages 1, 2 and 3 (1991–1993): Final Report', University of Warwick for the NCC, p. 1.

REED, M. and BEVERIDGE, M. (1993) 'Knowing ourselves: Practising a pluralist epistemology in teacher education', in VERMA, G.K. (Ed) *Inequality and Teacher Education: An International Perspective*, London, Falmer Press, p. 191.

ROSEN, H. (1982) 'The Language Monitors: A Critique of the APU's Primary Survey Report 'Language Performance in Schools', *Bedford Way Papers*, University of London, Institute of Education, p. 18.

START, K.B. and WELLS, B.K. (1972) *The Trend of Reading Standards: 1970–71*, Slough, NFER.

TURNER, M. (1990) *Sponsored Reading Failure*, Education Unit, Warlingham, IPSET.

VYGOTSKY, L.S. (1978) *Mind in Society: The Development of Higher Psychological Processes*, Cambridge, MA, Harvard University Press, pp. 86–7.

WEBSTER, A. and WOOD, D. (1989) *Children with Hearing Difficulties*, London, Cassell.

WOOD, D. (1988) *How Children Think and Learn*, Oxford, Basil Blackwell.

# Notes on Contributors

**Pamela Owen** has worked as a primary teacher and as a secondary English teacher before moving into literacy research at the Centre for Formative Assessment Studies, School of Education, University of Manchester. Here she worked on the development of a literacy assessment scheme and then moved into the development of SAT English material for the STAIR Consortium. From 1991 she has been senior lecturer at St Martin's College with responsibility for the design and delivery of reading and language courses in ITT and PGCE courses. She has run several courses on reading for serving teachers and was conference coordinator of the 1993 International Reading Conference held in Lancaster.

Contact address: English Department, University Sector College of St Martin's, Lancaster LA1 3JD. Fax: 0524 68943.

**Peter Pumfrey** is Professor of Education and Head of the Centre for Educational Guidance and Special Needs at the University of Manchester. He is a qualified and experienced teacher having been employed in mainstream schools and Remedial Education Services for fourteen years prior to training and working as an LEA educational psychologist.

His research and training interests are in the identification and alleviation of literacy difficulties in general and of reading difficulties in particular. In addition, he is concerned with the assessment and improvement of reading standards.

Professor Pumfrey is a fellow of the British Psychological Society and a chartered psychologist. He has served on the Committee of the Division of Educational and Child Psychology, and also on the Society's Committee on Test Standards.

He has published over 250 papers and written and edited fourteen books.

Contact address: Centre for Educational Guidance and Special Needs, School of Education, University of Manchester, Oxford Road, Manchester M13 9PL. Fax: 061 275 3548.

**Linnea Ehri** is a distinguished professor at the Graduate School, City University of New York, where she conducts research on literacy acquisition. She holds elected offices in the Society for the Scientific Study of Reading and the American Educational Research Association.

Contact address: The Graduate School and University Center, City University of New York, 33 West 42 Street, New York, U.S.A. NY 10036–8099. Fax: 0101 212 6422642.

**Rhona Johnston** is a lecturer in the School of Psychology, St Andrew's University. Her research interests are in the area of reading disorders and normal reading development.
Contact address: School of Psychology, St Andrew's University, St Andrews, Fife, Scotland KY 16 9JU. Fax: 0334 63042.

**Vincent Connelly** is completing a PhD in the School of Psychology, St Andrew's University. He is studying the influence of language experience and phonics teaching methods on how children read.
Contact address: School of Psychology, St Andrew's University, St. Andrews, Fife, Scotland KY16 9JU. Fax: 0334 63042.

**Joyce Watson** has worked as a primary school teacher for six years and just retired as a lecturer in the Primary Education Department, Northern College, Dundee Campus. In 1981 she was awarded an M.Ed degree from the University of Dundee, and is currently studying for a PhD at the University of St Andrews.
Contact address: School of Psychology, St Andrew's University, St Andrews, Fife, Scotland, KY16 9JU. Fax: 0334 63042.

**P. Papoulia-Tzelepi** is associate professor in Patras University, Department of Education, Greece. Her interests are in the emergence of literacy, teaching reading/writing in the primary school, and in the education of reflective teaching.
Contact address: Department of Education, Patras University, 261 10 Patras, Greece. Fax: 010 301 6917391.

**Rhona Stainthorp** is a psychologist working in teacher education at Reading University. Her research interests centre on the development of literacy within a cognitive psychological framework. Her main teaching focus is working with teachers undertaking In-service courses on literacy and literacy difficulties.
Contact address: Department of Educational Studies and Management, University of Reading, Bulmershe Court, Woodlands Avenue, Earley, Reading RG6 1HY. Fax: 0734 352080.

**Anna Adamik-Jászó** graduated from Eötvö Loránd University, Budapest, specializing in Hungarian and Russian language and literature, and Finno-Ugric comparative linguistics. She has more than 100 publications, among them books, on the history of reading instruction in Hungary. She is editor of the mythodological/periodical Magyartanitás/Teaching Hungarian. She is also a board member of HUNRA/Hungarian Reading Association.
Contact address: Budapest Teachers Training College, Budapest, Hungary. Fax: 010 361 2023859.

**Martin Turner** is head of psychology at the Dyslexia Institute. His acronymic form includes membership of the SEAC English committee (1992–3), the English advisory group of SCAA (1993–4) and CATE (1992–4). His collection of poems, *Trespasses*, is published by Faber and Faber.
Contact address: The Dyslexia Institute, 133, Gresham Road, Staines, Middlesex, TW18 2AJ. Fax: 0784 460747.

**Henrietta Dombey** is Professor of Education at the University of Brighton. Her interest in early literacy was first kindled when she taught 7-year-olds in Inner London. Since then this interest has been strengthened and her understanding deepened by her own children, by the gifted teachers and students she has worked with at the University of Brighton, and more recently by the teachers and researchers from mainland Europe she has met through IEDPE.
Contact address: Faculty of Education, Sport and Leisure, University of Brighton, Falmer, Brighton BN1 9PH. Fax: 0273 643390.

**Penny Munn** is a senior lecturer is Developmental Psychology at the University of Central Lancashire. Her research has included studies of young children in family settings, day care quality, and literacy and numeracy in the preschool years.
Contact address: Department of Psychology, University of Central Lancashire, Preston PR1 2HE. Fax: 0772 892902.

**Ros Fisher** is principal lecturer in language and literacy Rolle School of Education, University of Plymouth, Exmouth, Devon. She is involved in initial and in-service teacher education. Previously she was an infant teacher, including a year teaching first grade in USA. Her research interests are in the role of the teacher in early reading.
Contact address: Rolle School of Education, University of Plymouth, Exmouth, Devon, EX8 2AT. Fax: 0395 255303.

**Robin Campbell** is a professor of primary education at the University of Hertfordshire, with research interests in classroom literacy activities. Previously he worked as a primary-school teacher and headteacher. His two most recent books have been *Reading Together* and *Reading Real Books*, Open University Press.
Contact address: University of Hertfordshire, Wall Hall Campus, Alderham, Watford, Herts. WD2 8AT. Fax: 0707 285744.

**Morag Hunter-Carsch** is a lecturer in education at the University of Leicester school of education. She has experience as a primary teacher, researcher, lecturer in psychology and pioneer in teaching about specific learning difficulties in both Canada and the UK. She has edited two books on behalf of the United Kingdom Reading Association, of which she was president in 1988–9.
Contact address: University of Leicester, 21 University Road, Leicester LE1 7RF. Fax: 0533 523703.

**Malcolm Reed** lectures in education, training secondary-school English teachers, and researchers at the School of Education, University of Bristol.
Contact address: School of Education, University of Bristol, 35 Berkeley Square, Bristol BS8 1JA. Fax: 0272 251537.

**Alec Webster** is director of the Centre for Literacy Studies at the University of Bristol.
Contact address: School of Education, University of Bristol, 35 Berkeley Square, Bristol BS8 1JA. Fax: 0272 251537.

**Michael Beveridge** is dean of the Faculty of Social Science at the University of Bristol.
Contact address: Faculty of Social Science, University of Bristol, 35, Berkeley Square, Bristol BS8 1JA. Fax: 0272 251537.

# Index

Adams, M.J. 14, 26, 33, 37, 38, 69, 82, 84–5
Alegria, J. 40
Alexander, R. 164, 165, 166
alphabet 9, 20, 21, 22–3, 40
Apple, J. 147
Arter, J. 83, 84
assessment 171–3, 177; NCC 129, 166–7;
   SCAA 161, 174; see also tests
Assessment of Performance Unit 164–5
attitudes 106, 122, 151–2, 156–7
Austria 40
Aylwin, T. 82

Bacon, Francis 2–3
Baker, L. 11
Bakker, D.J. 151
Bald, J. 34
Balmuth, M. 26
Barrow, R. 146
Bassey, M. 83
Beard, R. 144
Beck, I. 15
Beech, J.R. 87
Benchmark School 25
Bennett, N. 119
Bettelheim, B. 144
Beveridge, M.C. 164, 184
Beverton, S. 144
Biemiller, A. 16
Blagg, N. 84
Boder, E. 26
books 99, 105, 106–14; attitudes to 122; in
   the home 105, 110–11, 113
Bradley, L. 40
Branwhite, A.B. 85
Brighton University 99–100
Brown, A. 11
Brown, Roger 89
Bruner, J. 121, 168
Bryant, P.E. 40, 65, 138, 154
Bullock Report 138, 141, 163–5
Burt Word Reading Test 36
Bussis, A. 99–100
Byrne, B. 20

Cambourne, B. 128
Campbell, R. 126, 128, 133, 183

Carnine, L. 16, 84
Carroll, J.B. 88
Carroll, Lewis 59
Carter, R. 147
Carty, G. 81
Cato, V. 166
Cattell, J.M. 13
Chall, J.S. 20, 25, 126
children: attitudes to reading 151–2; concepts
   of reading 107–8, 109–12, 143–4
China 155
Chomsky, N. 43
Clark, M.M. 127, 144
Clay, M. 24, 25, 43
Cochrane-Smith, M. 121
Cockburn, A. 115
cognitive psychology 87–9
Cohen, R. 101
Colmenares, C. 97–9
communication 70
computers 100–2
Connelly, V. 37, 39, 40, 182
Content, A. 40
context 16–19, 21, 33, 57–66
Corrective Reading Programme 85–6
Cortazzi, M. 147, 155
Cunningham, P. 26
curriculum 89–90, 170, 177–9 see also
   National Curriculum
Czukrász, R. 72

decoding 60, 61, 63, 65, 66, 80, 85–7, 145
Department for Education 161, 169, 178
DES 150, 151, 163, 168, 169, 174
Desforges, C. 115
development: proximal 170–1; stages 88
Diagnostic Prescriptive Remediation 84–5
Dictionary of Reading 68
Differential Diagnosis Prescriptive Teaching
   84–5
Direct Instruction Reading Programme
   144
Dombey, H. 99, 183
Donaldson, M. 61, 134, 138
Downing, John 69
Doyle, W. 116
Dyson, A.H. 23, 43, 54

# Index

*Economist* 83
Ehri, L.C. 11, 12, 13, 15, 17, 18, 19, 20, 21, 22, 23, 24, 26, 61, 88, 181
Elbro, C. 88
Ellis, A.W. 88
Engelmann, S. 85, 89–90
English, in NC 80, 161–2, 168–9, 174
environment 55, 127, 157; print in 20, 23, 35, 57–8, 96, 127
Exton, G. 39

Family Reading Groups 143–4
Feitelson, D. 26, 39, 40
Fernandes, C. 140–1
Ferreiro, Emilia 43, 44, 45, 49, 50, 51, 54
Fleiss, J.L. 174
Fox, B. 40
Frederiksen, J.R. 87, 88

Garnham, A. 86
Gaskins, I. 25
Gentry, R. 26
Gibson, E. 43
Goelman, H. 12
Golinkoff, R. 18
Gonczy, P. 71
Goodman, K. 16, 18, 32, 33, 82, 126, 129
Gorman, T. 140–1
Goswami, U. 15, 88, 138, 154
Gough, P. 9, 17
Graves, D. 152
Greece 45–51
Griffith, P. 9
Grundlach, R.A. 50
guessing 16–19, 21, 33, 60, 61, 65, 100
guidelines, national 148–51
Gursky, D. 9
Guttentag, R. 18

Hall, N. 58, 128
Halliday, M.A.K. 167
Hammill, D.D. 83, 84
Hannon, Peter 96
Harris, A.J. 26, 128
Harris, T.L. 68
Harste, J. 20
Hatcher, P.J. 40, 82, 84, 87
Henderson, E. 24 26
Henry, M.K. 22
heuristic programme 74–5
Hodges, R.E. 68
Holdaway, D. 23
home 96–7, 116, 121, 122, 127–8, 199; books in 105, 110–11, 113
Horkheimer, M. 152
Huggins, A. 14
Hughes, M. 116, 119
Hungary 67–78
Hunter-Carsch, C.M. 145, 153, 183

Illinois Test of Psycholinguistic Abilities 84
imagery 153–5
Institut Europeén pur le Développement des Potentialités de tous les Enfants 95–103
International Association for the Evaluation of Educational Achievement 3
Iversen, S. 82

Jacobson, Roman 70
Jansen, M. 145, 146
Jenkins, J.R. 83, 84
Johns, J.L. 14
Johnson, D.D. 83
Johnston, R.S. 35, 39, 40, 85, 182
Juel, C. 9
Juliebo, M. 116, 119, 122
Just, M.A. 33

Kehoe, E.J. 59
Kemp, M. 152
Key Phonics 37
key words 25
Kingman Report 145
knowledge 11–12, 16, 18
Kosztolányi, D. 70

Lake, M. 138
Laminack, L. 127
language 32–3, 89; development 164–5, 167; *see also* English; whole-language instruction
Language in the National Curriculum project 146–7
Lankshear, C. 170
Leicester 141–2, 145
'letterland' programme 23
letters (alphabetic) 9; mnemonics 23–4; recognition 12, 13, 22–3, 25, 35–6; -sound knowledge 13–14, 15, 20, 21, 23–4, 25–6, 33–4; *see also* phonics
Levin, I. 50
Lindamood, C. and P. 24
Link Up Reading Scheme 37
literacy 1–3, 161–79
Lloyd, S. 39–40
logical positivism 83
logographs 33

MacMartin, M. 152, 153
Malinowski, B. 167
Markman, E. 54
Marsh, G. 15
Mason, J. 21
Masonheimer, P.E. 20
mathematics teaching 115
Mathews, M. 70
McClelland, J.L. 88
McGee, L. 12
McKay, D. 152
McLullich, Helen 153

McNee, M. 39–40
meaning 44, 150–7
Medrano, G. 100
Meek, M. 83, 128, 144, 164
meta-analysis 83
Mexico 44, 50
Mitchell, D. 60
Moerk, E.L. 89
Morais, J. 40
Morris, D. 26, 138
motivation 151–2

National Curriculum 128, 177; English
  Order 80, 161–2, 168–9, 174; Guidelines
  148–51; Standard Assessment Tasks 129,
  166–7
National Curriculum Council 168–9;
  Consultation Report 148–9, 150
National Foundation for Educational Research
  (NFER) 163, 165–6, 169
national guidelines 148–51
National Writing Project 148
Neale, M.D. 33, 40, 87
New Zealand 36, 40
Newcomer, P.L. 83, 84
Ninio, A. 105
non-words (pseudo-words) 14, 15, 26, 36–7,
  61–5, 85
Northern Ireland 150
nursery schools 97, 98–9, 105, 106

Oakhill, J. 85, 86
Olssen, M. 82
O'Neill, G.P. 87

Palacio, Gomez 45, 49
Papandropoulou, I. 54
parents 96–7, 98, 99, 100, 102, 110, 111, 120,
  121, 127–8
Paris 101–2
Partnership School programmes 144
Patterson, K. 88
Pearson, P.D. 83
Perera, K. 58
Perfetti, C. 17, 18, 33
Perney, J. 26
phonemes 40, 69
phonetic-cue reading 21
phonetics 46–54
phonic-analytic-synthetic method
  71–4
phonics 9, 10, 27, 33–41, 137–8, 169
phonological recoding 14–15
phonological skills 84, 138, 154; *see also*
  decoding
phonomimics 72–3
Piaget, J. 44, 173
pictures 58–9, 75, 89, 99, 120; interpretation
  155
Pontecorvo, C. 45, 50, 51, 97

preschool experience 12, 19, 22–3, 55,
  95–103, 116; concept of literacy 104–14;
  writing 43–55
Pring, L. 61
pronunciation 21–2, 24–5, 27; of non-words
  61–5
Protheroe, P. 59

Raban, B. 169
Rabinowitz, M. 84
Rack, J. 15, 85
Read, C. 24
Readers 39; Hungarian 76
reading: ability 140–1, 156, 157; children's
  concepts of 104–14, 143–4, 156; definitions
  of 139–41; process 144–54
*Reading* 81
Reading Recovery programme 24, 25, 82
reading schemes 37
readings, shared 129–35
'real books' 137–8
Reed, M. 167, 184
Rego, L.L.B. 65
Reid, J. 61
Reitsma, P. 13
remedial teaching 84–5
research 10, 33, 80, 81, 82–3, 87–8, 115,
  162–3
Robbins, C. 12
Robinson, H. 16
Rome 97
Rosen, H. 164, 165
Routh, D.K. 40
routines 121–2
Ruddell, M.R. and R.B. 145
Rumelhart, D. 11

Schickedanz, J.A. 128
School Curriculum and Assessment Authority
  161, 174
schools: entry 95, 115, 116; inspection 166;
  primary 128–9, 174–6; reception classes
  115–24; secondary 174–7; *see also* nursery
  schools; teachers and teaching
Schools Examinations and Assessment
  Council 165–6
science 82–3; teaching 176
Science Research Associates 144
Scotland 34–5, 36, 38, 39, 40, 106–12, 149
Seidenberg, M.S. 88
semantics 45–54
Seymour, P.H.K. 88
Share, D. 20
Sheffield University 96–7
sight word reading 13–14, 15, 24–5, 27
signs 57–8; classroom 121–2
Sinclair, H. 54
Singh, N.N. 59
skills: literacy 33, 89, 167–8; prerequisite for
  reading 19–20, 84; reading 83–8, 165

Smith, F. 32, 59, 82, 126, 133, 135
Snow, C. 105
Snowling, M.J. 33, 61
social learning 117–19
Solman, R.T. 59
sounds 19–26; letter- 13–14, 15, 20, 21, 23–4, 25–6, 33–4; *see also* phonics
Spain 97–9, 100–1
speech 24, 32–3, 89
spelling 21–2, 24, 25–6, 35, 81, 175; patterns 15, 20, 21–2, 35, 88
Stahl, S. 15–16
stance 138–40
standards 137, 138, 161, 163–7, 177, 178
Stanovich, K. 9, 18, 19, 25, 33, 60
Start, K.B. 163, 164
Stevenson, H.W. 87
stories and storybooks 12, 71, 98, 99, 105, 106–14, 117, 119, 121
Stuart, M. 145
Sulzby, E. 12, 43, 104, 108
symbols 58, 155
syntax 88

teachers and teaching 10, 162–3, 177, 178–9; conceptual maps 168–70; effective 87, 166–8; proximation models 170–7; reading 22–6, 115–24, 166, 168–70; reception class 115–24; role 126–7, 128–35; training 39
Teale, W.H. 127
Templeton, S. 22
tests, reading 33, 36, 37, 38, 40, 86–7, 95–6, 140, 163, 164, 165–7; *see also* assessment
Thomas, G. 83
Thompson, G.B. 36, 40
Tizard, B. 116, 119
Tolchinsky Landsmann, L. 50, 51, 54
top-down reading model 2, 3, 59, 87, 145
Torgeson, J. 9
Torrey, J.W. 127

Treiman, R. 14, 15, 24
Turner, M. 85–6, 165, 166, 183

understanding, levels of 152–3
United States of America 137

Venezsky, R. 12, 15
Vincent, D. 85
visual cues 20, 153–5
Vogt, S. 154
Vygotsky, L.S. 170

Wagner, R. 9
Warwick University 169
Waterland, L. 130
Watson, J. 38–9, 182
Webster, A. 168, 184
Wells, G. 105, 116, 119, 127
Wendon, L. 23
West, R.F. 25, 60
whole-language instruction 9, 10, 18, 71, 75–6, 80–90
Wilce, L.S. 13, 15, 21, 23, 26, 61
Willinsky, J. 147–8
Wimmer, H. 15
words: key 25; predictability 16–17; pseudo- 14, 15, 26, 36–7, 61–5, 85; reading 12–26, 33–5; sight- 13–14, 15, 24–5, 27
writing 34, 145, 152; in Hungary 72, 128; preschool 43–55
Wu, H.-M. 89

Yaden, D. 54
Young, A. 88
Yuill, N. 85
Yule, V. 81

Zelan, K. 144–5
Zucchermaglio, C. 43, 50